To be successful, you need to accept the message

Your daily guide keeping you on track
Success is your one way road!

FRANCESCO VITALI

ISBN: 978-1-961028-61-6

To my always and forever partner,
Chris Siametis

About the Author

Never allowing himself the indignity of being a mere employee, Francesco Vitali has over thirty years of experience as a well-respected business consultant, manager, film producer, investor, and serial entrepreneur. He has led as a CEO for several companies and has been an advisor for many notable brands and celebrities.

With an unwavering passion for success and an innate ability to pivot and adapt to new challenges, Francesco has accumulated a wealth of knowledge and experience that he is now eager to share through his first book, *Message for Success*.

Preface

In the demanding and competitive landscape of today's world, success often appears as an enigmatic concept attainable only by a select few. However, I assure you that success is not an exclusive club—it is within your reach, and this book will serve as your unwavering companion on the path to achievement.

Message for Success is an inspiring daily guide that will propel you toward achieving your desired success. Composed of 365 brief chapters following a motivating quotation from an icon of success, this book is a daily reading practice and a purposeful resource created for business people, entrepreneurs, and individuals committed to achieving their goals. Every page contains insights and powerful reminders that will fortify your resolve, sustain your focus, and drive you relentlessly toward your desired outcomes.

Irrespective of whether you are a seasoned executive, a young professional, or an aspiring entrepreneur, this book cuts through the superfluous and offers direct messages that demand action and ignite an unwavering pursuit of excellence.

Success does not result from idle wishes or by passively waiting for opportunities to fall into your lap. It requires a proactive mindset, deliberate action, and an unwavering commitment to personal growth. This book will equip you with the attitude, habits, and strategies necessary to overcome obstacles, seize opportunities, and transcend your perceived limitations.

An indispensable companion for staying motivated, *Message for Success* is an unyielding resource providing a steadfast roadmap toward achievement. It will help you navigate the complexities of your journey and steer you toward greatness.

Be prepared to push beyond your comfort zone, embrace discomfort, and elevate your aspirations. With relentless dedication and unwavering determination, you will unlock your full potential and redefine the boundaries of what you believed was possible.

Francesco Vitali

Your Notes for Success

1

"It is hard to fail, but it is worse never to have tried to succeed." — Theodore Roosevelt

The journey of a thousand miles begins with a single step. And it is the first step we take that is the most important.

Sometimes, we let fear define us and hamper our growth. But remember that if you never try, you will never know what the results might be. Yes, there's a possibility that you might fail, but you can rest assured that you gave it your all. Also, don't give up when you experience failure. Those who have never failed have never tried anything new. Remember that failure is just another experience that helps one learn, and there are plenty of lessons we can learn from the mistakes we make. It's an opportunity for us to grow. Just because you've lost a battle doesn't mean you can't win the war.

Just like how a good friend corrects you and ensures you progress, failure can make you wiser. It can give you a new perspective and teach you how to bounce back when faced with adversity. In other words, failure is inevitable, and success is elusive. What matters is how you deal with it. Tenacity and resilience are the keys to success.

So, stay focused and face your worst fears head-on.

Your Notes for Success

2

"Eighty percent of success is showing up." — Woody Allen.

Success means different things to different people. For some, it means bagging that promotion at work they've been wanting. For others, it could be as simple as starting their day early or getting good feedback from a client.

But the most important ingredient for success is showing up. It's taking the first step toward your goals. It's getting back up when you fall, continuing to climb the ladder, even when your legs give in. It's focusing on the light at the end of the tunnel and continuing to walk toward it even when you want to turn back.

It's showing up for work on a Monday, even when we want to take a day off. Or staying late and wrapping up a project even though we want to be home early. When you walk an extra mile, you're doing your future self a favor. You're making things easier for yourself so later on, you won't stress over the amount of work you have.

The three fundamental elements of success are **passion, preparation, and persistence**.

Do what you're passionate about, plan out your goals, and keep pushing toward the finish line. You *will* impress that client. You *will* get that promotion. And you *will* exceed the expectations of your bosses.

All you need to do is trust yourself and the process.

Francesco Vitali

Your Notes for Success

3

"Don't spend time beating on a wall, hoping to transform it into a door." – Coco Chanel.

Often times what holds us back is our inability to move on from a setback or failure. We dwell on the past, forgetting that it is a part of us. Your mistakes make you who you are. But they don't define you or your capabilities.

At the same time, we can't wait for an opportunity to come knocking on our door. We need to seize it as soon as we get the chance. And remember that if one door closes, another opens. That means you should keep your options open and look at the bright side of things. If something doesn't go your way, remember that it's a bad day, not a bad life.

If you mess up one project, that doesn't mean you can't fix things. You can take your time, brainstorm ideas with your team, and try again. Don't be harsh on yourself. You've gotten this far for a reason, and success comes to those who don't throw in the towel.

Accept that you will experience failures, make mistakes, and feel like giving up.

The famous inventor Thomas Edison said, "I have not failed; I've just found 10,000 ways that won't work."

Remember, every exit is an entry somewhere else. You *will* figure things out. In the end, everything will be great. Just focus on your future, vision, and goals.

Francesco Vitali

<u>*Your Notes for Success*</u>

4

"Whatever the mind can conceive and believe,
it can achieve." — Napoleon Hill.

We are our own worst critics. But we often underestimate our true potential. There is not a single person in the world who does not possess talent.

Mozart was gifted with music. Picasso was gifted with painting. Michael Jordan was gifted with a basketball. But despite being born with so much talent, they worked hard to hone their skills. After all, practice makes perfect.

But remember that once you have a goal, you're already halfway there. Sometimes, things seem like they're out of our reach or a far-fetched dream. But once you start, you realize that you *do* have what it takes to move mountains and achieve your goals.

The Wright brothers believed in their flying machine when others said it was impossible, and now millions of people fly in an airplane every day. Don't think you don't have what it takes to get the promotion you've been dreaming of. Get the notion of "others are better than me" out of your head.

You've made it this far because you *have* what it takes to reach for the stars. Just visualize success in your mind, and you're on the way there!

Setting goals is the first step in turning the invisible into the visible. Tell yourself that you *can,* and you *will* get to the finish line.

Your Notes for Success

5

"Only those who dare to fail greatly can ever achieve greatly." — Robert F. Kennedy.

The sweetest victory is the one that is most difficult to achieve. Failure is an experience that is essential to growth. Without failure, we wouldn't be where we are today.

Thomas Edison is known for inventing the light bulb. But did you know that he failed over a thousand times before being able to do so?

"How did it feel to fail 1,000 times?" a reporter asked. "I didn't fail 1,000 times," Edison responded. "The light bulb was an invention with 1,000 steps."

Failure is not fatal. No matter how hard it may be, know that it simply means you get another shot to try it all again.

There are lessons in our faults that help us grow. Take failure as feedback on how you can perfect your craft. Nothing works unless you do. And while nothing will be perfect, if you're persistent, the easier it will be to deal with failures along the way.

The secret to success is perseverance and taking risks. You'll learn more than ever about your strengths, talents, and resolve, and you'll strengthen your will for the next big challenge.

So, grab the bull by the horns, be willing to take risks, and step out of your comfort zone!

Francesco Vitali

Your Notes for Success

6

"Success is stumbling from failure to failure with no loss of enthusiasm." — Winston Churchill.

It's not easy staying motivated. Whether it's going for an early morning run before work or working on a long-term project for a finicky client, sometimes we find ourselves needing a break. Success is about having the determination, perseverance, and resilience to keep going, even when everything else seems to be going against you.

Success is about believing in yourself, having the courage to face your fears, and the strength to go on. Success is stumbling from failure to failure with no loss of enthusiasm.

But remember that the road to success is paved with thorns. It won't be easy, but it will be ***worth it***. You've made it this far because you have the will, resolution, and adroitness to succeed. You kept going, even when things were tough. We sometimes forget that all successful people have failed, and they did not stop after their failures. The reason they succeeded is that they tried again and again until they got where they needed to be. Focus on *why* you started your journey, and you will find the drive and motivation to reach the finish line.

So do not be afraid of failure; it is a part of your road to success.

Your Notes for Success

7

"Failure is the condiment that gives success its flavor."
— *Truman Capote*

To grow, you need failure; it is life's ultimate lesson. Everyone fails at something at one point in their lives. But it's how you turn your losses into lessons that matter most.

There is value in failure. Through failure, you will get to know yourself better and learn from your mistakes. It makes us rethink, reconsider, and find new ways to achieve our goals.

There is nothing in the world you can't achieve once you set your mind to it. Remember that it only seems impossible because we undervalue ourselves. The word "impossible" becomes "I'm possible" when you face your worst fears head-on.

When you stop fearing the unknown and embrace your failures, that's when you will maximize your motivation, determination, and perseverance. And because of those failures, your success will be all the sweeter.

Thirty-six different publishers rejected Arianna Huffington's first book. But she didn't give up until her book was finally accepted by a publication, and she went on to found The Huffington Post.

Even the Huffington Post wasn't a success right away. It received negative reviews when it was first launched. But now it's one of the most powerful publications in the world. Sometimes, it takes time and patience to grow.

Be patient with yourself and try again and again until you are finally where you want to be.

Francesco Vitali

Your Notes for Success

8

*"It had long since come to my attention that people
of accomplishment rarely sat back and let things
happen to them. They went out and happened to
things." — Leonardo da Vinci.*

Actions speak louder than words. What we do has more value than what we say. We can make all the promises in the world, but unless we back them up with action, they are nothing more than empty words. Taking action shows that you are determined and committed to achieving a goal.

It's important to take action and follow through with what you say you are going to do. Taking action shows that you are reliable and trustworthy and can be counted on. It also shows that you have the courage and determination to succeed and make a difference. Taking action is the only way to make dreams a reality.

For example, delivering the work to a client before the deadline shows them that you're willing to go above and beyond to exceed their expectations. Or when you take on more responsibilities and prove you have what it takes to be a leader.

Action is how you show honesty, integrity, fairness, trust, respect, dependability, and genuineness. Don't be afraid to grab an opportunity when you see one. You are more than capable of succeeding in whatever you set your mind to.

You need to lead by example. Then, you will become an excellent role model your employees will take their cues from and genuinely strive to emulate.

Francesco Vitali

<u>*Your Notes for Success*</u>

9

*"Letting go means to realize that some people
are a part of your history, but not a part of your
destiny." — Steve Maraboli*

To climb the ladder of success, we need to put ourselves first. During your professional journey, you'll meet a lot of people whom you'll learn from. But only a few will stay for the remainder of the expedition.

It's people and the experiences we have with them that help shape and mold us. Every person who comes into our life teaches us a valuable lesson. Some of the lessons we learn can humble us; others can be life-changing. Let go of people who don't add value to your life and only focus on bringing you down. When we let go of people, places, and things that no longer serve us, we create space for new and beautiful things to come our way.

But remember that the person who will be there with you until the end of your journey is *you* and *you* alone. You will be there every step of the way. That's why it's important to trust and believe in yourself.

Your potential is limitless; it's unmatched and second-to-none. No one can take your place in this world. All you need to do is harness it so you can climb to the top of the Ladder of Success and achieve your goals.

Francesco Vitali

Your Notes for Success

10

"The only time you fail is when you fall and stay down." — Stephen Richards.

When life gives you lemons, make a lemonade. Opportunity knocks on every man's door, and it's up to us to grab it by the horns. It might feel like life is throwing curveballs your way from every angle, but that doesn't mean you're bound for failure.

Remember that opportunities don't just happen. We create them. If you get knocked down once, get up and try again. If one door doesn't open, try another one. It's only when we take chances and look for solutions that our lives improve.

We learn more from our failures than our successes. Don't let failure stop you; you are limitless. You are destined for greatness, and greatness can only be achieved through perseverance.

As the investor Arlan Hamilton said, "We don't just sit around and wait for other people. We just make, and we do."

Don't wait for success to come and find you. Find it first and show others who you are and *what* you're capable of. You have the tenacity, the brilliance, and the potential to trounce the world. You can overcome your biggest fears. You can take on difficult challenges and taste victory. And most importantly, you *can* do anything you set your mind to.

All it takes is for you to believe in your potential and get back up every time you're knocked down.

Francesco Vitali

Your Notes for Success

11

"Success does not consist in never making mistakes but in never making the same one a second time."
— *George Bernard Shaw*

We all make mistakes. We've all failed at something at some point in our lives. But that doesn't mean we're not capable or not good enough to achieve our dreams.

What's important is that we take the chance to learn from the mistakes we've made. Learning from failure is the key to success. Remember that everyone's definition of failure is different, and since people aren't perfect, mistakes are inevitable. But they don't define you. They *refine* you.

Even when things don't work out, they do—in different and better ways. We need to keep looking forward and remember our strengths more than our weaknesses. But keep in mind that your weaknesses can also be turned into strengths. There are lessons in failures, and instead of dwelling on what went wrong, use the opportunity to learn what can be done better.

No one can reduce mistakes to zero, but you can learn to harness your drive and channel it into better decision-making.

Failure is an opportunity to change our view and perspective of the world around us. Most importantly, it's an opportunity to take on new challenges, find out our strengths, and learn something new.

Think about it in terms of a video game if you are so inclined: failures are the resets necessary to eventually win the game.

Francesco Vitali

Your Notes for Success

12

"If you have a dream, don't just sit there. Gather courage to believe that you can succeed and leave no stone unturned to make it a reality." — Dr. Roopleen.

Everyone has a dream. But it's up to us whether we let our dreams stay as dreams or turn them into reality. People will tell you that what you want to do is impossible, but you need to remember that nothing is unachievable if you set your mind to it.

The first step to succeeding is believing in yourself and then going above and beyond to achieve your goals. Don't limit yourself to what you see now. The future can change at any given moment, and you have to muster up the courage to act. Do not delay anything, and take the first step.

Most of the things we have now seemed impossible a few years ago. But we have them now, and that means that if we set our mind to it, we can turn our dreams into reality.

Ask your boss for that promotion. You've been working hard and deserve it.

Pitch in your ideas. You're a brilliant individual with an amazing mind. You have what it takes to reach the sky.

Don't just dream, do. Chase after your dreams and turn them into reality. Do what it takes to bring your vision to life. And that's how you will get to the top!

Your Notes for Success

13

"To be independent of public opinion is the first formal condition of achieving anything great." — Hegel.

There will *always* be someone who will criticize you. But remember that it's their *opinion*, not a fact. What others say and think does *not* define you as an individual. You are worthy of praise; you are a valuable asset. Sometimes, people don't appreciate everything we bring to the table, and that is okay. That does not mean that we don't have the skills, expertise, or the talent to make it big.

Rejection is a way for us to understand the world around us. We can choose to stop doing what we love or choose to break through. The choice is always ours. We can let it break us or build us.

While we may be presented with different challenges and opportunities, it's what we do with these experiences that makes all the difference and sets us apart from others. The most successful people are the ones who take into account **constructive feedback** and not criticism. Not every individual's 'feedback' matters. Focus on the advice that will help you carve a better and brighter future for yourself.

Remember that every challenge is an opportunity to grow. So, don't let others hold you down or tell you that are you are not valuable.

Francesco Vitali

Your Notes for Success

14

"The way to get started is to quit talking and begin doing." — Walt Disney.

Too often, we keep thinking and talking about our goals; instead, we must learn to start taking action. Words and dreams alone will never get you where you want to be and will do nothing but waste your time. Taking action and getting started is a great way to move forward, and it can be incredibly rewarding. Taking action can help us better understand our goals and make progress toward them. If you don't take the first step, how will you know what you're missing out on? How will you reach your final destination?

So, the best thing for you is to stop talking about the goals you *will* make and start working on making them. It is the only path that will bring you success. Don't delay your goals and dreams.

No matter how hard it is to achieve your goals, you can do it. After you have reached the desired success in your life, no one will stop you from speaking; on the contrary, they will start listening to you even more. And then your words will become the inspiration for the rest of the world. It's time to stop talking and start doing what you talk about.

Francesco Vitali

Your Notes for Success

15

"There is no failure except in no longer trying."
— *Elbert Hubbard*

Sometimes, when things don't go our way, we think about throwing in the towel. But giving up on your dreams is the easy way out. Nothing compares to the feeling you get when you finally reach the finish line.

The only one getting in the way of achieving your dreams is yourself. It's about time you start recognizing the limiting beliefs that are holding you back. Take charge of your life and remind yourself that you have what it takes to change your story.

As long as we continue to strive and persevere, we can always overcome any obstacle and achieve success. There is no failure except in no longer trying. This is true in any endeavor we undertake. With hard work, perseverance, and dedication, we can always turn our failures into success. So, you need to keep your chin up and keep going. Remember that every failure is a stepping stone toward success.

Discover your ultimate purpose in life and connect every action you take and every decision you make back to that purpose. You need to take action today to begin getting what you want in life, and then you are guaranteed to find yourself where you want to be!

Your Notes for Success

16

"You may be the only person left who believes in you, but it's enough. It takes just one star to pierce a universe of darkness. Never give up."
— *Richelle E. Goodrich.*

When everyone is against you, you need to become your biggest supporter. Sometimes, the choices we make may not be popular with others. And that is perfectly okay.

But no one knows exactly what it is that you really desire deep down except yourself. You know yourself best, your strengths and weaknesses. You know who you are, what you want to do, and what you want to accomplish. Being your biggest support means committing to yourself and believing in yourself, even when times are tough. Even when you don't have the energy to carry on. It's about giving yourself the confidence and courage to take on any challenge and come out on top.

Of course, there will be people who *will* believe in you. But as nice as it is having others who support you, there's no one like yourself. The best thing you can do is also to depend on yourself first.

So, don't give up on yourself or your dreams. Who better to help you through a rough patch than yourself? Be your biggest supporter and your biggest fan because there is no one else like you. You have what it takes to take on the world and succeed.

Francesco Vitali

<u>Your Notes for Success</u>

17

"Vision without execution is just hallucination."
— *Henry Ford*

In order to achieve your dreams, you need to have a clear vision of where you want to be. But while it's important to plan everything, it's also important to take the next step.

Once you start planning and have an idea of where you want to be, take the steps to achieve your goals. Start small and then move on to bigger things. Remember that a clear vision is the spark that ignites the fire of innovation and progress. It is the foundation for creative problem-solving and making goals a reality. Without this combination, it would be impossible to make dreams a reality.

Having a clear vision of where you want to be is the key to success, as you must first set a goal and then work toward it. Vision is the motivation required to make change and overcome challenges.

As the saying goes, Rome wasn't built in one day, so be patient with yourself. Trust yourself and the process. But make sure you start doing things *now* so you don't have any regrets later. Don't delay anything. You can do amazing and incredible things once you set your mind to it.

So, don't hesitate to take the first step.

Your Notes for Success

18

"Success means we go to sleep at night knowing that our talents and abilities were used in a way that served others." — Marianne Williamson.

There's nothing more rewarding than doing right by those around you. The feeling that comes with helping others and genuinely putting a smile on their face is immeasurable.

To know that others can rely on and depend on you is not only rewarding, but it shows that you are a trustworthy individual with great integrity. It shows that you are honest, reliable, hardworking, and capable of making a difference in the lives of others. Remember that *you* matter, and you have what it takes to change the lives of those around you in a positive and beautiful way. When we strive to uplift others, we create a safe and comfortable environment for them to work in.

Success means we go to sleep at night knowing that our efforts were not in vain and that we have made a positive difference in the world. It is a reminder that our actions have meaning and that we are capable of making a difference.

Success gives us the courage to keep going and to strive for even greater successes in the future. So, do your part and help others achieve their dreams. Only then will you be able to understand the true meaning of success!

Your Notes for Success

19

"Success is … knowing your purpose in life, growing to reach your maximum potential, and sowing seeds that benefit others." — John C. Maxwell.

The best of us are those who share our success and achievements with others. Sharing the knowledge you've gained and helping others hone their skills is one of the best feelings in the world.

Nothing can replace the feeling of knowing that you have made a difference in someone else's life. Knowing your purpose, being willing to learn and grow, and taking responsibility are what make you an incredible individual, someone others can look up to and take on as a role model.

Success is about having the courage to take risks and make mistakes in order to learn, grow and improve. It's about pushing past self-imposed limits to reach your full potential. It's about recognizing and utilizing your unique gifts and talents to make a positive contribution to the world. It's about being passionate and determined in the pursuit of your dreams and ambitions.

Success is not just about the money and material goods. It's about having a sense of fulfillment and knowing that you have made a difference in the lives of others and that other people can count on you.

So, do your best to be the best version of yourself and help others on your way to success!

Francesco Vitali

Your Notes for Success

20

"The roughest roads often lead to the top."
— *Christina Aguilera*

Life isn't easy, and the journey to success is paved with speedbumps. But that doesn't mean it isn't worth it in the end. It's the challenges we face and overcome that transform us into extraordinary individuals.

A diamond is a rock that needs to be mined and molded to get its shape. A rosebud has to go through the process of blooming before it becomes a flower. And a caterpillar has to stay inside a cocoon before it becomes a butterfly.

Different conditions are required for different individuals to reach the point where they can be what they were meant to be. They respond to different stimuli and are unique in the ways their best qualities will come to the fore: do not, thus, compare your journey with others, but think about your own development and the difference between who you were, who you are, and the brilliance of whom you will one day become.

The challenges you are facing now might be tough, but nothing will be sweeter than the taste of success once you achieve your goals.

So, keep your chin up and don't give in to the pressures around you—they will be the ones that will form you into the brilliant diamond that you are destined to become.

Francesco Vitali

<u>*Your Notes for Success*</u>

21

"Doing the best at this moment puts you in the best place for the next moment." — Oprah Winfrey.

When you feel like giving up, remember that sometimes it's best to just show up. Show up to work, be there, and do your best to get through the day. You don't have to put in your 100 percent and make sure everything is perfect.

Putting in minimum effort is better than putting in no effort at all. Sometimes, you need to put yourself on 'auto-pilot' to get through. And remind yourself that you don't have to be perfect; you just need to *deliver*. Worry about perfection some other day.

Some days won't go as planned. But that doesn't mean every day is going to be the same. There are better days ahead, and just putting your best foot forward is more than enough. Don't push yourself to achieve things when you can't. Rest your body and mind so that later on, you can give it your all.

You have what it takes to shine. You have what it takes to outdo everyone. You just need to be patient with yourself. You are doing your best. Remember that it's a bad day, not a bad life, and you have plenty of things to look forward to in the near future.

Your Notes for Success

22

*"When your back is to the wall, and you are facing
fear head-on, the only way is forward and through it."*
— Stephen Richards

Fear is immobilizing. But remember that facing your fears head-on is the only way to move forward. Don't let your inner demons consume you; don't let them take over. Don't let your inner critic win or tell you you're not good enough. Because you know you are. You're better than good enough.

Instead of letting your doubts devour you, delve into why you're afraid. Sometimes, we're scared of something but can't pinpoint it. When we take apart our worst fears, we realize they're not as big as they seem. They're actually irrational thoughts trying to win over. You'll have to eventually face them, so it's best to do it immediately—in the moment, right now. Don't let them win; tell them who's boss!

We never know how strong we really are until being strong is the only option we have. You've got this. You were born to be great! You were able to get this far because you are an incredible individual who can take on any challenge and can achieve anything they sets their mind to.

So, face your fears head-on, and don't look back! Don't let anything or anyone stop you or get in the way of your journey and your success.

Francesco Vitali

Your Notes for Success

23

"The merit of all things lies in their difficulty."
— *Alexandre Dumas*

If things were easy, they wouldn't be worth it. The fruit of labor and patience tastes the sweetest. And once you've experienced the satisfaction that comes from hard work, there's no going back.

The blood, sweat, and tears you put into your work will all be worth it. It'll take you to great places. Climbing the ladder of success is difficult, but in the end, everything will pay off once you reach the finish line.

Remember that the Taj Mahal, or the Great Pyramid of Giza, wasn't built in one day. It took years for mankind to construct these great monuments. Now, they're known as some of the Seven Wonders of the world. Millions of tourists visit these heritage sites every year to marvel at their beauty. No one would have thought they would attract so much attention when they were being built.

Like a diamond in the rough, you need time to become polished, and, in the end, it'll all be worth the struggle. You need to be patient and trust the process. Don't doubt yourself because you are destined for greatness. You are resilient, hardworking, and committed. And that's all you need because these three traits will lead you to success!

Francesco Vitali

<u>*Your Notes for Success*</u>

24

"Each new day is a blank page in the diary of your life.
The secret of success is in turning that diary into the
best story you possibly can." — Douglas Pagels.

We all have twenty-four hours a day in our lives to make a difference in the world. What we do during those twenty-four hours is crucial. Every day is an opportunity to do something new.

Whether we choose to dwell on our past and mistakes or move forward and conquer our worst fears is up to us. But every individual has the same hours, and we need to make sure we use our time wisely and do things that will help us achieve greatness.

Make every day count by putting in everything you've got. Wake up with a smile on your face, ready to take on any challenge that comes your way. Plan things out, and make sure you get them done on time. Yesterday might not have been the way you expected, but that doesn't mean tomorrow won't be good. We have to make sure we make the present count. Believe in the power of positivity, and you'll see the difference it will make in your life.

So, keep your chin up and don't look behind you. Keep moving forward without ever stopping. Leave the past in the past and focus on your present and what the future holds.

Francesco Vitali

Your Notes for Success

25

"The level of success you achieve will be in direct proportion to the depth of your commitment."
— *Roy T. Bennett*

Everyone dreams of making it to the top. But only those who dare to chase their dreams are the ones who are successful. Actions speak louder than words, and in order to succeed, one must be willing to dedicate themselves to their goals. They should be willing to push their limits and work with fervor to realize their potential.

After all, it's through persistence, commitment, and dedication that we can overcome every hurdle that stands in the way of achieving our goals. You'll be surprised by how a strong work ethic, commitment, and positive attitude can take you far. These traits show that you're a team player and willing to put in effort to tackle any challenge thrown your way.

Having a commitment that is deep and unwavering will give you the courage and determination to reach the success you desire. It will also show others that you are someone who can be relied upon. It will show you are hardworking, trustworthy, and an excellent role model to others.

So, don't sit back and relax. Instead, get up and chase what you deserve to have most—*success*. Before you even know it, you'll be knocking on Success's doorstep in no time!

Your Notes for Success

26

*"Success nullifies. You then have to do it again,
preferably differently." — Karl Lagerfeld.*

Why settle for being the best when you can do better? When we achieve our goals, we become stagnant and forget to look at the bigger picture. It's human nature to stop trying after we've achieved what we've wanted all along.

But you need to remember that a new journey has just begun, and you need to find the drive and motivation to be greater than you were yesterday. Picture where you want to be in the future. Creating a vision for success gives us the confidence to know that no matter what, we overcome any obstacle that comes our way—even the obstacle of success. Being able to create a new vision gives us the motivation to keep going even when things get challenging. Or when we feel like throwing in the towel because we're mentally exhausted and on the verge of giving up.

Give yourself a new purpose and set new goals. Don't settle when you know you have the potential to do even greater things in life. Remind yourself that success is achievable if you stay focused and committed to your goals. Don't limit yourself to others' expectations of you.

So, set your aims higher than ever because there's no such thing as dreaming too big!

Your Notes for Success

27

"That some achieve great success is proof to all that others can achieve it as well." — Abraham Lincoln.

Just because someone is more successful than us does not mean that we can't shine as brightly as them. It's proof that through hard work, commitment, and perseverance, you can do anything you set your mind to! Other people's success can become a beacon of hope for us and motivate us to push ourselves beyond our limits. Nothing is impossible if you believe in yourself. With the right mindset and determination, anything is possible.

You were destined for great things; you are more than capable of achieving your dreams. Learn from those around you; take them as a role model. They were once in the same place as you. Think about what they did differently to be where they are now. They got where they are now because they persisted with their dreams. They never gave up, and neither should you. They took action and didn't put off their dreams for another day. The first step is always the hardest, but once you take it, you'll realize you're already closer to your dreams than you know. You'll realize that the challenges you thought were difficult to tackle were easier to overcome than you thought!

So, don't give up, and take the initiative you need to succeed! You can do this.

Francesco Vitali

Your Notes for Success

28

*"Never sit back and wait for an opportunity to find
you. Get up and search for one. It exists, find it!"*
— Victoria Addino.

If we let others take the front row, they'll have access to the stage. Don't let opportunities slip from your hands just because you want to wait for a better one. Someone else will snatch the opportunity you're letting slip away. Life is full of opportunities. Instead of sitting back and waiting for one to come your way, be proactive and seek one out. You never know when a great opportunity may arise, so don't let go of one if you find it. Don't wait for luck to find you—you need to create your own destiny.

Now is your chance to shine and outdo yourself. Grab opportunities when they come your way. And if they don't, create them. You are capable of achieving incredible things; you are capable of being great. Put time and effort into keeping up with the latest research in your field, make connections via networking, and keep yourself updated on the latest events.

Also, make sure you don't let anyone criticize you. You made it here for a reason. Don't let others tell you otherwise. Don't let anyone dim your light. There is no one who can be like you; you are unmatched! Believe that you can do anything, and find opportunities that work in your favor.

Francesco Vitali

<u>*Your Notes for Success*</u>

29

"Apply yourself. Get all the education you can, but then
... do something. Don't just stand there, make
it happen." — Lee Iacocca

Education is just the first step to achieving your goals and dreams. The second step is chasing after them.

Don't let your potential go to waste. Make the most of what you have, but hone your skills as well. Strive to do the unthinkable and the impossible. Don't let anyone get in the way of your goals. You are destined for remarkable things. You are meant to go far, both in your professional and personal life.

You might encounter challenges that will throw you off, but stay focused. Discipline your mind to concentrate only on the goals you want to achieve and ignore the rest. Visualize yourself achieving these goals. Look at the bigger picture; think about where you want to be in the future. Take small steps. But make sure you're consistent in your efforts. Surround yourself with people who want to see you succeed. Take constructive criticism as a chance to learn and grow, not as feedback to stop trying.

Once you realize your true potential, there's no going back. There's no looking back. There's no going back, either. There's only one path—the road forward.

So, make it happen. Chase your dreams, work hard, and make them come true.

Francesco Vitali

Your Notes for Success

30

*"Every failure is a chance to make things better
than ever." — Vishesh Panthi.*

Regardless of what people say, failure is not a bad thing. There are positive sides to it as well. Failure is an opportunity that allows us to learn from our mistakes and do better. It gives us insight into what we've done wrong. It gives us a way to change our actions, develop a new plan, reassess our goals, and figure out what our next move should be. Failure is a chance to gain a new perspective and grow.

There's not a single successful person in the world right now who has never failed. Failure makes us realize where we lack so we can overcome our weaknesses and turn them into strengths. Take out time to reflect upon your mistakes, and come up with an action plan for amendments. You'll be amazed by how much you can learn from your failures. You can use them to your advantage to become even better than ever. Every failure is a chance to set things right.

So, don't be scared to fail. Don't give up on yourself. There's not a single person in the world who hasn't failed at something. Instead, analyze your mistakes and learn from them so you can do better in the future!

Francesco Vitali

Your Notes for Success

31

*"If you want to continue to be the best in the world,
then you have to train and compete like you are second
best in the world." — Steve Backley.*

Never settle for anything other than becoming the best version of yourself. There will always be someone better than us. The point is to keep improving ourselves and competing only with who we were yesterday. If you want to make a place for yourself in this world, remind yourself that we can do more than what we have already accomplished.

There is always something we can do to improve. Set new goals, find a new purpose, and overcome obstacles that hinder your success. But don't settle. After you become number one, work even harder to maintain that position. You know you are capable of doing great things. But make sure you train yourself like you're still number two. It will help you stay motivated and help you push the limits you have set for yourself. Similarly, you should use the competition as a learning opportunity and use it to grow and improve. We can always do more, be more, and achieve more. There's always a new challenge awaiting us. There's always a new day to prove yourself and improve yourself.

So, why be the best when you can be 'better'? Why settle and become complacent when you can always strive for excellence?

Francesco Vitali

Your Notes for Success

32

*"The first step toward success is taken when you refuse
to be a captive of the environment in which you first
find yourself." — Mark Cain.*

We are *not* the situations we find ourselves in. You are not your circumstances. You are what you make of the situations. It all depends on your perspective and on your decisions.

If you choose to wallow about it, you will not be able to move forward. And if you choose to do something, then you have taken the first step toward success.

We can all do the impossible if we put our minds to it. Remember that every individual is capable of achieving greatness, and you are no stranger to this. We have the power to create our own paths in life, no matter the struggles we face. We are capable of so much more than we may think.

Look back at all the times you thought you couldn't make it—but you did. You're here now, in this moment, and you've achieved all that you don't think you could a few years ago. Your past self would be proud of how far you've come.

So, don't give up on yourself. Times may seem tough right now, but you have what it takes to overcome any hurdle that comes your way. You've done it before, and you can do it again!

Francesco Vitali

Your Notes for Success

33

"Success shuns the man who lacks ideas."— David Schwartz

Don't be a follower. You're meant to be a leader. Don't let anyone dim your light or hinder you from reaching your true potential. You are qualified, skilled, and talented. You are born to lead, not be led.

Don't be afraid to take risks or pitch in ideas. Innovation is the key to success, and it's those who take the lead and come up with something new who are true geniuses. It's individuals who are willing to take risks and think outside the box who are the ones who will find success. Those who are creative and think of new ways to do things will have the world cheer them on.

Taking risks and having the courage to try something new is the key to success. Giving up is never an option. The only way to success is to move forward and trust the process and yourself. Success shuns the man who lacks ideas, but it's the man who has the courage to stand against all odds and work toward achieving his dreams that taste the fruit of success.

Don't shy away from coming up with something new. Remember that the world needs powerful leaders with brilliant ideas to thrive.

So, get into the game and give it your best shot!

Your Notes for Success

34

"Someone's good fortune is not your misfortune."
— *Frank Sonnenberg*

A healthy competition can go a long way, but make sure not to take it too far. Celebrate those who deserve to be celebrated. A good leader doesn't compete with his team.

After all, just like you, they have worked hard to be where they are now. Learn from those around you, those who are best at what they do. Every opportunity is a learning experience, and you should never let go of the chance of gaining knowledge.

When we learn from the best, we will grow as individuals. Just because someone is successful does not mean that you will never be. Everyone's journey is different, and someone else's good fortune does not diminish your own. There is more than enough success to go around, and someone else's victory should be seen as an opportunity to learn and grow.

Remember that your team's success is your success, and vice versa. You are in this together. Take every failure and victory as a chance to reach new heights and grow with them.

It takes time, patience, and perseverance to reach our goals. You *will* be where you need to be. Have faith and trust yourself. Trust the process; trust time, and you'll reach for the stars.

Your Notes for Success

35

"The first step is to establish that something is possible;
then probability will occur." — Elon Musk.

Evaluation of risks is important when making investments. The most crucial step is figuring out whether something is possible. Then, once you've established it, work toward achieving your goal.

Don't just look at the bigger picture; look at the minute details as well. Set small goals so that there aren't any major obstacles you'll need to overcome later on. Focusing on the details will ultimately make things smoother and stress-free.

Don't waste time on saving a sinking ship; take control of the one that you *can* save. Invest your efforts and time in a goal that is not only achievable but beneficial to you as well. If you believe that it is possible to reach your goals, then you have already taken the first step. It takes courage, determination, and a positive attitude to move forward and make that first step happen. With those in place, the probability of success increases. And once you take that first step, you've already accomplished half of your goals!

So, don't delay something just because you're not sure. How do you know you won't get anywhere unless you try? Take that leap of faith, and you'll reach your destination in no time.

Francesco Vitali

Your Notes for Success

36

*"Move fast and break things. Unless you are
breaking stuff, you are not moving fast enough."*
– Mark Zuckerberg.

Don't confine yourself to one set of rules. Make your own if you have to, in order to succeed.

You have to be quick on your feet and make on-the-spot decisions. You need to prioritize and see what benefits you most. Time is crucial and of upmost importance. The faster you move, the more chances you have to make a breakthrough.

If you take things slowly and move at a slow pace, you will not be able to reach your goals. You have to move faster than your competition; take over before they take over you. Taking the initiative and not procrastinating can lead to the success that you desire. Quickly responding to emails, taking action when you see a problem arise, and utilizing resources can all be extremely helpful in achieving your goals. Having the confidence to act quickly and not be afraid of failure can put you miles ahead of the competition. When you move quickly and with purpose, you will find everything will fall into place on its own.

You have the skillset, power, and capabilities to take down any competition that comes your way.

So, don't lose focus, and keep moving forward. Be quick on your feet, and you will get where you need to be!

Francesco Vitali

<u>*Your Notes for Success*</u>

37

"Priority means to precede and proceed." — Richie Norton.

True leaders are those who pave the way for others. Be the change you wish to see in the world. Lead the way by setting an excellent example. You are born to lead, and you are born to be a role model for those who come after you. Become a visionary that everyone can rely on.

Don't let others dictate your destiny, and don't settle for anything less than what you deserve. This is the only way you can show those who look up to you what you are truly capable of.

Leaders lead. They are not meant to be led. Show the world what an incredible individual you are by prioritizing your goals, accomplishing them, and carving a way for others to succeed as well. They have the confidence to take risks, the ambition to reach for their goals, and the humility to acknowledge their mistakes.

Be the one who sets an example for others to follow. Be the one who stands up for what is right, even in the face of adversity. Be the one who puts the needs of others before their own.

When your team can rely on you and trust your decisions, that's when you've truly made a breakthrough.

Francesco Vitali

Your Notes for Success

38

"Don't be part of the people complaining about the problem you are born to solve instead, take action to solve that problem." — PuleSir

Complaining about the world and not doing anything about the problem is not the solution. You are born to come up with the elucidations that are the answer to every challenge that comes your way. You were born to push past your limits, challenge norms, and conquer the world.

Show the world what you are truly capable of. Lead your team to success by coming up with innovative and unique solutions to all of their problems. Remind them they can come to you with any challenge and leave with complete satisfaction. After all, you *are* the leader who is set to set the world on fire.

Believe in yourself, start small, and work your way up. Don't be afraid to fail, and don't complain when you do. Learn from your mistakes, use them as lessons, and keep going. Do your research, ask for help, and take calculated risks. Have the courage to take action and pursue your dreams.

When you have that courage, you become unstoppable. Together, with courage, resilience, and determination, you can make this world a better place. Be the one to take action and solve the problem you are born to solve. Make a difference and be an agent of change.

Francesco Vitali

<u>Your Notes for Success</u>

39

"Work hard enough, and your dreams will become memories." — *Arian Adeli Koodehi.*

We all have been there—dreaming of being at the top of the ladder of success. But if we work hard enough, we can turn our dreams into reality.

Nothing is far-fetched once you put in the effort and determination to make it real. It's important to give it your all and push yourself to the limit. If you work hard enough, you will eventually see the fruits of your labor. With dedication and hard work, your dreams will eventually become a reality. You'll be able to look back on all the hard work you put in and be proud of what you have achieved. With dedication and perseverance, you can make anything possible.

The saying "dreams don't work unless you do" is true. It's all about the hard work you are willing to put in that will see you living your dreams. Don't be afraid to take the first step, and don't be scared of failure. There are many lessons to be learned in getting up after failing.

So, go on ahead, dream big, and work hard! Don't give up on your passions and dreams, and one day, you'll look back and see it wasn't as difficult as you thought.

Your Notes for Success

40

"Never settle for trying to be less than the best." — Ken Sayles

You know you deserve to be at the top. You deserve to be recognized for your talents, skills, and accomplishments. Everyone has something they're good at; they have numerous strengths that they should be proud of. You are no different.

So don't settle for anything less than being the best. You *know* you have what it takes to conquer the world. You *know* you are more than what people know. Take the world by storm and show them your true potential. Never doubt yourself and how far you've come. You should never accept mediocrity. You should never accept being second place. You should be willing to put in the hard work and effort it takes to achieve your goals and never give up until you reach them.

Keep striving for excellence and keep working on improving until you reach your goals. Don't give up on your dreams. Don't give up on yourself; be your biggest support, and keep reminding yourself that you've been able to come this far because you have what it takes to take on any challenge that comes your way. Show the naysayers what you're made of and what you're capable of. Show them you have what it takes to reach the top!

Your Notes for Success

41

*"Communication—the human connection—is the key
to personal and career success."* — *Paul J. Meyer.*

Communication is the key to success. Without communication, we won't be able to connect with others and comprehend their needs.

In a professional setting, it's important to understand how different individuals in your team work. As a leader, understanding their mindset, personalities, strengths, weaknesses, as well as talents are what will help you lead them to success. You should know everything there is about your team so you can bring them together to work in harmony. With communication, we can build relationships, find common ground, and understand the needs and wants of others. Communication allows us to build trust, express our feelings, and share ideas. Communication is the essence of human connection, and without it, we would be unable to collaborate, problem-solve, and progress.

Achieving goals isn't about one individual. As a team, you need to work together to overcome and face challenges that threaten to stop you from reaching your goals. By understanding each other and aligning your goals together, you can form an unbreakable and unmatched connection with your team. Remember that there's a reason they say, "Teamwork makes the dream work!"

So, embrace communication with an open mind and an open heart, and you will be well on your way to success.

Francesco Vitali

Your Notes for Success

42

"Whosoever desires constant success must change his conduct with the times." — Niccolò Machiavelli.

To compete with people in this day and age, we need to let go of our traditional and conservative ways of thinking. We need to keep up with the times and learn to adapt.

Change can be good; it doesn't necessarily have to be bad. We have to learn to see the positive in everything and try something new.

So many people think that change is bad. But embracing change can open up new opportunities. Seeing change as an opportunity to grow instead of an obstacle can be a powerful motivator.

By embracing change and staying flexible, we can stay ahead of the competition and keep our success continual. Don't limit yourself, and don't hold yourself back. Let go of things you can't change so you can keep moving forward, striving for greatness.

Holding onto things will hinder growth, and you won't be able to catch up with others around you. It's essential to grab opportunities as they come so you can keep growing as an individual. Success comes to those who are willing to learn new things and aren't afraid of taking risks.

So, put your best foot forward and take charge! You know you have what it takes to take on any competition that comes your way!

Francesco Vitali

<u>*Your Notes for Success*</u>

43

"The harder the conflict, the greater the triumph."
— *George Washington.*

Often in life, we feel that our situation is our fate. We are powerless to do anything about it. But the best thing about time is – it keeps changing. Our struggles – every battle we fight – prepare us for what's to come. All we need is to continue working towards our goals. With each passing day, you'll realize that you're doing better than tomorrow. And if you remain consistent with your efforts, then there will come a time when you will feel that all the hardship you faced actually made you stronger and helped you achieve your goals.

The conflict before you might appear difficult – almost impossible in some cases. But remember that your success will make enough noise for you to get the recognition you rightly deserve. George Washington aptly encapsulated this secret of success in his quote, "The harder the conflict, the greater the triumph."

Success might appear to be a distant dream, like an unsurmountable mountain. But creating a plan and sticking to it will help you achieve your goal – no matter how impossible it may seem. And the moment you are successful – you'll be thankful for all the difficulties, roadblocks, and challenges you had to face.

Francesco Vitali

<u>Your Notes for Success</u>

44

"One of the lessons that I grew up with was to always stay true to yourself and never let what somebody else says distract you from your goals. And so when I hear about negative and false attacks, I really don't invest any energy in them because I know who I am." — Michelle Obama.

Don't ever change who you are for others. Other people have not walked in your shoes, so they will never be able to understand your struggles and the sacrifices you've made to be where you are today.

Always stay true to yourself because you are the only one who knows yourself well. You know what your needs and wants are. You know the compromises you've had to make to reach your goals. Don't let anyone tell you otherwise. You're a great individual with amazing potential who can take on any challenge that comes your way.

Everyone is different, and that is something to be celebrated. You should never feel like you need to change who you are for anyone else.

Focus on the things you can control and take time to nurture yourself. Do things that make you happy and that bring out the best in you. Focus on the positive, and don't let anyone tell you that you need to change. You are perfect just the way you are, and you should never feel like you need to be something you are not. Believe in yourself and be proud of who you are.

So, don't focus on negative things people have to say. They *always* have something to say. Focus on what *you* need to do to climb the ladder of success.

Francesco Vitali

<u>*Your Notes for Success*</u>

45

"If you're waiting until you feel talented enough to make it, you'll never make it." — Criss Jami.

Sometimes, we don't feel 'good enough' to do anything. And this leads to us looking for motivation or procrastinating. But you shouldn't wait for a 'miracle' to happen. You shouldn't wait for a superhero to save you. Be your own superhero.

Be the one you need when the going gets tough. No one knows you better than yourself. Look into the mirror and remind yourself that you have what it takes to make it that you're incredible, capable, and worthy of success. If you are waiting for the day to come when you feel confident enough to make it, don't wait any longer. You have the talent inside you now, and you have what it takes to make it. Don't let self-doubt hold you back from pursuing your dreams.

Yes, you may still have a long way to go, and you may not yet have the level of expertise that you desire, but you have the potential to get there. You have the passion, the drive, and the determination to make it. And that's all you need. All you need to do is keep going, keep believing in yourself, and keep at it.

Don't wait for anything; go get it yourself.

Your Notes for Success

46

"It is in your moments of decision that your destiny is shaped." — Tony Robbins.

Don't waste time when it comes to taking a stand for yourself or making a decision. Every moment counts. And you should always prioritize yourself and what's best for you. You are going to be the one living your life, not other people.

You are more than capable of taking the right decisions. You are more than capable of leading your team to success. The choices you make will impact the results you seek. That's why it's vital you trust your own judgment and yourself.

You've come this far for a *reason*. And that reason is that you have what it takes to lead your team to success!

In moments of decision, you may be faced with difficult choices and, at times, feel overwhelmed. However, it is important to remember that you are in control of your destiny and that you have the power to make positive changes in your life.

Every decision you make has the potential to shape your destiny and create a life of purpose and meaning. You can choose to live a life of adventure, passion, and fulfillment. Your decisions are a reflection of your character, and they define who you are. So remember, your decisions today create your tomorrow.

Your Notes for Success

47

"Never feel shame for trying and failing, for he who has never failed is he who has never tried."— *Og Mandino.*

Never fear failure because it gives us multiple opportunities to try something new.

No one is born with the ability to do everything right. It might seem that way for some people, but we all have our struggles and battles. That doesn't mean you won't be able to accomplish anything you set your mind to. Fear is immobilizing. But you need to grab it by the horns and face it head-on. If you conquer your fears, you'll be able to see the light at the end of the tunnel.

Adversity only teaches us about the things that don't work in our favor. But we need to find the things that do. When one door doesn't open, a dozen others will. And if those don't open, there's always the window!

By facing our failures, we can become more resilient and better equipped to handle whatever life throws at us. We can also use failure as an opportunity to look at our lives and make changes that will help us reach our goals. In a nutshell, don't be ashamed of failure—instead, use it to push yourself and grow into the person you want to be.

So, stand up to your worst fears and say, "I *can* and I *will*."

Francesco Vitali

Your Notes for Success

48

"Your goal should be just out of reach. But not out of sight." — Remi Witt

Having an ambitious goal can be incredibly motivating. In fact, having a goal that is just out of reach can be the perfect way to push yourself to try harder and reach farther.

When the goal is close enough to be visible, it can be inspiring to strive for something that feels attainable. It can be a reminder of how far you can go and how much you can accomplish. When a goal is just out of reach, it can give you a sense of purpose and show you that even when you are close, you can still reach farther. It can help you stay focused and give you something to strive for. It can also be a reminder that anything is possible and that no matter how difficult the task, there is always a way to achieve it.

Having a goal that is just out of reach can be a great motivator and a way to keep pushing yourself to reach your goals. It can give you the confidence to keep going and the determination to never give up. Having a goal that is just out of reach is a great way to challenge yourself and help you reach your full potential.

Francesco Vitali

<u>_Your Notes for Success_</u>

49

"Don't be afraid of failure. This is the way to succeed."
— *LeBron James*

Everyone is scared of something. It's natural to be scared of failure and rejection. But you shouldn't let it control your life.

Fear isn't the end. It's the beginning of something new, something *better*. If you've failed, it means that you have ruled out one road that is a dead end. This means there are a dozen other roads to try out, and eventually, you will find the one that will lead you to success.

Failure has negative connotations attached to it. But the truth is, failure isn't bad. It helps build character, grit, and resilience and gives us experience. It is a reminder that life is not easy and that working hard is necessary to achieve success.

Failure should be embraced and viewed as a learning experience. It should be used as motivation to work harder and to reach our goals. Failure isn't the end of the road. It's another step in the journey to success. By embracing failure and using it as a tool to learn and grow, we can become successful in life.

So, next time you feel down and are hard on yourself, remember that you haven't failed; you have opened the door to a thousand other ways to succeed!

Francesco Vitali

Your Notes for Success

50

"What seems to us as bitter trials are often blessings in disguise." — *Oscar Wilde*

When life hits us hard, don't say, "Why me?" but instead, say, "Try me!"

We might mourn the loss of an opportunity, but we often don't realize that there are hundreds of better opportunities awaiting us. You might think that life is unfair, but we often fail to see that sometimes things don't go our way because it's not the right time. Certain things that happen are a blessing in disguise.

Like not getting a promotion within six months might make you feel bitter. But there's probably an even bigger promotion waiting around the corner. You just need to be patient with yourself, and remind yourself that you are destined for better and bigger things. What may feel like bitter trials right now will turn into important lessons in the future. The challenges you face right now will help you grow and learn different things. These hurdles will teach you everything you need to know to be successful.

So, no matter how hard it seems or how tough things get, never give up on your goals! Times like these will pass, and you will get where you need to be. With patience, perspective, and optimism, you can conquer the world.

Francesco Vitali

Your Notes for Success

51

"Don't be afraid to give up the good to go for the great." — John D. Rockefeller

Don't let others tell you that you've missed out on a good opportunity when you *know* you deserve better.

Never settle for anything less than what you deserve and are capable of. You know what you need, and you are aware of what your true potential is. Not choosing an opportunity that is good for you does *not* mean that you won't get better opportunities. It doesn't mean you've missed out.

Sometimes, it's okay to wait for something better to come along. It's okay to want better things for yourself. Don't let fear of the unknown stop you from taking that leap of faith. At times, the great may require more effort and dedication, but the rewards can be life-changing. It takes courage to step out of your comfort zone and take a chance.

Believe in yourself and the great things you can achieve. Don't be afraid to go for it. Seize the moment, and don't be afraid to give up the good to go for the great! There are better things that are coming your way.

So, don't let what others say hold you down. Do what you feel is best for you and take the first step.

Francesco Vitali

Your Notes for Success

52

"Take your victories, whatever they may be, cherish them, use them, but don't settle for them." — Mia Hamm.

You deserve to celebrate yourself and your successes. You have come this far because you are talented and capable of great things.

Keep all of your achievements in mind, no matter how small they may be. Getting a new client, getting out of bed, or pitching in a good idea—all that you do *matters*. It makes a difference in your life and others around you.

But don't stop trying. Don't stop believing in yourself and your dreams. You are destined for great things, and you have what it takes to achieve all that you desire.

It's important to take pride in your accomplishments and recognize the hard work you have put in to achieve them. However, it's just as important to remember that your accomplishments don't define you and that you should never settle for them. You should always aim higher. There's always more you can do and strive for.

Celebrate your successes, but don't forget to keep pushing yourself and challenging yourself to reach new heights. Remember that this is *your* journey, and it's up to you to make the most of it. So, don't get complacent and stagnant; stay focused and motivated, and keep striving for greatness!

Francesco Vitali

<u>*Your Notes for Success*</u>

53

"Go as far as you can see, and you will see further."
— Zig Ziglar

Trust your guts and your instincts when making important decisions. When you think about your goals and dreams, envision success. How far do you see yourself going? What do you think you are capable of achieving?

Imagine driving up a hill or climbing up a flight of stairs. When you reach the top, you think, "This is it," and you're done. But are you really done? Is there more you can do? Can you achieve further success and greatness?

Yes, you can! When you achieve one dream, you'll see an even greater dream. Go as far as you can see. There will always be more to see along the way. Remind yourself that you *can* do it! Remind yourself if we take a few steps forward, we will soon see even greater possibilities open up in front of us.

We also need to take risks and challenges to push our limits and discover what we are capable of. By believing in ourselves and striving to go as far as we can see, we can open up a world of possibilities and challenge ourselves to become the best versions of ourselves. With determination and ambition, we can go even further than we could have ever imagined. By taking that first step and going as far as we can see, we can unlock our true potential.

Francesco Vitali

Your Notes for Success

54

*"No matter how good you get, you can always get
better, and that's the exciting part." — Tiger Woods.*

Don't stop trying just because you've achieved your goals. Keep dreaming; keep improving and growing. Never give up on learning something new. No matter how good you get at something, there is always room for improvement.

This can be both daunting and exciting. It is daunting because it can be difficult to learn new skills and take on new challenges, but it is also exciting because it keeps us motivated. We can continue to strive for excellence and push ourselves to be better. There will always be something new that we can learn and something that we can do differently. No matter how good we get, there is always the potential to get better. This is an exciting thought that should keep us feeling motivated and inspired.

You'll find out that there are a thousand things you're unaware of. There are millions of things you need to learn. And remember that you haven't tapped into your full potential yet. There's always something to do and, so much to experience, and so much to look forward to.

So, don't let yourself hold you back from greatness. Take the first step and remember that you have the power to achieve anything you set your mind to.

Francesco Vitali

Your Notes for Success

55

"The only guarantee for failure is to stop trying."
— John C. Maxwell

The worst thing you can do to yourself is to stop trying. Don't kill your dreams just because you failed once—or even a hundred times. Keep trying, and don't give up.

Remember why you held on for so long. The moment we give up, we've lost the war. Consistency, patience, and hard work are the keys to success. Don't settle for less than you deserve and what you're truly capable of.

One thing you need to keep in mind is that success is not always linear, and it often requires trial and error. Instead of giving up, you can use mistakes as sources of feedback and learning. With enough effort, you can turn any obstacle into an opportunity. There's no limit to what you can achieve when you keep pushing forward, no matter how hard the journey may be. When you break through the barriers, you open up a whole new world of possibilities.

Keep trying and never give up; you will eventually reach your goals. If you stop trying, you will never know how far you can reach. Aim for the moon. If you can't reach the moon, you'll land among the stars. Try again next time, and work hard, as this time you won't start from scratch. You'll start from experience!

Francesco Vitali

<u>*Your Notes for Success*</u>

56

"Success doesn't come to you; you go to it."
— *Marva Collins*

You'll never be successful if you expect success to come to you. You need to put in the blood, sweat, and tears to achieve your goals. Good things come to those who wait, but great things come to those who chase after them.

To be successful, you need to have faith in yourself and believe in your ability to make something happen. You have to take ownership of your destiny and understand that success won't just happen. It takes hard work and dedication. You have to have the courage to take risks and be willing to put in the effort and time to achieve your goals. Success is a journey, and it's not always easy, but it's worth it in the end. Remember, you are the captain of your own ship, and you have the power to make your dreams come true.

Go after that promotion you've been dreaming about. Figure out a way to get that car you've been eyeing. Pitch your ideas to your boss. Send a dozen emails to potential clients. But don't ever give up or give in. Keep chasing your dreams and keep envisioning success, and you *will* get there.

You have to chase success, and only then will you be able to grab it! So stay focused and don't give up, as success is just around the corner.

Francesco Vitali

Your Notes for Success

57

"Our greatest glory is not in never failing, but in rising every time we fail." — Confucius.

Life is like a rollercoaster—it's full of ups and downs. Sometimes, it's full of magical, happy little moments. Other times, we're greeted by failure and sadness. But picking yourself up when you're at your lowest is what matters most.

After all, if you're not going to be your biggest supporter, who will? Face adversity head-on. Remind yourself that you have been able to get through difficult challenges, and this is just one more obstacle you have to overcome.

You have what it takes to get through any difficulty and take on any challenge that comes your way.

There will come a point in your career where you will hit a slump or feel like nothing is going your way. But remember that you need to focus on your strengths and not your weaknesses. We should never let setbacks and disappointments bring us down; instead, we should look at them as opportunities to grow and develop. With each stumble, we can use it as a stepping stone to success.

We are resilient and have the strength to bounce back and make the most of every situation. We have the courage and determination to keep going and never give up. Our greatest glory is in our ability to persevere and carry on despite the odds.

Francesco Vitali

Your Notes for Success

58

"If you want to be successful, you must respect one rule. Never lie to yourself." — Paulo Coelho.

Don't try to convince yourself that you're someone different than who you truly are. Always be true to yourself, and don't try to be like others. You are unique, and there is no one else like you.

You know what you are capable of and what your true potential is. Don't let others define or set the path you need to follow. In the end, your journey is yours alone. Do what makes you happy, and do what's best for **you**. When you have a positive outlook and trust in your own decisions, you can take action with confidence. By setting realistic goals and taking consistent action, you will be able to create success in your life. Believe in yourself and never doubt your own potential.

Don't beat yourself up for things you can't do. Acknowledge and accept yourself for who you are. Remember that nobody can be perfect. But we can always strive to be better versions of ourselves. Take ownership of your mistakes and use them as learning experiences. With consistent effort, you can achieve anything you set your mind to. Remember, you've made it this far because you are capable of great things. The things that are troubling you now are temporary.

So, keep your chin up and face challenges head-on!

Francesco Vitali

Your Notes for Success

59

"Don't sleep too much. If you sleep 3 hours less each night for a year, you will have an extra month and a half to succeed in." — *Aristotle Onassis.*

A proper routine is essential for success. You've heard of the idiom "the early bird gets the worm," and it can't get any truer than this. Proper sleep means you'll wake up early and feel energized. Sleeping late means you'll wake up exhausted and won't be able to get to work on time.

You'll feel better mentally and physically once you've carved out a routine that works in your favor. Your brain will no longer feel fatigued and confused, and you will get more things done in a short amount of time.

Getting enough sleep and following a routine also helps improve critical and creative-thinking skills. It will help you become more productive during the day. Use this time to create, plan, develop, and strategize. Take advantage of your mind's alertness and creativity. Utilize your time and energy to work on projects, learn new skills, or start a new business.

Don't waste your potential by sleeping too much. Instead, use the time to study, network, and create something great. Make the most of your day with positive and productive activities. You have the power to achieve greatness, so don't waste it with too much sleep!

So, go to bed early and tackle the challenges that await you the next day with ease!

Francesco Vitali

Your Notes for Success

60

"If a craftsman wants to do good work, he must first sharpen his tools." — Confucius.

In order to get ahead of the competition and succeed, you need to keep improving yourself. You need to keep honing your skills so that you are the best of the best. We never stop learning and evolving, so we need to keep trying to become better than we were yesterday.

The world is rapidly changing, and we need to keep up with its pace. We need to keep up with others and make sure we come out on top. Remind yourself that you are more than capable of taking every challenge that comes your way. You are more than capable of achieving greatness.

The journey of a thousand miles begins with a single step. In addition, practicing the skills you already have is key. Practice makes perfect, so the more you can hone your existing skills, the better.

Finally, don't forget that networking is also essential for success. Building relationships with people in the same field and staying in touch with them can help you get ahead. By keeping improving yourself, you can make sure you stay ahead of the competition and achieve success.

So, take the steps necessary to become a better version of yourself and hone your skills!

Francesco Vitali

<u>*Your Notes for Success*</u>

61

"I haven't failed. I've just found 10,000 ways that won't work." — Thomas Edison.

Just because you fail once or twice or a hundred times doesn't mean you're incapable. There are a thousand ways to do one thing, and you've only tried one or two or a hundred methods that didn't work out in your favor.

Focus on things that *do* work and find out what's easier for you. The goal is to make things less stressful for yourself. And remember, there's no one way to do things. There are a thousand ways to achieve your goals. There are plenty of options and solutions you haven't tried out yet!

Every "no you receive is one step closer to a "yes." Every path that doesn't lead to success is one step closer to the right one. Every mistake is a lesson that will make you stronger.

Every failed attempt is a valuable experience that will help you become wiser. So don't be discouraged. Instead, be thankful that you get to learn and grow. With every setback, you can use it as an opportunity to become better and eventually achieve your goals. Remember, there are a thousand more opportunities awaiting you. You just have to step out of your comfort zone to see them.

So keep trying and never give up on your dreams.

Francesco Vitali

Your Notes for Success

62

"Big things begin with big thinking." — Kent Healy.

It's great to focus on minute details, but don't forget to look at the bigger picture. You should have a vision for where you want to be so you can work toward your goals.

Don't look at where others are; only focus on where you need to be—the top of the ladder!

No dream is too big or too impossible to achieve if you have a clear vision of what you need to do to accomplish it. So focus on the bigger picture and think about what you want from your future self. The time you have right now is what counts the most, so make it count!

Remember, people who think big are the ones who make their mark on the world, creating new opportunities and inspiring others to follow suit. When we think big, our minds come alive with possibility, and our potential is unleashed. We can look beyond our current circumstances and envision a future that is brighter and more fulfilling. Big thinking leads to big ideas, and big ideas have the potential to change the world. So, don't be afraid to let your imagination run wild and think big. The world needs more big thinkers who are brave enough to take on the impossible.

Francesco Vitali

<u>Your Notes for Success</u>

63

"Success awaits those who steadfastly commit to any requisite sacrifice." — Ken Poirot.

You need to be willing to make sacrifices to achieve your dreams. Nothing comes without compromise, perseverance, and hard work. You need to be dedicated to your own self to make your dreams a reality. Committing to the hard work and dedication that is required of any successful endeavor is paramount to achieving the result you want. Taking the time to focus on the end goal and pushing through the challenges that arise is how one can ultimately attain success.

It is important to remember that success does not come without sacrifice. One must be willing to make the necessary sacrifices for the sake of achieving their desired outcome. But with unwavering commitment, dedication, and sacrifice, success is sure to follow.

Moreover, don't think about what others say; they are not going to fight your battles for you. You need to think about how you're going to get ahead of the competition. You have what it takes to overcome all obstacles. Just don't lose focus on your goals and where you want to be! Make sure to always keep your eye on the finish line.

The blood, sweat, and tears you put into your dreams will be worth every hardship in the end.

Francesco Vitali

Your Notes for Success

64

"If you won't trust yourself, nobody else will."
— *Anamika Mishra*

We are our worst critics, but we can also be our biggest supporters.

Nobody knows you better than yourself. You know your weaknesses, flaws, strengths, and skills better than anyone else. You know what you are capable of achieving.

Don't let anyone tell you that you are unworthy of success. You need to believe in yourself and show the world what you are truly capable of. When you trust yourself, you will also be more confident, which will help you take on more challenges and opportunities.

People will notice your confidence and trust in yourself, and they will be more willing to trust you and your abilities. This will help you grow and develop, as you will be pushing yourself and challenging yourself to reach new levels.

Remember that everyone makes mistakes, and no one is perfect. No matter how many times you fail, you must trust yourself to get back up and try again. It is important to have faith in yourself and your capabilities, especially when things don't seem to go your way.

Show the naysayers that you have what it takes to prove them wrong. Remind yourself that you've gotten this far for a reason, and that reason is that you are a truly remarkable individual.

Francesco Vitali

<u>*Your Notes for Success*</u>

65

*"Opportunity doesn't make appointments; you have to
be ready when it arrives." — Tim Fargo.*

When you've got a chance to prove yourself, don't wait and let others take control. Take charge and grab the opportunities that come your way. You might not get them again! It could be a job offer, a challenge, or a chance to learn something new. We need to be ready to seize the opportunity when it comes our way. It's not something that is handed to us but something we have to actively pursue. We must be open to new ideas, take risks, and be willing to step out of our comfort zone. Opportunity is a special chance that, when taken advantage of, can open up a world of possibilities. We just have to be ready to seize it when it comes.

While it's great to let others shine once in a while, don't be selfless when it comes to your own success. You need to put yourself first. You need to make sure your goals align with your plans for the future. You are where you are for a good reason. You are a born leader who was given this role to lead your team to success. Make every moment count! Don't give up on your dreams, no matter what!

Your Notes for Success

66

"Every achievement is a servitude. It compels us to a higher achievement." — Albert Camus.

Once you taste success, you realize your true worth and potential. And that makes us want to achieve more. We *know* we can do better and accomplish more than we did yesterday. Tomorrow holds better opportunities and more challenges we need to face head-on.

Take those challenges at face value and work toward improving yourself and honing your skills. You've got what it takes to achieve anything you set your mind to, so never doubt yourself.

Think of it this way: Every achievement gives us a sense of purpose and pushes us to reach our goals. It allows us to appreciate the efforts and hard work that went into our success and to be grateful for the opportunity to keep growing and learning. Every achievement is an opportunity, not a limitation. It helps us to learn and develop our skills, become more confident, and find more success in the future. Achievement is the foundation of great personal growth and development and a reminder that nothing is impossible with the right attitude and effort. Every achievement is a stepping-stone to the next one and a reminder to never give up. So, don't hold back, and go after what you want to achieve!

Francesco Vitali

Your Notes for Success

67

"Every day, you can dress for smiles and success! Why hide your beauty when you are meant to shine and sparkle? It's your time to shine!" — Cindy Ann Peterson.

The way we present ourselves is extremely important. When you dress well, you feel good. And when you feel good about yourself, you're ready to take on any challenge that comes your way!

You owe yourself to look good and feel good. No matter how tough life gets or how hard it is to make it through the day, remind yourself that you outshine everyone.

Look in the mirror every morning and appreciate yourself. When you remind yourself that you have amazing qualities and that you have what it takes to take on the world, you will start your day on a good note. But don't just act the part. Dress the part as well!

A good leader needs to have impeccable fashion taste and dress in a way that inspires. People are attracted to those who present themselves well. When you dress well, you will emit positive energy. As you start your day, you can't help but feel energized and positive. You have dressed for success and smiles, and you are ready to take on the day. With your positive attitude and your beautiful outfit, you can spread your confidence to others, and you will be sure to achieve success.

Your Notes for Success

68

"Discipline is a prerequisite of greatness. Nobody becomes great by accident." — Henry Joseph-Grant.

Starve your distractions and feed your focus if you want to be successful. The people who are most successful aren't lucky. They have incredible focus and are dedicated to their craft. They know what they want to achieve and have the discipline to go after it.

Discipline gives you the gumption to stick with difficult tasks and allows you to overcome obstacles while helping you step out of your comfort zone. It requires hard work, dedication, and a commitment to stay focused on the goal. It teaches us to be organized, to prioritize our tasks, and to keep trying no matter how difficult the challenge may be. Discipline helps us to become more self-aware and to recognize our strengths and weaknesses. It gives us the strength to persist through difficult situations and to develop our abilities. Discipline also instills in us the courage to take risks and to learn from our mistakes. Learning from our mistakes is the key to success.

You have to put in the effort, show up to work every day and push yourself to new heights. Only then will you be able to achieve your goals? Remember that nothing is impossible once you set your mind to it and develop the discipline to make it happen!

Francesco Vitali

Your Notes for Success

69

"Don't prioritize your schedule, schedule your priorities." — *Ryan Serhant*

If you stick to one schedule and ignore other responsibilities, you'll end up compromising on things that are important in your life.

Spending time with your team, taking a short break, or taking a day off from work when you need it should be on top of your list. When you're in a good place mentally and are well-rested, the results will speak for themselves!

You matter, and *you* are an important part of the company you work for. Therefore, prioritize your needs before anything else. *You* will have to fight your own battles, so make sure you're always doing right by yourself!

You deserve recognition and appreciation for the hard work you do, so start by praising and prioritizing yourself first. When we make sure that our priorities are fulfilled, we are more likely to feel fulfilled and successful. This is a great way to stay motivated and inspired to pursue our dreams and make a difference in the world. With dedication and hard work, anything is possible.

It is important to remember that life is full of joys and challenges. By making sure that our priorities are met, we can experience the joys of life to the fullest and face the challenges head-on.

Francesco Vitali

<u>*Your Notes for Success*</u>

70

"You are always one decision away from
victory or defeat." — Erol Ozan.

Making on-the-spot decisions isn't easy, but that's what separates managers from leaders. You have to quickly decide your next step and ensure minimal damage to the team. We're always one step away from victory or disaster. But it's crucial that you trust your instincts and yourself.

You *know* you were chosen for this role because you *are* an exceptional leader. You're the reason your team is where it is today. Your team has been able to reach its goals and objectives because of your relentless effort and determination.

Opportunities come and go, but it's imperative that we believe in ourselves and trust our gut when making important decisions. We have the capacity to create our own destiny and make the most of any opportunity that comes our way. With self-confidence and courage, we can make decisions that will open doors and provide us with valuable experiences.

So, embrace the challenges that come your way and trust that you have the power to make the right decision. Your team looks up to you for a reason—they have placed their trust in you. Believe in yourself and know that with the right decision, you can achieve anything you set your mind to.

Francesco Vitali

Your Notes for Success

71

"Success is a lousy teacher. It seduces smart people into thinking they can't lose." — Bill Gates.

Just because you've reached the top and achieved some of your goals doesn't mean you should stop trying. There's always more to do and more to achieve.

Keep your eye on the goal, but remind yourself that you can *always* improve and do better. You are always going to be one step away from achieving something even greater, and it's imperative that you don't lose focus.

Improving yourself is a key factor to success. It's important to never stop striving to be better, grow, and learn. With each day comes a new opportunity to become a better version of yourself. You should never be afraid to challenge yourself and take risks. You should stay curious and motivated in order to keep improving.

When you take the necessary steps to better yourself, you will find that you will soon reach success. You should stay focused, determined, and goal-oriented. Believe in yourself and your unique skills and talents, and work hard to achieve your dreams. Look in the mirror every day and remind yourself there is no one like you. You are capable of so much more than you think.

You have what it takes to achieve anything you set your mind to, so don't stop now!

Francesco Vitali

Your Notes for Success

72

"Success doesn't just happen; it doesn't pop out on its own. Success is all about the choices you make. It's a balancing act between what to choose and what not to."
— *Bhuwan Thapaliya*

Unlike what movies want you to believe, success doesn't happen overnight. You need to be persistent, focused, and dedicated to your dreams to turn them into reality.

You have to make tough decisions but analyze each and every step that you take. To be able to climb the ladder of success, you need to prioritize, act fast, and face your worst fears.

It takes courage, strength, and dedication to make the right choices. With the right choices, you can create a better future for yourself and those around you. Staying focused on the goals you set for yourself and believing in yourself is key. Setbacks may occur, but you can overcome them with a positive attitude and determination. Success is possible when you work hard, strive for excellence, and practice resilience.

Celebrate the small victories and keep striving for the big ones. Don't be discouraged by failures, but rather use them as learning experiences. Be confident in your abilities, be open to new ideas, and take the necessary steps to achieve success. With effort, dedication, and the right choices, success will be within reach.

Moreover, you need to keep believing in yourself and keep reminding yourself that you are destined for greatness. Don't give up, and don't give in. Make the right choices, and you will conquer mountains!

Francesco Vitali

Your Notes for Success

73

"Failure is the prerequisite to success, not the elimination of it." — *Craig D. Lounsbrough.*

Despite what people think, failure is not something to be ashamed of. In fact, the most brilliant minds failed before they found success.

From Thomas Edison to Nikola Tesla and Albert Einstein, nobody is born perfect. But like them, we can perfect our craft through practice and learning from our mistakes. Each one of us must try and fail a thousand times before we can find the success that we're looking for.

Failure teaches us what we can do differently, *how* we can do it differently, and methods that work better in our favor. We should not fear failure but instead embrace it. We should take risks and be willing to fail in order to learn and grow. We should also be willing to accept our mistakes and use them as a motivation to do better.

Failure is a part of life, but it does not have to define us. We should use our failures as a stepping stone toward success. With the right attitude and approach, failure can be the key to unlocking the door to success.

So, don't ever feel down if you don't succeed the first time; remember, there are a dozen other ways you can achieve your goals! You just need to figure out what works best for you!

Francesco Vitali

<u>Your Notes for Success</u>

74

"Some people will never be highly successful not because of their lack of competence but because of the lack of welcoming new ideas and new people into their lives." — Anuj Jasani

Though it's important to believe in yourself and your ideas, it's also crucial to celebrate others. Give way to others to succeed as well; give them a chance to prove themselves. Your team's success is your success, after all!

It is important to be willing to take risks and try something new, even if it goes against the grain of what you are used to. When you are open to new ideas, you create opportunities for yourself to grow, learn, and improve. You become more innovative and creative, which can lead to success.

Moreover, having an open mind to new ideas can help to foster collaboration and create better relationships with your colleagues and customers. By being open to new ideas, you can create an environment that encourages creativity and growth. You become more aware of the needs of those around you and can create solutions that meet those needs. By not being afraid to take a chance on something new, you can open yourself up to new possibilities and opportunities for success.

This includes being open to meeting new people so that you can form new relationships and expand your network. Remember, no one achieves success alone!

So, don't be afraid of welcoming new ideas, meeting new people, and taking risks!

Francesco Vitali

Your Notes for Success

75

"Your success lies into your thought process."
— *Santosh Kumar.*

A positive and confident mindset is crucial to achieving your goals. If you have a negative outlook toward everything, the results will be the same.

But if you're willing to overcome obstacles and challenges in your way and step out of your comfort zone, you'll find yourself at the top of the ladder of success. A positive outlook creates positive results.

Having a positive mindset can be one of the best assets in your professional life. It can help you push through difficult moments, stay motivated, and be productive. When you have a positive mindset, you are more likely to see the good in difficult situations, be resilient, and stay on track, even when the going gets tough. A positive mindset also helps you to be more creative and open to new experiences, which can lead to professional growth and development.

We must recognize that success starts with our own thoughts and beliefs. We must have the right attitude and believe in ourselves. We must be determined to succeed and have faith in our abilities.

Believe in yourself and remind yourself every day that you have what it takes to achieve greatness. You *are* incredible; you *are* great, and you *are* destined for success!

Your Notes for Success

76

"Kindness is the key to success." — Jason Naylor.

While the qualities of a leader include powerful communication and negotiation skills, there's one thing people forget—*kindness*. Many people think that achieving success requires a harsh, even rude attitude. But many of the most successful people are also the kindest.

Kindness toward others, especially your team, will help you establish beautiful and long-lasting relationships. It will also help build an empowering work culture where people are not only productive and happy but they have the space to grow. Kindness is a skill that can be learned and practiced, and it is one of the most powerful tools for success.

When we show kindness to others, we open the door to new opportunities and possibilities. Kindness can create a ripple effect, spreading positivity and good vibes throughout our lives.

But it's equally important to be kind toward ourselves as well. When we are kind to ourselves, we understand our limits and learn to be compassionate with ourselves. When you're compassionate with yourself, you'll be compassionate with others.

You, as a leader, have the power to make this happen. Be understanding and patient with your team. That doesn't mean you shouldn't be strict where necessary. But by promoting a kind work culture, you can create a team of empowered individuals.

Francesco Vitali

Your Notes for Success

77

*"Do not say a little in many words but a great
deal in few." — Pythagoras*

Communication is the key to great workplace relationships
and success. But it's also important to know what to say and when
to say it. It's important to know when to communicate a little and
when to communicate a lot. Good communication also increases
our ability to problem-solve and work together to find solutions.
It strengthens our relationships and encourages us to see each
other's perspectives. When communication is open and honest,
it can create a supportive and collaborative atmosphere, which is
essential for a successful workplace.

But most importantly, communication must be clear. Clear
communication helps to ensure that everyone is on the same
page and working toward the same goals. This helps to build trust
and respect in the workplace, which are essential ingredients for
successful relationships and achieving results. Trust and respect
will help create a sense of belonging in the workplace and boost
employee morale.

Don't criticize others unnecessarily; instead, give them
feedback and encourage a positive workplace through kindness
and empathy. Positive affirmations should become a part of your
work environment, and remember that the best kind of leader
is someone who proves himself through his actions, not just his
words. Speak less, do more. And you will find yourself making an
amazing impact on others.

Francesco Vitali

<u>Your Notes for Success</u>

78

*"Once you have found out what you love to do,
there is only one goal: how can you be the best in
the world at it." — Mark Cuban*

Find out what you're passionate about and stick to it. It's okay to not know what you want in life; there's no time limit when it comes to following your dreams. This doesn't necessarily mean that you have to quit your day job and give up the security of a steady income, but it does mean that you should make sure that your passion always remains at the forefront of your mind.

You can do this by setting aside time each day to do something related to your passion, whether it's reading, writing, or working on a project. By doing this, you will always be reminded of what it is that makes you happy and why you should continue to pursue it.

The best part about having a single goal in life is that it gives you a sense of purpose and direction. Knowing what you want to do and how you want to do it gives you the motivation to keep pushing forward no matter what obstacles come your way.

Great people do great things because they never stop believing in themselves. When you love something and are passionate about it, don't give up because though things will be tough, they'll get easier over time!

Francesco Vitali

Your Notes for Success

79

"If you run, you stand a chance of losing, but if you don't run, you've already lost." — *Barack Obama.*

The truth is, we never know where life will take us. There's no guarantee. But if something *is* guaranteed, it's the regret we'll feel if we don't follow our dreams.

It's better to try and fail than to never try at all. Taking risks can open up new opportunities you never thought were possible. Maybe you'll be able to break a personal record or start a new business. Maybe you'll be able to explore a new place or make a new friend. Life is full of possibilities, and if you take a chance, you can make the most of them.

When you take a risk, you're investing in yourself and your dreams. You're showing yourself that you're brave and capable of overcoming obstacles.

Failure is inevitable, but not trying is worse. Don't lose a golden opportunity just because you feel like you won't win. Because what if you tried and won? All it takes is a single step. Don't lose out on an experience of a lifetime because of fear. Fear will immobilize you, but courage will set you free.

So, take the chance to do something great today and tap into your full potential. After all, you *are* destined for greatness!

Francesco Vitali

Your Notes for Success

80

"You can have the best technology, you can have the best business model, but if the storytelling isn't amazing, it won't matter. Nobody will watch." — Jeff Bezos.

Even with the best resources and tools, we should not forget the most important thing—creating an exceptional company image and work culture through telling its story. Your employees are your greatest asset, and they should be happy with the environment. Everything else comes secondary.

Humanize the experience; be patient, flexible, understanding, and, most importantly, *considerate*. Treat your clients and employees the way you want to be treated by others—with respect.

Storytelling can be used to inspire and motivate, to teach and enlighten, and to entertain and engage. It can be used to build trust and foster relationships, to create a shared experience, and to influence and persuade. In business, storytelling can help to build a narrative that resonates with customers and helps to build loyalty. It doesn't matter if you're selling a product, pitching a business idea, or recruiting a new hire—great storytelling can help you achieve your goals. It can create the right atmosphere, build relationships and trust, and drive people to take action.

You have the power to build an extraordinary empire. Make sure you take the right steps and make the right decision by investing in those who understand the art of storytelling and learning how to become a great storyteller yourself.

Francesco Vitali

Your Notes for Success

81

"I'm convinced that about half of what separates the successful entrepreneurs from the non-successful ones is pure perseverance." — Steve Jobs.

You know the phrase: When the going gets tough, the tough get going. During challenging times, you need to show the world around you that you have what it takes to persevere and succeed. You are born to be great; you are destined to set an example for those who will come after you.

When you work toward your goals and dreams, there will be obstacles and setbacks. However, the ability to remain determined through challenging projects will help you get ahead and will lead to better opportunities.

Successful entrepreneurs understand that failure is inevitable, but they don't let it stop them. They use failure as a learning opportunity and use it as fuel to keep going. They are willing to take risks, make mistakes and, learn from them, and keep striving for success.

The road to greatness isn't easy to tread, but the journey will be worth it. No one ever achieved greatness without continuing to try, even in the face of failure. It's about pushing forward, learning from your mistakes, and never giving up. Success takes hard work, dedication, and a willingness to keep going even when it feels impossible.

So, don't give up, and you'll make it to the finish line of success!

Francesco Vitali

Your Notes for Success

82

"The best revenge is massive success." — Frank Sinatra.

Don't waste your time and energy on those who try to bring you down. You are better than this; you have to focus your time and energy on making your dreams a reality.

The best response to criticism is to work in silence and let your success make noise. Think of your critics as obstacles that you need to overcome to reach your final destination. Success is the ultimate way to show those who underestimated you that you are capable of achieving your goals. It is a way to show that you have the power to overcome all obstacles and that you have the strength to take on anything life throws your way.

By achieving massive success, you can prove that you are strong enough to let go of the past and create a better future for yourself. When you focus on becoming successful and growing in life, it can become a powerful form of revenge against those who have tried to belittle or bring you down. You know you're better than all the naysayers!

Focus on the positives and ignore the negatives; you know what your strengths are, and you know you have what it takes to be the greatest of them all!

Francesco Vitali

Your Notes for Success

83

"Develop success from failures. Discouragement and failure are two of the surest stepping stones to success."
—Dale Carnegie

Failure doesn't define you until you let it. Take criticism as an opportunity to motivate yourself and do better. Your naysayers are your biggest support.

Criticism and discouragement are the background music you need to reach your goals. Don't give up; don't stop trying. Take risks and dedicate your time to your dreams. It is important to remember that failure is not permanent, and it can be used as an opportunity to learn and grow. Learning how to cope with failure and how to use it to your advantage is key to developing success from it. It is important to recognize the lessons that can be learned from your failures and to use those lessons to build a more successful future. Failure can have a positive outcome, as it can help us to experience life from a different perspective. It can also give us the chance to try something new and to push ourselves out of our comfort zone.

By understanding that failure is a part of the process and that we can use it to grow and develop, you can start to create a more positive outlook on life and use it to develop success.

Don't let others stop you from achieving greatness!

Francesco Vitali

Your Notes for Success

84

"Success is peace of mind, which is a direct result of self-satisfaction in knowing you made an effort to become the best of which you are capable." — John Wooden.

Half of your success depends on your mindset. If you *are* satisfied with yourself and the work you put in, you will be unstoppable. But that means you must put in the work.

Success is the state of mind that results from the self-satisfaction in being confident that you have done your best and achieved your goals. It is about feeling contentment and joy for the accomplishments you have achieved and for the journey that has taken you to get there. It is about having a sense of fulfillment and knowing that you are truly living your life to the fullest. When you have found success in this way, it is something that no one can take away from you.

Work hard to make sure *you* are happy. The goal is to be proud of yourself. There's no fruit that tastes sweeter than the fruit of self-satisfaction. In the end, you feel accomplished and content that you never gave up, even when things got tough. You'll give yourself a pat on the back for getting through. Give it your all, and you will feel proud of yourself for putting your best foot forward and never giving up. You deserve to feel proud of where you are today.

Francesco Vitali

Your Notes for Success

85

"I never dreamed about success. I worked for it."
— *Estée Lauder*

Just dreaming of success will not do. You need to put in the effort to get there as well. Work hard to achieve your dreams; don't let them stay dreams.

You have what it takes to become successful. Don't worry about accomplishing your goal in one go or all the work it'll take. Just take things one step at a time. Working hard can also lead to personal growth as you develop new skills and knowledge, and build relationships with colleagues. It can also help you achieve your goals and dreams and make a positive impact on your professional life. Therefore, it's essential for success.

If we are determined to succeed, we should not be afraid to take risks and try new things. We must be persistent in our efforts and never give up. We should also be open to new ideas and learn from our mistakes. It is important to focus on the present and accomplish the tasks at hand. Even though success is not achieved overnight, it is something that we can achieve if we persevere.

Take baby steps and do what you need to do in order to keep going. Focus on one goal at a time.

Francesco Vitali

Your Notes for Success

86

"Opportunity is missed by most people because it is dressed in overalls and looks like work." — *Thomas Edison*

Don't wait for the opportunity to knock on your door. Seize it when the time is right. You need to put in the effort and work to find success.

Work is hard, and if it isn't, then you aren't doing it right. So don't shy away from putting in the elbow grease! Make every day count. The reason most people miss a golden opportunity is because you need to put in a lot of effort. But remember that patience is a virtue. Do the work, don't expect it to be easy, and opportunities will find you.

Opportunity can be the most rewarding experience of all, and the only way to get there is to put in the effort. Taking advantage of the opportunities that come your way can help you grow and reach heights you never thought possible. So don't let the overalls fool you; take the time to recognize the opportunity and give it your all. Having the right attitude, a desire to learn, and a willingness to help can take you a long way. Even if you are not the most skilled person in the room, you can still contribute significantly by being a hard-working team player and offering your support!

Francesco Vitali

Your Notes for Success

87

"Setting goals is the first step in turning the invisible into the visible." — Tony Robbins

Life is too short to not chase after your dreams. Don't hesitate to take risks. But make sure you play it smart. Plan everything out; take baby steps.

Goals give us something tangible to work toward and a way to measure our progress. Goals should be realistic and achievable, with a clear timeline and measurable steps. It's also important to break your goals down into smaller, more manageable chunks. This will make it easier to stay motivated and on track.

Focus on achieving one goal at a time so you don't rush through anything. Remember that you can't achieve success overnight. It takes time, perseverance, and patience. Failing isn't an option, it's a challenge to keep going until the goal is achieved. Patience is key when it comes to success, as it can take time for the fruits of one's labor to be realized. Perseverance is also essential because it takes repeated effort to overcome any obstacle that may stand in the way. Do not let the fear of failure stop you from trying. Do not give up on the dreams you want to achieve—turn the invisible into the visible! Have faith and patience, and you can achieve anything.

Francesco Vitali

Your Notes for Success

88

"Great things are not accomplished by those who sit and wait; they are achieved by those who take action and make them happen." — Thomas Jefferson

Opportunities are present all around you as well; you just need to learn how to identify and step into them.

Whether you're an entrepreneur embarking on your next business idea or a visionary simply wanting to start a new quest in your professional life, you don't need to wait for an opportunity to knock on your door. You need to create that opportunity.

By knowing yourself and making a conscious effort to push forward, you can create your own opportunities or find ones that fit what you're looking for. In order to create opportunities in life, you must be proactive and take action. You can do this by setting goals, taking risks, reaching out to people, networking, and being persistent. You must be willing to put in the effort and take advantage of any situations that arise. It is important to remain open-minded, flexible, and willing to try something new.

Opportunities are out there, but you must be willing to put in the work and create them. If you don't prepare for opportunities, you'll miss out on a chance of a lifetime when they arrive. Tackle every challenge by giving it your all, and before you know it, success will be at your feet.

Francesco Vitali

Your Notes for Success

89

"I do not know anyone who has got to the top without hard work. That is the recipe. It will not always get you to the top, but should get you pretty near." — Margaret Thatcher

When it comes to success, there are no shortcuts. You have to be ready to give it your all. The main ingredients you need are hard work, perseverance, and dedication. Along with a positive attitude, there is nothing we can't do once we put our mind to it. Once you take the first step, don't look back! The only way is forward. You won't always succeed even if you put your best foot forward, but remember that if you try your best, you won't have any regrets either.

Giving it your all will open the Gates of Opportunity for you. Success doesn't come easy; you need to be patient with yourself and keep working hard. But once you taste it, all of your struggles will be worth it. Celebrate each and every milestone. Remind yourself that you have come this far because you are capable and there is no one else like you.

Create clear goals that will lead you to your destination. But don't falter; don't get distracted. The journey to success will not be easy and you will come across thorns. But as long as you don't give up and keep moving forward, you can take on any hurdle that comes your way!

Francesco Vitali

Your Notes for Success

90

"He who conquers himself is the mightiest warrior."
— Confucius

He who conquers himself is the most successful, because the only person you're truly in competition with is yourself. It is a challenge to overcome our own fears and doubts. It is a battle to break the chains of our own negative thoughts. But when we finally break those chains, we have conquered our own inner demons and can truly experience success. We can then use our newfound strength to take on any challenges thrown our way and be better equipped to tackle them. It takes courage and determination, but the reward is worth it.

When we take the time to focus on the positive and choose to believe in our own potential, we can reach great heights. A positive mindset is incredibly powerful and can open up many possibilities. When we conquer our negative mindset, we unlock our true potential. This is the key to success. This is why it is so important to focus on positive thinking and be mindful of our thoughts. We have the power to create a better world, and it starts with conquering our own internal fears and doubts. When we do this, we open the door to a world of possibilities and a successful future.

Francesco Vitali

<u>*Your Notes for Success*</u>

91

"However difficult life may seem, there is always
something you can do and succeed at."
— Stephen Hawking

Just because one thing didn't work out for you doesn't mean there won't be other opportunities. When one door closes, a dozen others open. Look for those other doors.

There is *always* something we can do and excel at. Don't stick to one plan. Make Plan B, C, and D.

It's not enough to just dream about success; you have to take the necessary steps to make it a reality. This includes setting realistic goals, making an action plan, and then taking consistent and persistent action. You need to be prepared to work hard and make sacrifices, but the rewards of achieving your goals will be worth it. Don't just think about success; work for it, and you will achieve it. However difficult a situation may seem, there is always something you can do and succeed at. It just takes hard work, dedication, and a positive attitude.

Through hard work and dedication, you can develop the skills and confidence to tackle even the most difficult of situations. It's important to remember that even if the outcome isn't what you expected, you still have the power to take control of the situation and come out better on the other side.

Francesco Vitali

<u>Your Notes for Success</u>

92

"Action is the foundational key to all success."
— *Pablo Picasso*

Don't just dream about success, work for it!

Your dreams won't come to life until you put work into them. Don't lose focus. Manifest positive thoughts so you remember you're powerful, capable, and destined to achieve greatness. Once you take the initiative to change your mindset and routine, the rest will come easy.

You have to take the necessary steps to make it a reality. This includes setting realistic goals, making an action plan, and then taking consistent and persistent action. You need to be prepared to put in the effort, even when you feel you can't go on, but the success you'll achieve will be all the sweeter in the end.

Don't just think about success; achieve it by making it happen. Believe in yourself and set goals that are attainable. Break down these goals into smaller, more manageable steps, and work diligently toward them. With every step, you will be one step closer to your goal. Surround yourself with positive people and stay focused on the end goal. Be patient with yourself and trust in the process. Remember, success does not happen overnight and is a result of hard work and dedication. In the end, what matters is what we do, not what we say we will do.

Your Notes for Success

93

"Success is no accident." — Pele

Success is never an accident; it is the result of hard work and dedication.

Those who seek success must be willing to put in the work and make the necessary sacrifices. Success requires a sustained effort, and it is the result of remaining disciplined and focused on the long-term goal. It is possible to achieve success despite any obstacles or challenges one may face. Success is most often earned through dedication and perseverance, and it is a reward that can make all the hard work and dedication worth it. Success is not something that can be accomplished overnight; it requires commitment and a strong work ethic.

It takes the willingness to take risks and make sacrifices to reach the top. It is a journey of self-discovery, one that requires a person to challenge themselves and push their boundaries. The rewards of success are immense, and it is often the satisfaction of achieving a goal that is the most rewarding part. Success is not something that happens easily; it requires patience, perseverance, and a strong sense of purpose. It is a journey that requires one to take calculated risks and remain focused on the end goal. With a combination of hard work and dedication, success is within reach.

Francesco Vitali

Your Notes for Success

94

"The real risk is doing nothing." — Denis Waitley

The journey of success is not a straight line. There will be obstacles in your way. Sometimes, we'll need to take a step back before taking two more forward. That's why it's important to take consistent and deliberate action—no matter how small—in order to move forward. There is no secret recipe for success, but with hard work and dedication, you can create a life of success and fulfillment.

Taking action is the only way to make progress and turn dreams into reality. When you take action, you are no longer a passive bystander in your own professional life, but an active participant. You learn from your mistakes, take risks, and have the courage to persist no matter what obstacles may come your way. You have full control over everything and you can turn any situation into a victory.

Taking action is the only way to prove yourself and to move closer toward your goals. Success is not something that can happen overnight, but with a consistent effort, it can be yours. You can make it through the situations that are testing you mentally. You can overcome the difficulties and challenges you are facing. The only thing you can't do is do nothing.

Francesco Vitali

Your Notes for Success

95

"Success is most often achieved by those who don't know that failure is inevitable." — *Coco Chanel*

Those who have achieved great success in life have often done so by embracing the idea that failure is inevitable. They understand that in order to succeed, you must be willing to take risks and accept the fact that failure will happen along the way. They also strive to learn and grow from their mistakes, using each failure as a stepping stone to reach their goals. By being open to failure and learning from it, they have been able to achieve levels of success that they may not have otherwise.

Success is an attainable goal for anyone who is willing to put in the effort. It is most often achieved by those who don't accept failure as an option and use it to their advantage. Instead of being discouraged by short-term setbacks, they use them as an opportunity to learn and grow. Those who strive for success understand that failure is inevitable, and use it as a valuable lesson on the path to their goal. They take risks, push their boundaries, and never give up, even when the going gets tough.

So, don't be scared of taking risks; don't be scared of rejection. Your perseverance will take you to the finish line and help you achieve greatness!

Francesco Vitali

Your Notes for Success

96

"Failures are the stairs we climb to reach success."
— *Roy T. Bennett*

Failure is something we should never fear. It is part of the journey to success and should be embraced. But we must learn from our failures, so that we don't make them again.

Failures are simply stepping stones on the path to success. Every time we fail at something, we learn a valuable lesson and gain knowledge that we can use to do better next time. When we experience a failure, it's a chance to learn, reflect, and refocus our energy on what we need to do to make sure it won't happen again. Each failure is an opportunity to do better, and to gain new knowledge and insight. We learn from our mistakes and grow stronger, wiser, and more resilient. Ultimately, it is these failures that will help us reach our ultimate goal of success.

So, never give up. Keep climbing. Every step taken is one step closer to the top. Each step taken is one more step closer to achieving the ultimate goal. Having the right attitude and mindset is key to getting the results you want. Have faith in yourself and be sure to celebrate each step taken, because it means that you're the closest to victory you've ever been.

Your Notes for Success

97

"If you really look closely, most overnight successes took a long time." — Steve Jobs

No matter what the world wants you to believe, remember that it's hard work, grit, and perseverance that leads to success. The successful people we look up to today were in our shoes not that long ago. The difference is that they continued to not only chase after their dreams, but put in the effort to make them come true.

It's not just luck that plays a crucial role in success; it's also grabbing the right opportunity, making on-the-spot decisions, and taking risks. It's not always rainbows and butterflies. Feed your focus and starve your distractions. Don't let anything that isn't going to contribute to your success slow you down. Remember that you are bound for greatness and this journey is yours, and yours alone. Set small goals, minimize distractions, manage your time efficiently, and define your purpose. You need to have clarity and figure out where you want to stand in the future. When you have a clear vision of where you want to be, things will become streamlined and easier. Before you know it, success will be at your feet.

So don't look at just the big picture and what's in front of you. Look at what's behind the curtains, and dedicate yourself to achieving your dreams.

Francesco Vitali

Your Notes for Success

98

*"The successful man will profit from his mistakes and
try again in a different way." — Dale Carnegie*

The successful person has the courage and resilience to not only learn from their mistakes but to use them as a way to propel themself forward. They know that there is always a way around a problem and will use their experiences to come up with a different solution. They will use their mistakes as a learning experience and will not let mistakes define them. Instead, they will use them as a platform to build upon and as a source of inspiration.

Mistakes will become fuel to strive for greater success. Success only comes through hard work and dedication, and the successful person will use their mistakes to get there. They have the courage and resilience to not only learn from their mistakes, but to use them as a way to propel themself forward. They understand that failure is a part of life, and that it can be an opportunity to grow and become better. They know that every challenge is an opportunity to prove themself and that nothing worthwhile is ever achieved without taking risks. They are always willing to take the initiative and try something new, and they are always open to learning and improving. The successful person is confident in their abilities, and they are determined to reach their goals no matter what the obstacles may be.

Your Notes for Success

99

"The test of success is not what you do when you are on top. Success is how high you bounce when you hit the bottom." — *George S. Patton*

Success is not only about achieving greatness, but also about overcoming challenges and bouncing back from failure. The test of success is not just what you do when you are on top, but how resilient you are when you hit the bottom. It is about the courage and strength to pick yourself up and move forward, despite the challenges and obstacles in your way. No matter how far, deep, or dark the bottom is, the real measure of success is the resilience and determination you show in the face of adversity.

Successful people never give up on their dreams and aspirations. They keep bouncing even when the world is pushing them down. They have a clear vision of what they want to achieve and refuse to be deterred by any obstacles or setbacks. They stay focused, work hard, and stay motivated even when faced with challenging times. They are able to stay positive, even in the midst of failure and disappointment. They understand that failure is part of the process and use it as an opportunity to learn and grow. They never stop trying, no matter how difficult the goal may seem.

So, forget about what the rest of the world has to say. Do what you need to do to make your dreams come true.

Francesco Vitali

Your Notes for Success

100

"Success will be within your reach only when you start reaching out for it." — *Stephen Richards*

Success is something that can only be achieved by those who are willing to put in the work. It is not something that will come easily and is not for the faint of heart; it requires dedication, hard work, and commitment. But when you start reaching out for it, you will find that success is within your reach. You must be willing to put in the time and energy to get what you want.

Don't be afraid to take risks and try new things; you never know what may come of it. With each step, you will gain experience and knowledge that will help you move closer to your desired outcome. With the right mindset, you can achieve anything you set your mind to. Surround yourself with colleagues who will motivate and inspire you to keep working hard.

Believe in yourself and your dreams, and success will be within your reach. Have faith in yourself and the world around you. Know that you can achieve anything you set your mind to. Believe that you can be successful in life and you will be. You are capable of greatness and you will be unstoppable. Follow your heart and trust in your vision.

Your Notes for Success

101

"It's failure that gives you the proper perspective on success." — Ellen DeGeneres

It's not about how much we can achieve, but how much we learn from our mistakes. Failure teaches us that we need to be patient and stay focused on our goals, no matter how difficult it may seem. Not only that, but failure can serve as a stepping stone to success. Every failure is a lesson, and every lesson can help us take one step closer to our ultimate goal. Success is not about never failing, but about learning from our failures and developing a positive attitude and resilience to keep pushing forward.

When you fail, you can assess what went wrong and how you can do things differently in order to be successful. You can also learn to appreciate the successes you had along the way, as well as the successes of others. Remember that the only person you should compete with is yourself. You are always trying to do better than you did yesterday. It's important to stay resilient and to keep pushing forward after a failure, because that is what will ultimately lead to success. Failure is not the end, it's the beginning of the journey toward success. So, don't give up, don't stop, and you will reach your destination!

Francesco Vitali

Your Notes for Success

102

"A successful man is one who can lay a firm foundation
with the bricks others have thrown at him."
— David Brinkley

A successful person is one who can take even the most difficult of challenges and turn them into opportunities. They are able to see the potential of each challenge and use it to their advantage.

They are resilient and confident in their abilities, never giving up on their goals. They are able to take the bricks that others have thrown at them and build a strong and reliable foundation. They are determined, focused, and have the courage to take risks when necessary. They are a leader and an inspiration to those around them. They strive for excellence and are driven by their passion to achieve great things. They understand that success is not a destination, but a journey that requires hard work, dedication, and resilience.

In order to succeed, one should be able to turn any challenge into a victory. Make use of the tools and resources you have available, and work toward turning your weaknesses into strengths. Focus on the skills you need to hone and keep improving yourself. But remember to be patient with yourself; there's a reason why it's called "the journey of success." You won't get there overnight, but when you *do* reach your destination, it will all be worth it!

Francesco Vitali

<u>*Your Notes for Success*</u>

103

*"The backbone of success is hard work, determination,
good planning, and perseverance." — Mia Hamm*

Without hard work, determination, skillful planning, and perseverance, you won't get where you want to be. These are the four major components that are needed to achieve long-term success. Hard work is essential as it requires dedication and effort to push through difficult times. Determination is crucial as it allows one to stay focused and motivated. Skillful planning is necessary to ensure that the desired outcome is reached in the most efficient and effective way. Perseverance is the foundation on which success is built and the only way to make progress.

Take the initiative to push yourself, stay focused and motivated during difficult times, and never give up. Don't listen to the criticism from others, unless it's constructive feedback.

Remember that you are capable of doing anything you set your mind to. Remind yourself of your strengths and use them to your advantage. Celebrate the small successes along the way, as they will motivate you to keep going. Develop a positive attitude and never give up, no matter how hard it gets.

Lastly, skillful planning ensures that one is organized, prepared, and able to handle any obstacles that may arise. With skillful planning, hard work, determinization, and perseverance, success is attainable.

Your Notes for Success

104

"Hustle is essential for sensational success." — Anuj Jasani

Hustle is the spark that ignites the flame of success and the fuel that keeps it burning. It is the drive that moves us forward, the ambition that propels us to reach our goals, and the passion that keeps us motivated. Without hustle there is no success, and without success, there is no happiness.

Hustle is the force that pushes us to go above and beyond in order to get the reward we seek. So, no matter what you do, make sure that you give it your all and always hustle, every day.

Every day is an opportunity to work hard and strive toward success. It is essential to believe in yourself and have faith that hard work will pay off. Hustling always eventually leads to success. It helps build self-confidence and can make us feel more capable of tackling any challenge. It instills a sense of discipline and perseverance, which are key components of success. The effort we put in is what we get out in the end, and the hustle is the foundation of any success.

So don't give up; don't stop chasing after your dreams, and keep pushing forward so you can get to the finish line!

Francesco Vitali

Your Notes for Success

105

"Rest to refresh yourself but do not stop until you find a way to succeed." — Lailah Gifty Akita

Taking a break from your work can help you focus better and find creative solutions to any obstacles that you may face. When we make time to rest, it gives us an opportunity to re-energize and refresh ourselves. It helps us to stay motivated and focused on our goals. Taking time to rest allows us to gain perspective, find new solutions, and have the energy to tackle the challenges ahead. When we take time to rest, we are able to think more clearly and come up with creative solutions to problems. We also have more energy to devote to the tasks that matter. Resting allows us to take a break from the hustle and bustle of life and just relax.

However, it is important to remember that rest is not an excuse to avoid confronting challenges. Instead, use it as an opportunity to recharge and come back with a fresh perspective and renewed determination to find a way to succeed. Your mental well-being is just as important. When your mind is well-rested, that's when you'll be able to give it your all. So, take the time to rest, but don't stop until you find a way to reach your goal.

Francesco Vitali

<u>*Your Notes for Success*</u>

106

"Progress is not always rapid, in fact, sometimes it moves at a 'snail's pace.'" — Dr. B

Progress is never easy, and rarely is it fast. It's as if each step forward is a struggle, and you have to push against the wall of resistance to move ahead. At times, progress feels like it's moving at a snail's pace, and it can be extremely frustrating. But it is still progress, and if you remain vigilant and focused, you will eventually get to the finish line. It doesn't matter if it's slow. What matters is that it's steady.

It takes time to build something great, and it takes even more patience to see it through. Every day, we are actively striving to become better versions of ourselves and collectively, as a team, we are making progress. We may not see it right away, but each action we take—whether big or small—is helping to move us forward.

Don't be discouraged by the slowness of progress, instead embrace it, for taking your time to do things right will only make your end product that much better. We can be proud of the progress we are making and encouraged that the future holds even more.

As long as we keep our eyes on the prize, no matter how long it takes, we will eventually reach our goal.

Francesco Vitali

<u>*Your Notes for Success*</u>

107

"Your success is your responsibility, nobody else's."
— *Brajesh Kumar Singh*

Nobody else can be responsible for your success. You are the only one who can make it happen. Taking responsibility for your own success means that you are willing to go the extra mile and put in the hard work to achieve your goals. You are the only one who can determine how much effort you put in and how much you get out. It means taking ownership of your decisions and understanding that the outcome of your choices will be dependent on your own actions.

Success is not something that is given to you. It is something that you create for yourself. It takes dedication, consistency, and a positive attitude to make it happen.

Having a good attitude and a positive mindset are key components to success, as well as having a good support system. Take the time to reflect on your progress and celebrate your successes. Every small victory should be celebrated, as it will bring you one step closer to your ultimate success.

Taking ownership of your success is the key to unlocking your full potential. You have the power to make your dreams come true, and success is within your reach. All you have to do is take the first step and never look back.

Francesco Vitali

Your Notes for Success

108

"The route to success often has a pariah phase along the way." — Steven Magee

The route to success is often filled with unexpected twists and turns and sometimes even a pariah phase. That is, sometimes, people you know may turn against you. However, it is important to remember that this pariah phase is just a part of the journey and it should not be seen as a sign of failure. Instead, it should be seen as an opportunity to learn, grow, and eventually find our way back to success. Don't feel discouraged; use it to your advantage. Use it to self-reflect and figure out ways to improve yourself.

It is a time when you must be focused on your goals and be resilient in the face of adversity. With this in mind, the pariah phase should be embraced as an opportunity to learn and grow, to build strength and character, and to ultimately become successful. Believe in yourself, in your goals, and in your vision. You'll be able to tackle any obstacle that comes your way. You have what it takes to make it through anything. No matter what anyone says, don't give up hope. The road to success has a lot of twists and turns, but it's worth every challenge.

With hard work and dedication, you can turn hurdles into a positive experience that leads to lasting success.

Your Notes for Success

109

"Failure is a part of life. Success teaches you nothing, but failure teaches you resilience. It teaches you to pick yourself up and try again." — Sarah Morgan

Success is fleeting, but failure can be a powerful teacher. It teaches you to be resilient and to never give up. Failure shows you that it's okay to make mistakes and that you can still come out the other side. It helps to build character and it encourages you to take calculated risks. Failure also makes success even better, as it makes you appreciate it more and gives you the motivation to continue striving for your goals.

It is only through failure that you can truly reach your highest potential. Failure teaches us to accept ourselves the way we are and not be harsh or critical of ourselves. It's a catalyst for professional growth, and reminds us that we can do a lot more than what we believe we are capable of doing.

Failure can also be a reminder that even when things don't go our way, we can still remain positive and keep going. Failure builds character and helps us to grow as individuals. It can be a great opportunity to learn something new and use it to create success in the future. Most importantly, it's how we develop resilience. So, don't be afraid of failure, embrace it and use it to reach your goals.

Francesco Vitali

Your Notes for Success

110

"We learn from failure, not from success!" — *Bram Stoker*

We learn from failure, not from success. Failure allows us to explore our limitations, push our boundaries and gain valuable insight into what we can do differently in the future. By taking risks and not being afraid to fail, we can grow and become better in our endeavors. By understanding the lessons failure can teach us, we can become more successful by learning how to better manage our expectations and take calculated risks. We can never be perfect, but we can get close to perfection!

Failure is not something to fear, but rather an opportunity to learn and grow. There isn't a single successful person who hasn't made a mistake in their life. They are where they are today because they were able to learn from their mistakes and improve. From Bill Gates to Jeff Bezos, the people who are on top of the world right now started from the bottom. They made their way up by constantly improving themselves. They kept pushing their limits and working toward getting better and better.

By understanding that failure is just a part of our professional life, we can develop the strength to keep going and push through our struggles in order to achieve our goals.

Francesco Vitali

Your Notes for Success

111

"Failure is not the opposite of success, it's part of success." — Arianna Huffington

Failure is an essential part of success. It is a valuable lesson in life that can teach us important things. Through failure we learn how to grow, how to be better and stronger, and how to strive for success.

We figure out things that don't work in our favor and we learn to prepare for tougher challenges that will come our way in the future. We learn to take risks, to believe in ourselves, and to have faith in our abilities.

No one ever achieved success without any failures. In fact, successful people have a higher chance of failing than other people.

With each failure, we gain a better understanding of ourselves and what we are capable of. By embracing failure and viewing it as an important part of our journey to success, we can make mistakes, learn from them, and continue to reach our goals. The more we experience failure, the more confidence we gain in our resilience and ability to overcome any obstacle.

So, don't give up on achieving your goals just because you failed once. Or twice. Or a hundred times. You can do so much better than you think! Get back up, get into the game, and try once again!

Francesco Vitali

<u>*Your Notes for Success*</u>

112

"Failure is simply the opportunity to begin again, this time more intelligently." — *Henry Ford*

Failure is a powerful teacher and should be embraced, not feared. Failure is simply the opportunity to begin again, this time more intelligently. It gives us the chance to reflect on our mistakes, learn from them, and make adjustments to our approach. Failure is a necessary part of growth and development and a way to gain valuable insight into ourselves and our goals. It allows us to adjust our course and change our path.

With each failure, we become more experienced, more aware, and more capable of succeeding in the future.

Instead of seeing failure as a negative experience, it's important to embrace it as an opportunity to grow, learn, and ultimately become more successful. A lot of people have negative feelings about failure, but it is not a sign of weakness. Instead, it's a sign of strength—so long as you keep going. It means we have the courage to take risks and try new things. If you fail, don't give up. There is no greater feeling than pushing through failure and achieving success.

So, don't be afraid to take risks and to make mistakes. With the right attitude and an open mind, failure can be a powerful tool for growth.

Francesco Vitali

Your Notes for Success

113

"A minute's success pays the failure of years."
— *Robert Browning*

Success can be hard to come by, but it is always worth striving for. One minute of success can make up for the failure of years. It might not erase all the hardships and struggles, but it can remind you that success is possible, and that everything was worth it. Every small victory is a reminder that you can achieve anything, no matter how long it takes. Keep pushing forward, and never give up on your dreams. With hard work and dedication, you will reach your goals eventually. Remember, years of failure will be wiped away in one minute of success.

Believe in yourself and the power of small successes.

One successful moment can be the key to opening the door to many more successes in the future.

Those who are successful are known for having a positive mindset. They don't believe in giving up or giving in to their failures. They believe in taking each challenge as an opportunity.

Even when we stumble and fail, it is important to keep going and to remember that success will come. With every setback, we should learn and grow, and strive to become greater than we were before.

So stay motivated and keep pushing forward—success is within your reach!

Your Notes for Success

114

*"I can accept failure, everyone fails at something. But
I can't accept not trying." — Michael Jordan*

Failing is inevitable in life, but never let it stop you from trying. You can learn a great deal from failure, and it can be a great motivator to push you to do better and be stronger. Remind yourself that failure is part of the process and it is simply a necessary step on the path to success. Don't be afraid of it or let it drag you down. Instead, use it as a learning experience and an opportunity to grow and become even better. Remember, you can always try again, and you can always succeed. Success comes from persistence and hard work, and it's important to never give up. Even if you fail, you can draw strength from the fact that you tried.

Find ways to stay motivated and focused, and keep pushing forward. Believe in yourself and your abilities, and you can make anything happen. Visualize your success, and take small steps each day to get closer to achieving your goals. Persevere, stay resilient, and never give up! Even if you feel like you are failing, keep going, and eventually you will find success.

As long as you keep trying and never give up, you are well on your way to success.

Francesco Vitali

Your Notes for Success

115

"Impossible is just an opinion." — Paulo Coelho

Completely remove the word "impossible" from your dictionary. A few years ago, you didn't think it was possible to be where you are right now. But here you are, standing tall, unstoppable and successful. We are the ones who set a limit to our abilities and our mind. Don't for a second think or believe that you don't have what it takes to be successful. Every person has a unique set of abilities, strengths, and skills. You are no different—and yet, you are. Don't let anyone tell you that your ideas are impossible to achieve. Don't let anyone's opinion distract you from pursuing your goals. Remember that that's all they are—opinions. They are not set in stone; they are not hard facts. Nobody knows you better than yourself!

If the Wright Brothers, Elon Musk, Steve Jobs, and Jeff Bezos listened to others, they wouldn't have changed the course of history. Like them, you will always encounter naysayers. You will always have people doubting you. What's important is that you don't doubt yourself.

So don't let anyone tell you you're not capable, because you know you are. Don't give up; there's always light at the end of the tunnel.

Francesco Vitali

Your Notes for Success

116

"We all have a few failures under our belt. It's what makes us ready for the successes." — *Randy K. Milholland*

We all have experienced failure at some point in our lives. Every single one of us. But these disappointments should not be seen as a negative thing. Instead, they should be seen as an essential part of life that prepares us for success. They provide us with valuable lessons in resilience and determination. Through our failures, we gain the courage and strength to face our future successes. Failing is not the end of the world, but it can be the beginning of something great. Everyone has the capacity to learn from their mistakes and push forward with a positive attitude. With each failure, we gain the courage, wisdom, and strength to take on whatever the future throws our way.

In the end, it's our mistakes that will be the driving force that leads us to success. Our mistakes give us valuable lessons and insights that can be used to better ourselves and our work. We must believe in ourselves and our abilities, for it is our failures that will help us reach our goals. So, don't belittle yourself every time you fail; remind yourself that it is human to err, and what matters is that you get back up after tumbling!

Francesco Vitali

Your Notes for Success

117

"Just because you fail once, doesn't mean you're gonna fail at everything. Keep trying, hold on, and always, always, always believe in yourself, because if you don't, then who will?" — Marilyn Monroe

Failing can feel like a setback, but it doesn't have to define you. Just because you fail once doesn't mean you're going to fail every time. Even if you fail ninety-nine times, you can achieve success on the hundredth. Failure is a part of life and it is important to learn from it. Instead of being bogged down by it, use it as an opportunity to grow and become a better version of yourself. Everyone makes mistakes and has to learn from them.

If you have the courage to keep trying, you'll eventually get it right. You never know what lies ahead, but you can trust that your effort will pay off. No matter what, never give up on yourself. Hold on to your faith and always believe in yourself. You can accomplish what you set your mind to, and prove to yourself that you can do it.

It's okay to make mistakes and stumble along the way, it's all part of the journey. It may take time and effort, but you can do it! Don't let your failures define you—use them as motivation to keep going and never stop believing in yourself. You can do anything you put your mind to!

Francesco Vitali

<u>*Your Notes for Success*</u>

118

"You always pass failure on your way to success."
— *Mickey Rooney*

On our way to success, we'll pass by many failures. And that's how we should think of them: as things we move beyond. It's a reminder that you don't always have to get it right the first time, that it's okay to make mistakes, and that you can always use those experiences to grow, and make better future decisions. It's also a reminder that there's no one single path to success. Every journey is different, and even when things don't go as planned, you can still reach your goal if you keep pushing and never give up.

Don't be afraid of failure. Don't let it get you down; instead, use it as a stepping stone to success. Think of it as something natural that happens to everyone. It's important to stay motivated and never give up—even if it feels like you're not making any progress.

Instead of allowing failure to discourage you, use it as a stepping stone to achieve your goals. Every time you come up against a setback, take it as a sign that you are getting closer to success. No matter how many times you fail, you will always come out stronger and wiser on the other side. You will eventually become invincible!

Francesco Vitali

Your Notes for Success

119

"Successful people don't fear failure but understand
that it's necessary to learn and grow from."
— *Robert Kiyosaki*

Successful people know that failure is an inevitable part of the journey to success. Rather than fear failure, they use it as an opportunity to learn and grow, knowing that it will make them a better person in the long run. They understand that failure is not a sign of weakness, but rather a necessity in order to reach their goals. They also use failure to help identify their weaknesses and work on improving them. With this mindset, successful people are able to take risks and stay motivated, knowing that failure is not the end, but part of the process of reaching their ultimate goals.

Moreover, ambitious and successful people understand the importance of failure in their journey to success. They know that failure can be a valuable lesson and an opportunity to learn and grow. They don't let it interfere with their goals and ambitions, but rather use it as an opportunity to become stronger and wiser. With the right attitude and a positive mindset, failure can be a stepping stone to success. So, don't be afraid of failure—embrace it, learn from it, and use it as a catalyst to achieve success.

You need to be resilient and resourceful, turning each mistake into an opportunity to learn and improve. With this, you'll be on your way to achieving greatness.

Francesco Vitali

Your Notes for Success

120

"Failure will never overtake me if my determination to succeed is strong enough." — Og Mandino"

Disappointment is a natural part of life, but it doesn't have to stop you from achieving your dreams. With determination and perseverance, you can turn any setback into an opportunity for growth. When you are determined to succeed, disappointment will never overtake you, no matter how hard you try. Your determination is the fuel that propels you forward, no matter how many times you stumble or how often you are met with challenges or resistance.

You are making a conscious effort to move forward and that is the most important thing. You must believe in yourself and never give up. Even when the odds are against you, keep pushing forward. Even if you experience severe disappointment, know that it's just a step on the way to success.

It might take a bit longer than you imagined, but you will get there. Believe in yourself and your goals. No matter how many times you experience disappointment, never give up on yourself. You have the power to keep going and to make your dreams come true. You can be successful if you stay focused and never stop believing in yourself. So, don't give up; be proud of your efforts and have faith in your abilities. With enough determination, disappointments will never overtake you.

Francesco Vitali

Your Notes for Success

121

"Do not judge me by my successes, judge me by how many times I fell down and got back up again."
— *Nelson Mandela*

We all have successes and failures, but what separates us is our ability to not give up when things get tough. Everyone has an idea of what success looks like, but it's important to remember that success can come in many different forms. Instead of judging others by their successes, look at the times they didn't give up even when their success seemed impossible. Those moments will often tell you more about a person than their accomplishments ever could. People who keep going despite difficult circumstances are often the ones who have the most meaningful and lasting impact.

Those moments of persistence, courage and strength are what truly make someone strong and show their resilience. We all have the capacity to make something of ourselves, no matter our circumstances. It is those who have the courage to keep going despite the odds who will eventually achieve greatness. We must remember to celebrate that perseverance and strength, and not only the achievement. Everyone should be appreciated for the effort they put in and the difficulties they overcame to get there.

So never judge someone by what they achieved, but rather by how they kept going in the face of adversity.

Your Notes for Success

122

"It's fine to celebrate success, but it is more important to heed the lessons of failure." — Bill Gates

The road to success can be long, winding and tough, but it's important to always remember that it's just as important to learn from failure. Celebrating successes is a great way to stay motivated, but it's also important to take a step back reflect on any failures and use them as a learning experience. Failure can be a great teacher, providing us with valuable insights and motivation to reach our goals.

By seeing failure in this way, you open yourself up to better understanding yourself and your capabilities, as well as the potential of what could be achieved. Learning from mistakes and failures helps to develop resilience, and it is this resilience that is key to achieving success.

Failure can provide us with valuable insight and help us to develop our skills and knowledge. With failure, we can learn where we need to improve, and become better equipped to take on future challenges. Ultimately, it is essential to recognize and celebrate successes, but learning from failure is just as important.

So, it's fine to celebrate success and achievements, but don't forget that it is more important to heed the lessons of failure. This is the perspective you'll need to succeed.

Francesco Vitali

Your Notes for Success

123

"Success or failure is caused more by mental attitude than by mental capacity." — Walter Scott

Your attitude is like a spark that ignites the fire of success within you. It shapes the way you think, feel, and act in various situations. A positive attitude gives you the enthusiasm and courage to take on the challenges of your career head-on and to make the most of every opportunity. On the other hand, a negative attitude will make you feel defeated and alone, hindering your progress in your professional life.

The right attitude can take you to unimaginable heights. You can achieve anything you set your mind to, provided you have the right mindset and outlook. It is important to remember that success or failure is ultimately determined by one's own mindset. No matter what life throws at us, if we stay focused and keep a positive attitude, we can overcome any obstacle and reach our goals. As long as we keep pushing forward and don't give up, nothing is impossible. We can reach new heights of success and fulfill our dreams if we stay positive, stay motivated, and never lose sight of our goals.

Believe in yourself, focus on your goals, and stay determined to make it happen. This is the key to success and achieving your dreams.

Your Notes for Success

124

"If you are afraid of failure, you don't deserve to be successful." — Charles Barkley

Failure should not be feared, but welcomed as an opportunity to learn and grow. It takes courage to try and fail in order to come out on top.

Whenever you are faced with a challenge, don't let the fear of failure stop you from pushing forward. Instead, focus on the potential success you could achieve if you take the risk. Even if you are disappointed in the result, the experience will provide you with invaluable lessons that will help you succeed in the future.

Don't be afraid to take chances and learn from your mistakes. To be successful means to take risks, learn from your failures, and never let fear stop you from aiming higher. Remember that fear is a natural part of life and it should never stop you from pursuing your goals. That is how you will find success and become a better version of yourself. By taking risks, learning from your failures, and never letting fear stop you, you can become a successful individual and an inspiring leader.

Believe in yourself and your abilities and you will be able to conquer any obstacle that comes your way. All you need to do is embrace challenges and never give up!

Francesco Vitali

Your Notes for Success

125

"People who avoid failure also avoid success."
— *Robert T. Kiyosaki*

Failure is not something to be feared or avoided. In fact, it can be your greatest teacher. When you fail, you learn from your mistakes and use that knowledge to create a more successful path. With each instance of failure, you become more resilient and determined to succeed. You also become more creative in your problem-solving and more focused on what works and what doesn't.

Failure can be your greatest asset on the road to success.

You can also gain valuable insight into your strengths and weaknesses, allowing you to make more informed decisions in the future. In short, if you're willing to take risks and accept the possibility of failure, you can set yourself up for greater success down the road. Don't avoid failure—use it to your advantage. It is a valuable tool that can be used to learn, grow, and become stronger.

By embracing failure and using it to our advantage, we can unlock our potential and reach new heights. The key is to never give up and to use failure as an opportunity to improve and become better. With the right attitude and the right mindset, failure can prove to be a powerful motivator in helping us reach our goals.

Your Notes for Success

126

*"If you set your goals ridiculously high and it's a
failure, you will fail above everyone else's success."*
— James Cameron

If you set your goals ridiculously high, it can be a daunting task to reach them. But if you put in the hard work and dedication, you will be able to achieve the impossible. Even if you fail to reach your goals, you will still have achieved more than the average person; you will have failed above everyone else's success.

Professionalism is all about taking risks and learning from your mistakes. When you set goals that are too ambitious, you are taking a risk that could lead to great success. On the flip side, it can also be a huge learning experience if it doesn't go as expected. No one said that achieving these goals would be easy, but with the right attitude and mindset, you can do anything.

Take a deep breath and start working toward your goal. Anything is possible if you put your heart and mind into it. Remember, goals are not meant to be easy; they are meant to challenge and push you out of your comfort zone.

You will gain invaluable insight into what strategies and techniques work best for you. So, go ahead and set those high goals, and rise above all the other successes out there.

Francesco Vitali

Your Notes for Success

127

"One fails forward toward success." – Charles Kettering

Each failure presents the opportunity to learn and grow, allowing one to become wiser and more resilient. With every mistake, one is presented with a unique chance to take a step back assess the situation, and decide how to improve it. This is failing forward.

The process of failing forward encourages one to develop new strategies, gain new skills, and build a strong network of support. As one continues to push forward, the successes start to pile up, and the road to success becomes more and more attainable.

Failure doesn't mean that you're defeated, it just means you have to try something different. Success isn't a straight line but rather a series of small wins, losses, and lessons learned. By pushing through the hard times, you can start to see the light at the end of the tunnel. Change the way you view failure and you'll find yourself one step closer to success. Instead of seeing it as a wall, we should view it as a bridge that we can build on.

Let us all take this mindset and use it to our advantage so that we can reach our ultimate goals. With a positive attitude and perseverance, we can find success.

Your Notes for Success

128

"Success is the result of perfection, hard work, learning from failure, loyalty, and persistence." — *Colin Powell*

Success is not a destination but a journey, and it is the result of a perfect blend of hard work, learning from failure, loyalty, and persistence. It takes a great deal of dedication, determination, and resilience to work toward success, and these are qualities that cannot be learned overnight. Successful people have an unwavering commitment to their goals and never give up.

In order to be successful, you need to be committed to the cause, remain loyal to your goals, and persist in spite of the obstacles you may face. Learning from failure is a crucial part of the process, and you must use the lessons learned to make sure that you don't repeat the same mistake in the future. With the right attitude and mentality, success can be achieved, and the result will be something that you can be proud of. People should be determined to do whatever it takes to reach their goals. They should also be willing to learn from their mistakes and apply new strategies to achieve success. It is important to believe in oneself and to never give up. So, don't give up on your hopes and dreams, and eventually, you will get where you need to be.

Francesco Vitali

Your Notes for Success

129

"The difference between average people and achieving people is their perception of and response to failure."
— *John C. Maxwell*

Success can be elusive, but it starts by changing your perspective of failure. Rather than being something that should be avoided, failure should be understood as a chance to learn and grow. It can be a chance to identify our weaknesses and make positive changes that can help us reach our goals. Recognizing our mistakes, understanding why we failed, and learning from them can lead to success.

Think of failure as part of the path to success. Every mistake provides you with an opportunity to improve and become even more successful. With the right attitude and determination, failure can be a stepping stone to success.

It's important to always keep in mind that failure can be a valuable part of the journey to success. It doesn't have to be a negative experience. By embracing failure and using it to our advantage, we can become more successful in the long run. By learning from our mistakes and taking on new challenges with an open mind, we can make mistakes, learn from them, and move forward to achieve success. Failure can be a teacher, and with the right mindset, it can become a powerful tool to help us reach our goals.

Francesco Vitali

Your Notes for Success

130

"A person who never made a mistake never tried anything new." — Albert Einstein

Trying something new can be intimidating, but it's worth it in the end. Making a mistake is part of the learning process and gives you the opportunity to grow and become more confident in your abilities. So don't be afraid to make mistakes, because it gives you the chance to explore new things, find hidden talents, and discover new possibilities. Don't let fear or the fear of making a mistake hold you back from reaching your goals. Mistakes can be fun and even exciting; they help you learn and grow and push you out of your comfort zone.

Making mistakes can open up possibilities you never even knew existed. One mistake can lead to a new idea. So don't be afraid to take risks, and don't be too hard on yourself if you make a mistake. It's all part of the adventure of life. Taking risks can lead to incredible opportunities and amazing experiences.

Embrace the uncertainty and don't be too hard on yourself if you make a mistake. And don't be afraid to take the plunge and make bold moves. The rewards can be great; they can be better than you expected, and you may even surprise yourself by where they take you!

Francesco Vitali

<u>Your Notes for Success</u>

131

*"Stay away from those people who try to disparage
your ambitions. Small minds will always do that, but
great minds will give you a feeling that you can become
great too." — Mark Twain*

When it comes to achieving your ambitions, it is important to stay away from those who try to disparage them. Such people have small minds and will only bring you down, but those with great minds will have the power to inspire you to reach your goals. They will provide you with the motivation and support you need to make your dreams a reality. You don't need to prove yourself to the right people. Find the great minds who will help you become great too.

With the right kind of people in your corner, no matter how ambitious or difficult the task, it can be accomplished. So, seek out those who will lift you up and make sure to stay away from those who will try to bring you down. People who support and understand you can open up a world of possibilities and potential that would have otherwise been out of reach. With their help and support, you can reach heights you never thought were possible. Life is a team effort, and it is important that you surround yourself with people who will uplift and encourage you to reach your highest potential. So, only make room for those who have your best interest at heart!

Your Notes for Success

132

"It is only when we take chances, when our lives improve. The initial and the most difficult risk that we need to take is to become honest." — Walter Anderson

When we become honest with ourselves, we create a foundation for taking risks and ultimately improving our lives. By being honest with ourselves and with others, we open ourselves up to possibilities we may have never imagined. We can embrace new opportunities and make decisions that may have otherwise been too overwhelming to consider. We can see the world from a new perspective and uncover the potential for growth, development, and success.

When we take chances and become honest, we can ultimately create a career path that is more fulfilling and rewarding. We can become role models to those around and show them that it's honesty and integrity that paves the way for success. It's honest people who reap the benefits of the fruit of their labor.

That's the best way to improve ourselves, climb up the ladder of success, and open up our minds to the possibilities that await us. It is a risk that is definitely worth taking. It's the best way to reach the top. Be honest not only with others but with yourself as well. Analyze where you stand and what you need to do to improve, and before you know it, you'll be on your way to the top!

Your Notes for Success

133

"The pessimist sees difficulty in every opportunity.
The optimist sees opportunity in every difficulty."
— *Winston Churchill*

The saying that the optimist sees opportunity in every difficulty is so empowering and inspiring. It reminds us that no matter how tough the situation may be, there is always a way to turn it around and make something positive out of it. There is no challenge too great, no obstacle too difficult that we cannot overcome with the right attitude, optimism, and creativity. With the right perspective, we can take any difficulty and turn it into an opportunity.

An optimist looks at the bigger picture and strives to make the most of every opportunity. They are willing to take risks and explore new ideas without fear of failure. An optimist is a problem solver who is always looking for solutions and growth. They are resilient, open-minded, and passionate about life, which helps them face every challenge.

This optimistic mindset is invaluable, as it can help to shape our professional lives in ways that lead to success and happiness. By embracing an optimistic perspective, we can see solutions to difficult challenges from a new angle. So, the next time you come across a challenge, take a deep breath, and remind yourself that the optimist sees opportunity in every difficulty.

Francesco Vitali

Your Notes for Success

134

"Either you run the day or the day runs you." — Jim Rohn

We are in charge of our lives and we have the power to be the masters of our destinies. We have the opportunity to make the most of our days and make the most of our lives. It's up to us to choose how we spend our time and energy, so choose wisely! We have the power to prioritize, stay organized, and make the most of our time. When we take charge of our day and don't let the day take charge of us, we can focus on the things that are most important. We can set goals, make plans, and take steps toward achieving our dreams.

With this in mind, we can choose to take charge of our days at work, setting our own agendas, and making sure that our days are spent in ways that are meaningful, productive, and enjoyable. With a positive mindset, an ambitious outlook, and a willingness to take risks, we can choose to be the ones running our days, making the most of every moment and ensuring that we make the most of our professional lives. So, remember that no matter how hard things are, you are still in control. You're still the captain of your ship!

Francesco Vitali

Your Notes for Success

135

"When we strive to become better than we are,
everything around us becomes better too."
— Paulo Coelho

When we strive to become better than we are, we become empowered to create positive change in our lives and in the lives of those around us. As we strive to be our best selves, we inspire those around us to do the same. When we make a conscious effort to improve ourselves and work toward our goals, it positively impacts our environment, creating a ripple effect that spreads to those around us.

Through our own hard work, determination, and commitment, we set an example for others to follow. We show that with dedication, we can all have a positive impact on our coworkers. We can open doors to new opportunities, inspire others to pursue their dreams, and help create a world in which everyone can thrive. When we strive to become better than we are, everything around us becomes better too. We can make the world a better place by striving to become better people.

Together, this small, collective effort can make a big difference in the lives of not just others, but ourselves as well. By striving to make ourselves better than we are, we are actually making the world a better place, one person at a time.

Francesco Vitali

Your Notes for Success

136

"You've got to get up every morning with determination
if you're going to go to bed with satisfaction."
— *George Lorimer*

Waking up each morning with a determined attitude is one of life's most powerful habits. When you face each day with a positive outlook, you increase the chances of achieving your goals. On the flip side, when you wake up with a negative attitude, you're likely to be disappointed in the end.

With determination and commitment, you can make the most of every day and be satisfied when you drift off to sleep at night. When you make the effort to set your intentions and stay focused, you can be proud of yourself for all the hard work you put in. When you look at the effort you've been putting in, you're more likely to become motivated. With motivation, you can look forward to a day of progress and satisfaction at the end of it.

We can take the steps necessary to improve our lives and reach our goals. The satisfaction we will feel when we look back at our accomplishments will be worth the effort. Determination, commitment, and perseverance are the keys to unlocking our potential and achieving our dreams.

So, no matter what happens, don't give up. Stick to your plans and your dreams, and you will make it.

Francesco Vitali

<u>Your Notes for Success</u>

137

"The elevator to success is out of order. You'll have to use the stairs, one step at a time." — Joe Girard

Sometimes, the elevator to success may be out of order, but that doesn't mean your journey has to be. Instead, you can start your ascent up the stairs, one step at a time. While it may take more effort and dedication to climb the stairs, the view from the top will be all the more rewarding.

By taking our tasks one step at a time, you can appreciate each accomplishment and savor the feeling of accomplishment. With each step, you'll gain strength, courage, and confidence. With each step, you'll be closer to success.

It's important to remember that success is a long-term process and it won't happen overnight. You must be willing to make sacrifices and put in the effort to reach your goals. Taking shortcuts may be tempting, but in the long run, it won't bring the same level of success as putting in the effort to do things the right way.

No matter the goal, success is achievable through dedication and hard work, and there is no shortcut to get there. So, don't lose sight of the staircase to success. Keep climbing and be patient with yourself. Once you reach the top, it will all be worth it!

Your Notes for Success

138

"Be a positive energy trampoline—absorb what you
need and rebound more back." — Dave Carolan

Positive energy brings out the best in you and those around you. By having a positive attitude, you will be able to tackle any challenge that comes your way with confidence. You will also be able to build strong relationships with your colleagues, which will enable you to reach your goals and objectives. Additionally, having a positive outlook will help you stay motivated and focused on accomplishing your goals. Overall, having a positive energy will help you to achieve success in your professional career.

When you have a positive attitude, you will attract more opportunities, build stronger relationships, and have a greater chance of success. People are drawn to those with a positive outlook and energy, as it is a sign of optimism and hope. A positive attitude also improves your outlook on life and allows you to remain optimistic even in difficult situations. This can open up more doors and create more possibilities for you.

Not only will you be more successful, but you will also be happier and more fulfilled in your work. You'll look forward to taking on new responsibilities and challenges.

So make sure to be a positive energy, and you will be rewarded with a successful career.

Francesco Vitali

Your Notes for Success

139

"I am not a product of my circumstances. I am a product of my decisions." — Stephen R. Covey

You are not a product of your circumstances; you are a product of your decisions. When faced with adversity, you can choose to be a victim of your circumstances, or you can choose to rise above and make decisions that will lead you to success. You can choose to be proactive in finding solutions and choose to make positive changes to your life and circumstances. You can choose to be successful.

When you make the conscious decision to take responsibility for your life and decisions, you will have the power to create a better future for yourself. You have the power to choose courage over fear, to choose growth over complacency, and to choose resilience over defeat. You are the master of your own destiny. You are more in control than you realize. Don't let others tell you otherwise. What others say or think about you doesn't matter. What matters is that you don't stop moving forward and working toward achieving your goals, choice by choice.

Each step you take toward success is a step away from the grips of your current circumstances. Believe in yourself and your decisions, and you will be able to create a better future for yourself.

Your Notes for Success

140

"One of the differences between some successful and unsuccessful people is that one group is full of doers, while the other is full of wishers." — Edmond Mbiaka

Successful people are doers—they don't just hope and wish for things to happen, they make things happen. They are always on their feet, waiting for the next big challenge to come their way. You'll always find them on the lookout for the next adventure.

They are ambitious, driven, and focused. They don't sit and wait for things to happen; they create their own opportunities and take advantage of them. They have the courage to take risks and have the determination to overcome any obstacle in their way.

They take charge of their lives and don't wait for good luck to come their way. They set long-term goals and work hard to achieve them. They are not afraid to ask for help when needed, nor are they afraid to fail. They see failure as a learning opportunity and use it as a stepping stone to reach their goals. They do, not wish.

Successful people understand that success is the result of hard work, dedication, and perseverance. They know that success doesn't come easy, but that it is possible to achieve with the right mindset and attitude. With the right attitude and dedication, anyone can be a doer and reach their goals.

Francesco Vitali

Your Notes for Success

141

*"Progress has little to do with speed, but much to
do with direction" — Timber Hawkeye*

Progress is the result of taking purposeful action toward a
well-defined goal. It is a process that requires thought, care, and
dedication toward the goal. Progress is not achieved through a
single effort but by consistently and persistently pursuing the goal.
One step at a time, step after step.

Success is not achieved by merely taking the first step, but by
taking the next step after that. It is not achieved by setting the bar
low, but by consistently striving to surpass it. It is not achieved
by taking a shortcut but by taking the long and winding road. It's
all about making steady, measurable progress toward a desired
outcome.

Progress is about taking small steps every day and reflecting
on the results to make informed decisions about future actions. It
is about having the courage to take risks, the willingness to accept
failure, and the courage to try again. It is about being resilient in
the face of adversity and continuing to move toward the desired
outcome. It is about learning from the past and leveraging it to
create a better future. It is about making a difference, even if it is
only one small step at a time.

Francesco Vitali

Your Notes for Success

142

"Don't bunt. Aim out of the ballpark. Aim for the company of immortals." — David Ogilvy

Push yourself to reach for the stars and take risks that will set you apart from everyone else. Set yourself up for success by dreaming big and pushing yourself to be the best. With hard work and dedication comes the potential for greatness and the chance to become immortal in your chosen field. You have the potential to become a legend and make a lasting impact, so don't let the opportunity pass you by. Embrace the challenge and aim out of the ballpark.

When you are willing to take that risk and go for something big, you become part of something special. You become part of a community of achievers, of people who have done the impossible and made their dreams come true. You become one of those who not only have their goals aligned but have envisioned success and are not afraid to go after it.

Surround yourself with those who exude positive energy and are always motivated to improve themselves. The acceptance of mediocrity is the death of hopes and dreams. That's something you want to avoid at all costs.

So, don't hold back; give it your all and you will become the successful individual you wish to be!

Your Notes for Success

143

"Set your goals high, and don't stop till you get there."
—Bo Jackson

Setting your goals high is the first step in achieving success. When you aim ambitiously high, you push yourself to strive for greatness and reach the highest level of success you can. You challenge yourself to reach for the stars and work hard to make your goals a reality.

Think about where you want to be. Create a vision for yourself and look at the bigger picture. It's not enough to just think about setting goals; you need to plan them carefully. Make an action plan and stick to it.

Once you set your goals, don't give up until you get there. It will be tough in the beginning but hang in there!

Even when you face obstacles, you stay determined and keep pushing forward. Having this attitude will help you stay motivated and focused on your goals. When you set your goals ambitiously high and don't stop till you get there, you will not only be rewarded with the satisfaction of achieving your goals, but the joy of knowing that you have accomplished something great.

Don't give up, no matter the obstacles you encounter. Set your goals high, and don't stop till you get there! You can do it!

Francesco Vitali

Your Notes for Success

144

"If you really want to do something, you'll find a way.
If you don't, you'll find an excuse." — Jim Rohn

If you really want to do something, you'll find a way. No matter how tough things get, remind yourself that you started this journey for a reason. This is a great way to stay motivated and focused on achieving your goals. It's a reminder that you have the power and the determination to make your dreams come true. It's a reminder that no matter what obstacles you may face, you can find a way to overcome them. It's a reminder that there is always a solution to any problem and that no matter how hard something may seem, you can always find a way to get it done.

This is a reminder that excuses won't get you anywhere and aren't an effective way to achieve your goals. If you want to get something done, you have to put in the work and the effort to make it happen. Some of the greatest leaders of the world are where they are right now because they never gave up or gave in. They found a way to make things work. And so can you! You can be where you want to be. All you have to do is have faith in yourself and keep going.

Francesco Vitali

Your Notes for Success

145

*"The greater the difficulty, the more the glory
in surmounting it." — Epicurus*

Difficult tasks can seem daunting, but when we take the initiative to rise to the challenge and overcome what may seem impossible, the feeling of accomplishment is truly indescribable. It is in these moments of success that we find ourselves capable of far more than what we could have ever imagined. The glory in conquering a difficult feat is something that can never be taken away, and will always stay with us as a reminder of our strength and determination.

You never know what you're truly capable of until you find yourself in a tough situation. That's when you have to utilize your strengths and give it your all. That's when you realize that you have what it takes to take on anything and everything.

With every difficulty overcome, you not only gain the satisfaction of having conquered something seemingly insurmountable, but also gain confidence in your own skills and resilience. Challenges should be embraced and not feared, as they build your character and provide you with invaluable life experience. The rewards of striving to overcome hardships are bountiful, and the greater the difficulty, the more the glory. So, give it your all and never give in to anything or anyone.

Your Notes for Success

146

"If the decisions you make about where you invest your blood, sweat, and tears are not consistent with the person you aspire to be, you'll never become that person." — Clayton M. Christensen

Investing your time and energy into the things that will help you reach your goals can be difficult and challenging, but it is worth it in the end. Having a plan for the future and making decisions that will put you on the right path to achieving your aspirations will help you stay motivated and focused on reaching your goals. With dedication and hard work, you can become the person you've always wanted to be.

But you have to make sure you are consistent when it comes to your goals. Don't doubt yourself. You have to be clear about everything; you have to be clear about what you want to achieve and the steps required to get there. Only then will you be able to be where you wish to be? Envision yourself there and you're halfway to the finish line!

Each decision you make about where to focus your time and energy allows you to become closer to achieving the life you have always envisioned. Each step you take builds on the decisions you make today.

So make the commitment to be consistent, and dedicate yourself to your goals and dreams, and you will be able to make the changes you desire to become invincible.

Your Notes for Success

147

*"I will not lose, for even in defeat, there's a valuable
lesson learned, so it evens up for me." — Jay-Z*

No matter what the outcome of the situation, do not give up. Even if you experience a defeat, there is still a valuable lesson to be learned, making it a win-win situation for you. You get to experience the satisfaction of learning something new, which can be applied to future scenarios. In addition, you can take comfort in the fact that you put in your best effort and can be proud of the work you have done.

With this attitude, you can see every situation as a chance to grow and develop into a better version of yourself. This ensures that no matter what, you will always gain something from the experience. But if things don't work out the first time, don't be afraid of restarting if you have to. Sometimes, we need to start again from the beginning to get to the end. There will be a hundred obstacles in your way, but you shouldn't be discouraged by it.

Embrace each challenge and failure as a chance to learn and grow, because in the end, you will be successful in one way or another. So, keep this in mind: even if you fail the first time, you will find success as long as you don't give up.

Francesco Vitali

Your Notes for Success

148

"Success is a science; if you have the conditions,
you get the result." — Oscar Wilde

Success is like a recipe; you need to combine the right ingredients and follow the right steps in the right order to achieve it. When these conditions are met, success is sure to follow. It's not a matter of luck; it's a matter of knowing what you need and taking the necessary steps to get the desired result.

We can create success when we have a clear vision of our goals and a plan of action to reach them. When we take consistent action toward our goals and stay committed, we increase our chances of achieving success. Success is a science: so long as you follow the right steps, you'll get there.

The science of success is based on the idea that if you have the right conditions and take action in the right way, then success will be yours. This means having an understanding of your goals, having a plan on how to reach them, and putting in effort every day. It also means having faith in yourself that you can achieve your goals despite any obstacles that might come your way. Success is not something that happens overnight; it takes time, dedication, and hard work, but with these three things combined, anything is possible!

Francesco Vitali

Your Notes for Success

149

*"When everything seems to be going against you,
remember that the airplane takes off against the wind,
not with it." — Henry Ford*

When everything seems to be going against you, remember that there isn't a single person in the world who hasn't faced adversity. This is a powerful reminder to stay persistent, even when the odds seem insurmountable. Don't let what others say get you down or make you discouraged. They're not in your shoes and they will never be. They won't know what it's like for you; they won't struggle the same way. They have their own journey, just like you do. Only focus on things that really matter—your goals and dreams. Don't let anyone stop you, and don't lose sight of your goals.

It takes a lot of courage and strength to stay focused and to move forward despite the obstacles and challenges that come our way. As long as you have the will and determination to continue, nothing can stop you. Believe in yourself and remember that it's the power of positivity and perseverance that will lift you up against the wind and help you reach your goals. Don't let anything stand in your way—you've got this! You can do it! You have what it takes to take on the world. Keep reminding yourself of that and keep pushing forward!

Francesco Vitali

Your Notes for Success

150

"Start where you are. Use what you have.
Do what you can." — Arthur Ashe

Start where you are. Use what you have. Do what you can. These three phrases are incredibly powerful, and when taken together, they can create a sense of possibility and hope. They remind us that progress is possible, even when resources are limited, that it's possible to make a difference, even if we start from a place of disadvantage. We can begin to take action, no matter where we are or what we have; by focusing on what we can do, we open up an exciting new world of opportunities.

Accepting where we are and doing what we can with what we have is an empowering message that can help us to unlock our inner potential and to make a real difference in the world. These three simple phrases are a powerful reminder that there's always something we can do, and that by taking action, big things can happen. Whether you're starting your own business, launching a charity, or helping out your neighbor, you can make a difference by getting creative with what you have. It's important to recognize that we are capable of creating something new, even if it's not perfect. You were born to make a difference in the lives of others! You have what it takes to create a ripple of change.

Francesco Vitali

<u>*Your Notes for Success*</u>

151

"Ideation without execution is delusion."
— *Robin Sharma*

Ideation without execution is like having a dream without ever taking the first step to make it a reality. Without proper execution, ideas remain ideas and can never become anything more. Execution is the only way to make an idea come to life and turn it into a tangible result. If you have an idea, you must take action and put in the hard work to make it happen.

Work hard to turn your ideas into reality. Wake up each day and commit yourself to putting in the work and staying focused on your goals and objectives. Take action, be consistent, and never give up even when things are tough. When the path is difficult, it can be tempting to give up, but the rewards that come from persevering are worth the effort. Being consistent is the secret to success—it will help you stay on track and focus on the goals you have set for yourself.

Finally, never give up. No matter how tough things get, having the courage to keep going is what sets apart those who succeed from those who don't. Believe in yourself and trust that you can make your ideas a reality. You have what it takes to make it big!

Francesco Vitali

Your Notes for Success

152

"It is a rough road that leads to the heights of greatness." — Lucius Annaeus Seneca

It is a rough road that leads to the heights of greatness. The road is often full of obstacles, but those who persevere will eventually reach a summit of success. The road to success may be paved with thorns, but it is all worth the hardships you will face.

Along the way, you will face hardships, and you will be tested. But you must be willing to put in the effort, to make sacrifices, and to keep going, even when you feel like giving up. With dedication and courage, you will eventually reach the top, where your efforts will be rewarded with the joy of accomplishment.

The journey may not be easy, but those who are determined to reach the heights of greatness will eventually find their way. Remember that a diamond goes through a lot of pressure for a long time before it can be molded into a diamond. You have to be willing to take on challenges, deal with setbacks, and face naysayers if you want to become successful. The journey ahead is tough but it will get easier with time.

So, don't give up even if the journey is difficult. The reward of success is well worth it!

Francesco Vitali

Your Notes for Success

153

*"For the great doesn't happen through impulse alone,
and is a succession of little things that are brought
together." — Vincent van Gogh*

Success doesn't happen overnight; it takes hard work, dedication, and determination to get to where you want to be. You can't expect to achieve success without putting in the work. It's not easy, but it's worth it. You need to be willing to take risks, learn from your mistakes, and find ways to stay motivated and focused on your goals. It takes time and effort, but if you stay the course, success will follow.

It is okay to take breaks in between bouts of hard work, but make sure you remain consistent with your efforts. You have to stay persistent in the face of adversity and not give up when things get tough. Never give up on your dreams, and continue to strive to be the best version of yourself. With the right attitude, you can achieve anything you set your mind to. You can make positive strides in life by taking on challenges and staying optimistic. Your attitude can help you stay on track and make wise decisions. It will be the defining factor in how people perceive you. In the end, having a positive attitude and outlook will help you to reach your goals and succeed in life.

Francesco Vitali

Your Notes for Success

154

"It's not the will to win that matters—everyone has that. It's the will to prepare to win that matters."
— *Paul Bryant*

It's not enough to simply have the will to win; it takes more than that to be successful. The will to prepare to win is just as important and often overlooked. Preparation is the key to success, as it provides the knowledge and skills needed to reach victory. It requires dedication, commitment, and hard work, but the effort will pay off in the end. With the right preparation, you can achieve anything you set your mind to. When we are prepared, we are more confident, and our chances of winning increase exponentially. We are able to tackle any and every challenge that comes our way.

We must be willing to invest the necessary time, energy, and resources to lay the foundation for our success. With the right combination of planning and persistence, we become capable of achieving great things. Preparation and success are correlated. It gives us the edge in any situation. It gives us the certainty that we are ready and able to handle whatever comes our way. We can take on any challenge and navigate through any situation.

So, if you want to be victorious, make sure to put in the preparation and effort necessary to reach your goals.

Francesco Vitali

Your Notes for Success

155

"If there is no struggle, there is no progress."
— *Frederick Douglass*

It is through challenge, difficulty, and hardship that we have the opportunity to grow and become stronger. Without these obstacles, we would never have the opportunity to reach our full potential, or to learn from our experiences and become a better version of ourselves. It is the struggle that allows us to realize the value of our accomplishments and to appreciate the victories that come with it. No matter how difficult the journey, it will eventually lead to success. It is only when we are pushed beyond our comfort zone that we have the opportunity to grow and develop.

Struggle can be seen as a positive thing, as it allows us to push our limits and gain new skills and knowledge. It teaches us to be resilient, to adapt and grow, and to not give up in the face of adversity. Struggle can also be a source of motivation, as it gives us something to strive for. It allows us to recognize our own strengths and weaknesses, and to develop our character.

We must embrace our struggles and challenge ourselves to become better. With perseverance and courage, we can make progress and create a better work culture for ourselves and for others.

Francesco Vitali

<u>Your Notes for Success</u>

156

"If you don't like the road you're walking, start paving another one." — Dolly Parton

If you don't like the road you're walking, start paving another one. It won't be easy, but it will be worth it. You have the power to make your own choices and create your own paths. If you don't like the direction you're heading, don't be afraid to take the initiative and start paving a new path. Take the risk and start paving a road that will lead you to success and happiness. Take the initiative and don't be afraid to try something new. Whether it's learning a new skill, taking a chance on a new job, or even starting your own business, the possibilities are endless. With dedication and hard work, you can create the life you want.

Start thinking outside the box, be brave, and take the initiative to create something new and different. When we do this, we open ourselves up for new opportunities, experiences, and a chance to grow in ways we could never have imagined. Life is full of possibilities. When we take action and create our own path, we can create something new and exciting that will bring us joy, success, and a sense of fulfillment.

Remember, the only person who can make a difference is you, so take the first step and start paving your own path today.

Francesco Vitali

Your Notes for Success

157

"Some people want it to happen, some wish it would happen, others make it happen." — Michael Jordan

Don't just sit around wanting and wishing for your dreams to come true. Turn that wishful thinking into action and make them come true. The world is what you make of it, and if you want to achieve something, you have to take the initiative to make it happen. Wanting alone won't do it. Take the first step and break down the goal into smaller tasks that you can handle. This way, you can take it one step at a time and eventually reach your goal.

Put in the effort, be consistent, and stay motivated. Don't let anyone or anything stop you from making your dreams a reality. You have the power to achieve anything you set your mind to.

Believe in yourself and never give up, and you will make your dreams come true. Making our dreams come true is a matter of believing in ourselves and having the courage to take the necessary steps. It is not easy, but it is achievable. With a positive mindset and the right attitude, anything is possible. We must be willing to work hard and persevere when the going gets tough. With the right perspective and determination, we can make our dreams come true.

Francesco Vitali

Your Notes for Success

158

"Success is the sum of small efforts—repeated day in and day out." — Robert Collier

Success is not something that can be achieved in a day, but rather through the cumulative effort of small actions that are repeated day in and day out. It is the little things done consistently that add up to meaningful change and progress. Success is not a single event but a series of accomplishments that are achieved through a consistent pattern of effort.

The small, daily actions taken to reach a goal are the most important and often the most difficult part of the journey. It takes tremendous dedication and perseverance to stay focused on the end goal, but it is the sum of these small efforts that can lead to great success.

In other words, achieving success is a marathon, not a sprint. Success is not measured by how quickly you reach the finish line, but by how well you manage to stay on track and remain consistent throughout the journey. It is important to remember that a successful journey is made up of small but meaningful steps, and that it is often these small steps that make the biggest impact. It takes time, effort, and consistency to reach your goals. Remember, through determination, you can achieve anything you set your mind to.

Francesco Vitali

Your Notes for Success

159

"Ordinary people think merely of spending time; great people think of using it." — *Arthur Schopenhauer*

Great people recognize that time is one of the most valuable resources we have, and that it should be used wisely. Instead of wasting time on trivial matters, great people strive to make the most of every second. They don't spend time, they use it. They know that time is a finite commodity and that it will not come again, so they strive to fill it with activities that will bring them closer to their goals.

Great people spend their time actively, whether it is through reading, taking up a new skill, or simply reflecting on their life and goals. They also use their time to help others, whether it is through volunteering, donating to a charity, or doing something as simple as reaching out to a friend. Great people understand that time is a precious gift and that we should use it to make the world a better place. They strive to make the best of every second, knowing that the time we have is limited and that it should be used in the most meaningful way possible.

So, use the time you have wisely and don't waste it. Focus on what really matters and you will reach new heights!

Francesco Vitali

Your Notes for Success

160

*"Success depends upon previous preparation, and
without such preparation there is sure to be failure."*
— *Confucius*

Success doesn't come easily and it certainly doesn't happen overnight. It requires preparation, dedication, and hard work. This is a lesson that has been taught over time and is often forgotten in the hustle and bustle of everyday life. However, those who are successful understand that without preparation, there will surely be failure. To achieve success, one must be prepared to put in the necessary effort to reach their goals.

Whether it's an individual or a team working together toward a common goal, by taking the time to prepare thoroughly, one can achieve their goals. Ultimately, success is not just about luck or having an innate talent; it's also about your mindset. Having a positive mindset helps you to believe in yourself and take the necessary steps to achieve success. It allows you to take risks and be open to opportunities. It also encourages you to learn from your mistakes and keep on trying. It helps you focus on the goals you want to achieve, and motivates you to work hard and stay disciplined.

So, believe in yourself and remember that you *can* do anything you want to. Don't give up, make the proper preparations, and keep chasing your dreams.

Francesco Vitali

Your Notes for Success

328

161

"Success isn't a result of spontaneous combustion. You must set yourself on fire." — Arnold H. Glasow

Success is something that we all strive for, but achieving it is not something that happens by itself. It takes hard work, dedication, and a strong will to never give up.

It's easy to get discouraged and to doubt yourself, but it's important to remember that success won't come easy. Just like a fire needs a spark, you must set yourself on fire with motivation and ambition to succeed. Believe in yourself and your dreams, and you will be able to push through any obstacle that comes your way. You have to leave your comfort zone and push yourself to the limit. You have to be willing to take risks, try new things, and push yourself further than you ever thought possible.

Achieving success is a process, and it requires consistent work and effort. It is not a destination that one can reach quickly. Success comes from taking small, achievable steps toward a larger goal. Success never happens spontaneously, but is a result of consistency. It is important to recognize and build upon small successes, as they will eventually lead to bigger and more meaningful accomplishments.

So, don't be afraid to set yourself on fire and reach for the stars.

Francesco Vitali

Your Notes for Success

162

*"The ladder of success is best climbed by stepping
on the rungs of opportunity." — Ayn Rand*

The ladder of success is often seen as a challenge to climb, but the truth is that it can be best scaled by stepping on the rungs of opportunity. Every step taken on the ladder of success requires careful consideration of the choices available and the determination to reach the next rung.

When one takes the time to evaluate each opportunity, it can be used as a stepping stone to greater heights. Each rung is an opportunity to learn and grow, to find creative solutions, and to make the most of every chance. Taking advantage of these opportunities can lead to success, regardless of the difficulty of the climb. With the right attitude, the ladder of success can be climbed one step at a time.

When you take the time to appreciate the small successes and milestones achieved along the way, you can stay positive and motivated to continue striving for bigger and better things. Looking at successes that have been achieved by others can also help to inspire and remind you that anything is possible. They, too, used the rungs of opportunity to climb the ladder of success.

So, don't stop climbing; keep going and you will get to the top before you even know it!

Your Notes for Success

163

*"If you believe something needs to exist, if it's
something you want to use yourself, don't let anyone
ever stop you from doing it." —Tobias Lütke*

If you believe something needs to exist, then don't let anyone stop you from making it happen! Even if it's something you want to use yourself and no one else does, you should never give up on your dreams or your goals.

You have the power to make a difference and create something new and exciting. Take the necessary steps to bring your idea to life and be proud of what you create. Don't let fear or doubt get in the way. Don't let anyone discourage you or make you feel like your idea is not worth pursuing. You can make a difference and create something that adds value to the world.

Believe in yourself and that anything is possible, and don't let anyone tell you otherwise.

Don't be afraid to try something new and take risks, because that's how progress is made. Take ownership of your dreams and never give up. Take a leap of faith and create something extraordinary and remarkable. If you envision it, make it.

Take the time to plan and create your vision, and then put your plan into action. With hard work, dedication, and a never-give-up attitude, you can make anything you desire become a reality.

Your Notes for Success

164

"Be sure you put your feet in the right place,
then stand firm." — Abraham Lincoln

Be sure you put your feet in the right place, then stand firm. It's a simple statement, but it's full of meaning. It's a reminder to all of us that life is full of choices and it's important to make sure we make the right ones. Taking the right steps is crucial in making sure that we are on the right path and that our lives are filled with meaning and purpose. It also reminds us to be confident in our decisions and to stay true to our values and beliefs.

When we make the right choices, have the courage to stand by them, and strive to be our best selves, we can achieve anything. It's an encouraging reminder that no matter the situation, we can always stay on the path of success by being sure of our choices and standing by them. We have to look at the bigger picture. We can be sure that if we put our feet in the right place, we can stand firm and have the confidence to make the best of any situation.

So, trust yourself and have firm faith in the decisions you make. Get yourself going in the right direction, and then keep going!

Francesco Vitali

Your Notes for Success

165

*"I can't tell you how many times I've been given a no.
Only to find that a better, brighter, bigger yes was right
around the corner." — Arlan Hamilton*

You may hear a no more often than a yes, but don't let that stop you from pursuing your dreams. Don't give up because a brighter future awaits you. Keep pushing and don't stop until you reach your goals. There will be obstacles along the way, but you can overcome them with hard work and determination.

Don't give up even if you face rejection or failure. Don't let one setback stand in the way of what you want to achieve. But it's important to remember that it's all part of the process. It's a sign that you are pushing yourself to be better and reach for something greater. And you never know what great yes lies around the corner from a no.

Take a moment to reflect and then move forward with determination and courage. Just keep going and you will eventually reach your destination. Don't be disheartened by the setbacks—use them as an opportunity to grow and find success. It may take time and effort, but you will be glad you never gave up. A brighter future is within your reach; all you have to do is keep believing in yourself and keep going. Don't look back; the only way to success is moving forward.

Francesco Vitali

Your Notes for Success

166

"We need to accept that we won't always make the right decisions, that we'll screw up royally sometimes— understanding that failure is not the opposite of success, it's part of success." — Ariana Huffington

We need to accept that we won't always make the right decisions, that we'll sometimes make mistakes, and that failure is just a part of life. Making mistakes is part of the journey, and it's important to realize that it's okay to fail. Failure doesn't mean you are a failure, it means you are learning and growing. We can learn from our mistakes, and use them to become better and stronger. When we make a mistake, it gives us an opportunity to reflect on our decisions and think about how we can improve. Mistakes can lead us to greater understanding, as well as help us identify our weaknesses and strengths. With each mistake, we can gain valuable insight that can help us become more successful.

Failure can be an opportunity to learn and grow, as it teaches us important lessons that can be applied in the future. It can also be a source of motivation, as it encourages us to persevere and strive to reach our goals. It also encourages us to take risks, as it gives us the confidence to try something new and the strength to push through challenging times.

So, instead of looking at failure as an enemy, we should embrace it and use it as a stepping stone to success.

Francesco Vitali

Your Notes for Success

167

"If A is a success in life, then A equals x plus y plus z.
Work is x; y is play; and z is keeping your mouth shut."
— Albert Einstein

If A is a success in life, then it can be said that A equals hard work plus play plus discretion. Hard work, or x, is the foundation of any successful life. Though work can be difficult, it is ultimately necessary to achieve success. Alongside hard work is play, or y.

Work is a form of discipline that helps us to develop ourselves and to build a better future. It helps us to learn more, to be more organized and to be better at problem-solving. Through hard work, we can become more successful in our endeavors and achieve our goals. Work can be a great way to practice perseverance, hone our focus, and develop resilience.

But also keep in mind that taking time to relax is essential in order to maintain a healthy work-life balance and keep motivation high. Don't forget to play.

The final ingredient in this equation is keeping your mouth shut, or z. In a professional environment, it is important to think before you speak and practice discretion in order to avoid any unnecessary conflict or drama. This will help create a safe work culture where every individual feels comfortable working.

All together, these components become the formula for success.

Francesco Vitali

<u>Your Notes for Success</u>

168

"Never let your mind become the greatest obstacle to success. To get your mind on the right track, the rest will follow." — *Roy T. Bennett*

Our minds are powerful tools, and they can either propel us toward success or become our greatest obstacle.

It is important to focus on the positive and use our minds to our advantage. We can take control of our thoughts, and shape our minds to think positively. When we focus on the positive, we can be more productive, and we can stay motivated to reach our goals.

If we let ourselves be overwhelmed with worry, doubt, and fear, our minds will become an obstacle to success. Often the only obstacles we face are those that we create. We must take time to nurture our minds, to focus on positive thoughts, and to recognize our worth. With a positive outlook, we can see the good in any situation and make the best of it.

Once we recognize our own potential, we can start to recognize opportunities for growth and success. When our minds are in the right place, we can capitalize on those opportunities and work toward our goals. With a positive attitude and determination, we can overcome any obstacle and move closer to success. Never let your mind become the greatest obstacle to success; instead, use it to your advantage.

Francesco Vitali

Your Notes for Success

169

"At the end of the day, let there be no excuses, no explanations, no regrets." — Steve Maraboli

At the end of the day, let there be no excuses, no explanations, and no regrets. Let there be only the gentle peace of a job well done, a sense of satisfaction and accomplishment, and the knowledge that you did your best with what you have.

Celebrate the small wins and always strive to do your best. Each small win should be celebrated and savored. It's a reminder of the progress you're making and a motivator to keep going.

Don't let anything hold you back from achieving your goals. Believe in yourself and don't let anyone tell you otherwise.

Let there be the joy of knowing you worked hard, pushed yourself, and made the most of the day. Let your efforts and hard work be your reward, and let your actions be the only thing that speaks for you. Be proud of what you have accomplished today, and look forward to the successes that tomorrow will bring. Don't be afraid to take risks and push yourself out of your comfort zone. Doing your best is about more than just achieving success; it's about learning and growing. With each success, you will gain confidence and be one step closer to achieving your goals.

Francesco Vitali

Your Notes for Success

170

"If you hang out with chickens, you're going to cluck,
and if you hang out with eagles, you're going to fly."
— *Steve Maraboli*

If you surround yourself with negative people, it's easy to become one of them. Spending time with people who are constantly putting you down can lead you to adopt a negative mindset and outlook on life. This can prevent you from reaching your full potential and achieving success.

However, if you spend time with ambitious and motivated people, you can benefit from their positivity and energy. You can learn from their successes and failures, and be inspired to set and reach your own goals.

The right people can encourage you, inspire you, and help you to develop the skills and mindset needed for success. By surrounding yourself with ambitious people, you will be able to unlock the power of positive thinking and be successful. When you are surrounded by people who have similar goals and ambitions, it encourages good habits and a positive outlook. It can also help you to stay focused and motivated, which is key to achieving your goals. Not only will you benefit from the positive energy of your peers, but you will also have access to their knowledge and experience. Ultimately, having ambitious people around you can help you unlock the power of positive thinking and be successful.

Your Notes for Success

171

"The difference between a successful person and others is not a lack of strength, not a lack of knowledge, but rather a lack in will." — *Vince Lombardi*

A successful person has an unwavering belief in themselves and the ability to push through difficult times.

They face challenges head-on and don't shy away from them. They understand that perseverance and resilience are key to achieving their goals. They are willing to take risks and try new things. They view mistakes and failures as an opportunity to learn and grow.

They understand that it takes hard work and dedication to achieve success, and they are willing to put in the effort to make their dreams a reality. They have the strength and knowledge, but they also have the will to make things happen.

They have a clear vision of what they want to achieve, and they are not afraid to take risks in order to make it happen. They understand that failure is a part of life and that success is just the result of hard work and dedication. They have the will to persevere, to keep going even when the odds may be stacked against them. They understand that success isn't something that is handed to you, it's something that you have to earn.

So, in order to become successful, you need to have all of these qualities.

Francesco Vitali

Your Notes for Success

172

"Always bear in mind that your own resolution to succeed is more important than any one thing."
— *Abraham Lincoln*

It's easy to become overwhelmed by the magnitude of the task ahead, but by reminding yourself daily that your own determination to succeed is the most important factor, you can stay focused and motivated. You must take ownership of your own success, and never forget that no matter what the odds, you have the power to make your dreams come true.

It's up to you to create your own success, and your determination to succeed is the biggest factor on the path to achieving your goals.

It is important to stay motivated and remember that hard work and dedication are what will bring us closer to our dreams. We should use our energy to make positive choices and work hard to achieve our goals. We should also remember to be patient and stay consistent. Success may not happen overnight, but with enough determination and perseverance, we will eventually reach our desired destination.

It is only through your own hard work and dedication that you will be able to reach the heights you desire. Keep this in mind when times are tough, and you will be able to push through and make your dreams a reality. Resolve to succeed, and you will succeed!

Francesco Vitali

Your Notes for Success

173

"In order to succeed, your desire for success should be greater than your fear of failure." — *Bill Cosby*

In order to achieve success, one must have a strong desire to succeed that is greater than their fear of failure. Having a positive outlook and an unwavering ambition is essential for pushing through the obstacles that may stand in your way. You must be willing to take risks and have the confidence to trust yourself and your abilities.

When faced with a challenge, remind yourself that it is simply an opportunity to learn and grow, and use it as motivation to keep going. You have to have an unshakeable belief in yourself and your abilities. You should set realistic goals and take action to achieve them. You must be willing to take risks and face challenges head-on. Your desire to succeed must be greater than your fear of challenges. Facing challenges head-on allows you to develop skills and learn how to overcome difficult situations. It also gives you the opportunity to grow and learn from your experiences. Taking risks and facing challenges can open up new doors and opportunities. It can also help you become a better problem-solver and leader.

Believe in yourself and the power of your ambition, and you will become an unstoppable force everyone will look up to.

Your Notes for Success

174

"The three great essentials to achieve anything worthwhile are, first, hard work; second, stick-to-itiveness; third, common sense." — Thomas Edison

Everyone has the potential to achieve something worthwhile in their professional life, but the path to success is never easy. It is essential to develop a positive attitude and to focus on the end result. It is also important to have faith in yourself and your abilities, and to stay motivated even when the going gets tough.

It takes dedication and determination to stay the course and not give up, no matter how difficult the journey may be. However, hard work alone is not enough. It's important, but there are other factors you need to consider as well. It is important to stay focused and motivated and never give up, even if the journey seems long and difficult. You need to create an action plan and break it down into achievable goals. Set yourself deadlines and identify the steps you need to take to reach your goals.

One must also have the ability to use common sense and make the right decisions in order to make progress. Stick-to-itiveness is key in order to stay on track and reach one's goals. Together, these three great essentials are the key to unlocking any door of opportunity and achieving anything worthwhile. Everyone has the potential to reach their goals, and it all starts with believing in yourself and having the courage and willingness to take action.

Francesco Vitali

Your Notes for Success

175

"Rich people have small TVs and big libraries,
and poor people have small libraries and big TVs."
— Zig Ziglar

Knowledge is the key to success. It is the foundation for achieving your goals and ambitions. It is the knowledge you gain through education, experience, and exploration that allows you to excel in whatever you do. It is the knowledge you gain that allows you to think critically and make informed decisions. When you have the knowledge, you have the power to open doors that would otherwise be closed. The more you know, the more you can do and the greater the chances of achieving success. So don't waste your time and potential by playing around.

Instead, focus on gaining knowledge and use it to your advantage. Don't let the opportunity to hone your skills and learn new things slide. With knowledge, you will be able to unlock a world of possibilities and achieve success. Learning is a lifelong journey, and it's important to take advantage of every opportunity to gain knowledge. Whether it's learning a new language, taking a class, or reading a book, every bit of knowledge will help you grow and move forward. Taking the time to develop your skills and learn new things will lead to personal growth, increased confidence, and success. Don't let these opportunities slide by—take them and grow!

Francesco Vitali

Your Notes for Success

176

"You're not obligated to win. You're obligated to keep trying. To the best you can do every day." — Jason Mraz

You're not obligated to win. You're obligated to keep trying. To the best of your ability, every single day. There is no greater freedom than knowing that you are in control of your own future and success. You have the power to decide how hard you will strive and the dedication you will put in to achieve your goals. Even if you don't achieve them, you can know that you have done everything you can and have given it your all.

There is nothing more satisfying than knowing that you have not given up, no matter what life throws at you. As long as you continue to stay motivated and never stop learning, you will find success in your own unique way. When you believe in yourself, you have the power to achieve anything. Trust in your skills, be consistent, and stay determined. The more you learn and challenge yourself, the more you will grow. With hard work and dedication, you will be able to reach your goals and make your dreams come true.

So keep going, never look back, and never stop. Keep trying and never give up. There is nothing you can't accomplish if you stay motivated and keep learning.

Francesco Vitali

Your Notes for Success

177

"Don't confuse poor decision-making with destiny. Own your mistakes. It's okay; we all make them. Learn from them so they can empower you!" — *Steve Maraboli*

Making mistakes is part of the human experience. Own your mistakes and you will be empowered to correct them, and in the process, you will gain a greater understanding of yourself. Mistakes can teach us valuable lessons that we can apply to future decisions. Take the time to reflect on your mistakes and learn from them. Understand why it happened, what was the cause, and how you can avoid making the same mistake again. Because that's the important thing: not that you made a mistake, but that you don't make the same mistake twice.

When you own your mistakes, you have the power to make better decisions in the future. It's okay to make mistakes; it's a part of life. Don't let your mistakes define you. Your mistakes can be a learning experience and give you the opportunity to grow. Embrace your mistakes and use them as a tool to help you become a stronger and wiser person.

Acknowledge what you have done wrong and use it to learn and progress. You are more than your mistakes, and you are capable of great things.

Learn from them, use them as a stepping stone to grow, and make your future better. So, don't let anyone ever tell you otherwise!

Francesco Vitali

Your Notes for Success

178

*"Winners are not afraid of losing. But losers are.
Failure is part of the process of success. People who
avoid failure also avoid success." — Robert T. Kiyosaki*

Winners know that the only way to keep going is to try and try again, even if they fail. They have the courage to face their losses and learn from them so they can become better every time. Winners don't give up when they fail—they get back up and try again. This is why they are so successful; they don't let their fears of failure stop them from achieving their goals.

Failure is an essential part of the success journey. Those who have failed and kept trying have eventually achieved success. The famous saying "If at first, you don't succeed, try, try again" is a great reminder that failure is part of the process of success.

It is important to take a step back, reflect on what went wrong, and adjust your strategy. Many successful people have seen failure as an opportunity to learn and grow. They use their experiences to become better and to reach their goals. Failure can be a great motivator. It can help you to stay focused and driven. People who avoid failure also avoid success. Don't be afraid to take risks and don't be discouraged when you don't get the results you want. Failure is just a step on the path to success.

Your Notes for Success

179

"Failure is a bend in the road, not the end of the road.
Learn from failure and keep moving forward."
— Roy T. Bennett

Failure is a natural part of life and can be a valuable learning experience. Every time we fail, we can look at it as an opportunity to learn, grow, and become better. We must remember that failure is a bend in the road, not the end of the road. We must use our failures as motivation to keep pushing forward and never give up.

Every time we fall, we can get up, dust ourselves off, and keep moving forward. We must learn from our mistakes and use them to our advantage. This way, we can develop the resilience and strength to continue our journey and ultimately achieve our goals. We must believe in ourselves and have the courage to keep moving forward, even when we experience failure.

It is important to understand that failure is not a sign of weakness, but instead a sign of courage and strength. By continuing to strive, even when we experience failure, we can reach our goals and make our dreams come true. Believing in ourselves and having the courage to keep going will help us grow and become better people.

So, don't be afraid of failure—embrace it as a natural part of life and use it to fuel your motivation and drive toward success.

Francesco Vitali

Your Notes for Success

180

"Keep your friends for friendship, but work with the skilled and competent." — Robert Greene

Keep your friendships thriving in your social life, but surround yourself with the skilled and competent in your work life. This is an important lesson to keep in mind when building relationships and creating positive outcomes. Having strong friendships is important for our well-being, but when it comes to achieving success, it is important to choose the right people for the job. Working with people who are skilled, competent, and reliable will give you the best results. When you're surrounded by like-minded individuals who are passionate about what they do, it can be very inspiring and motivating.

Not only will you have a successful outcome, but you will also have the opportunity to build meaningful relationships with people who have the same goals and values as you do. By surrounding yourself with competent and skilled people, you will be able to grow, learn, and excel in your chosen career. These are the people who can help you take your career to the next level. As you progress, you can also offer guidance and help to those starting out, creating a supportive and collaborative circle of success.

Ultimately, you will be able to take your success to the next level.

Francesco Vitali

Your Notes for Success

181

*"The universe doesn't give you what you ask for
with your thoughts—it gives you what you demand
with your actions." — Steve Maraboli*

The universe is like a giant factory; it's always producing something. It doesn't simply give us what we ask for with our thoughts; it gives us what we demand with our actions. We have the power to create our own future, to shape our reality. If we take action, if we take steps toward our dreams, the universe will respond with the resources and opportunities we need to make it happen. If we are determined and persistent, the universe will provide us with what we need to succeed. It won't be easy, but when we demand our actions, the universe will be there to help us make our dreams a reality.

With the right attitude, hard work, and dedication, we can achieve anything we set our minds to. The universe has given us the power to make our dreams a reality—all we have to do is take action. The universe is always there to support us, and if we pay attention to our intuition, we can tap into its wisdom and guidance. Taking action is the key to unlocking our potential and making our dreams come true. When we stay focused on our goals, stay committed to our vision, and take action, we will be able to find success.

Your Notes for Success

182

"You were put on this earth to achieve your greatest self,
to live out your purpose, and to do it courageously."
— *Steve Maraboli*

You have the power to achieve greatness and the courage to become your best self. You were put on this earth for a reason and it's up to you to find it. The world is full of opportunities for you to explore and grow. The journey won't always be easy, but it will be worth it. You have the strength to face any challenge that comes your way and the courage to reach for your dreams. It doesn't matter what others may say, they won't walk in your shoes.

You were put on this earth to live out your purpose and do it with bravery and determination. Believe in yourself and never give up, for the greatest version of yourself is only one brave step away. No matter what life throws at you, you must never give up on yourself. It is easy to become discouraged and overwhelmed by the obstacles in life, but when you believe in yourself and your capabilities, you can achieve anything. Have faith in yourself and keep pushing forward. Believe that the best version of yourself is within reach and all success takes is courage and determination. Don't worry about how hard it will be; focus on the end result and what you will be able to accomplish.

Francesco Vitali

Your Notes for Success

183

"Success is determined not by whether or not you face
obstacles, but by your reaction to them. And if you look
at these obstacles as a containing fence, they become
your excuse for failure. If you look at them as a hurdle,
each one strengthens you for the next." — Ben Carson

Success is all about how you approach and manage the obstacles that come your way. Rather than cowering at the thought of them, look at them as an opportunity to grow. With each hurdle you jump, you become more confident and more resilient. You learn to take risks, to think outside the box and to push yourself further.

Obstacles become the building blocks of your success, allowing you to reach greater heights. Each obstacle you face is a challenge, but with the right mindset, each challenge can be conquered. Success is determined not only by the obstacles you face, but also by your response to them.

Acknowledge the challenges and use them as an opportunity to learn and grow. Stay positive and your obstacles can become the stepping stones to success.

Francesco Vitali

Your Notes for Success

184

*"If you care about what you do and work hard at it,
there isn't anything you can't do if you want to."*
— *Jim Henson*

If you care about what you do and work hard at it, you will find that you will excel and achieve more than you ever thought possible. You will gain confidence in yourself and your abilities, and you will have the satisfaction of knowing that you put your best effort into something and achieved success.

With dedication and perseverance, you can turn your dreams into reality, no matter what obstacles you may come across. Put in the work and you will be rewarded with a sense of accomplishment and pride. You will be inspired to continue to strive to reach new heights and even bigger goals. It all starts with caring about what you do, pushing yourself to work hard and never giving up. When people care about their work and are willing to put in the extra effort, the results can be incredible.

Working hard is not always easy, and there are times when giving up seems like the best option, but if you care about what you do and never give up, you will find success. It is all about having the passion and dedication to do something and never giving up. With hard work and dedication, anything is possible.

Francesco Vitali

<u>Your Notes for Success</u>

185

"To be successful you need friends and to be very successful, you need enemies." — Sidney Sheldon

It is essential to understand that having a good team and enemies can be integral to success. Colleagues can offer invaluable support and guidance as you strive to reach your goals, while enemies can act as a source of motivation. When you are surrounded by people who are trying to outdo you, it can help you stay focused and strive harder to be the best. It is important to learn to find the balance between the two, as both can help you succeed. Make sure you have a team that can help each other out, lift each other up, and celebrate each other's successes.

Having a good team who can understand and encourage you, as well as a few adversaries who can push you to be better, can be the perfect combination for success.

A team that knows you, loves you, and supports you is invaluable. When you have a group of people around you who understand you and have your back, it can make a world of difference in your success and happiness. They can hold you accountable and help you to stay on track, while at the same time providing you with the emotional and mental support you need to stay focused.

Francesco Vitali

Your Notes for Success

186

"The way of success is the way of continuous pursuit of knowledge." — Napoleon Hill

The way of success is the way of continuous pursuit of knowledge. Knowledge is the key to success, and the more knowledge you acquire, the more successful you become. When you strive to learn more, you open the door to new opportunities and experiences, allowing you to reach your goals and achieve success. By continuously learning and expanding your knowledge base, you can continue to grow and find new avenues of success. It takes dedication and determination, but with a commitment to learning, you can unlock the door to success.

Moreover, knowledge can open up new perspectives and possibilities, allowing us to think more creatively and come up with innovative solutions. Therefore, the way of success is the way of continuous pursuit of knowledge, and is the surest path to success. With more knowledge, one can make better decisions, think more critically, and have a better understanding of the world. Knowledge can help one open doors to success that were not previously accessible. It is a lifelong process that requires dedication and hard work. The right attitude and determination can help one achieve success in whatever they set out to do.

Francesco Vitali

<u>*Your Notes for Success*</u>

187

"It is well known that a vital ingredient of success is not knowing that what you're attempting can't be done." — Terry Pratchett

It is well known that a vital ingredient of success is not knowing that what you're attempting can't be done. This is a powerful reminder that we should never let fear or doubt stop us from pursuing our dreams. After all, if we never try, we'll never know if we could have achieved something extraordinary. All too often, we let our own perceptions of what is possibly get in the way of our potential greatness. Instead, we should always remember that the only real limit is our own minds.

Believing in ourselves and our potential, no matter how far-fetched or outlandish, can open up a world of possibilities that can propel us to success. When we have faith in our own abilities, it can give us the courage to take risks and explore new opportunities. We can let go of our doubts and embrace our dreams, knowing that our potential is limitless. With the right mindset and hard work, we can unlock our true potential and bring our aspirations to life.

With this kind of attitude, there is no limit to what we can accomplish and no challenge too difficult to overcome.

Francesco Vitali

Your Notes for Success

188

"A quitter never wins and a winner never quits."
— Napoleon Hill

This popular phrase serves as a reminder that success requires hard work, dedication, and perseverance. It encourages us to never give up, no matter how difficult the situation may seem. Quitting is not an option, so we must be willing to push ourselves further and challenge ourselves to reach new heights. With the right attitude and mindset, we can overcome any obstacle and reach our goals.

Quitting will only lead to disappointment and failure, so it's important to keep pushing forward with our eyes on the prize. A winner never quits because they are determined and motivated to achieve their dreams. Quitting is not an option for a winner, so keep pushing forward and don't let anything stop you from achieving success.

Winners never let anything stop them from achieving success. They keep striving for excellence and keep pushing even when the going gets tough. They don't let anything stop them from reaching their goals, and they don't quit until their goals are achieved. Quitting is not an option for a winner, so keep pushing forward and don't let anything stop you from achieving success. You have what it takes to make it big!

Francesco Vitali

Your Notes for Success

189

"Amateurs sit and wait for inspiration, the rest of us just get up and go to work." — Stephen King

Amateurs sit and wait for inspiration, but the rest of us just get up and go to work. This is not to say that inspiration is not important, but it is only the first step in the creative process. Going to work means taking the initiative, proactively seeking out opportunities, embracing challenges, and pushing yourself to reach your goals. It is an attitude that leads to success, not only in the creative world but in all aspects of life.

Working hard and pushing yourself to reach your goals is rewarding, as it leads to a sense of satisfaction, accomplishment, and pride. Hard work also means staying focused and determined, no matter how difficult the task may seem. It gives us the strength to remain positive and keep going even when the going gets tough. It gives us the courage to take risks and the patience to see things through to the end. Hard work pays off and is the foundation for true success.

When we work hard and stay focused, we show that we believe in ourselves and our abilities. We prove that we are capable of achieving our goals and dreams, no matter how difficult or far-fetched they may seem. Working hard is the key to success, and it is never too late to get up and go to work.

Francesco Vitali

Your Notes for Success

190

*"Don't let what you cannot do interfere with
what you can do." — John Wooden*

Don't let what you cannot do interfere with what you can do. Too often, we get caught up in the things we are unable to do and let that frustration or disappointment stop us from exploring the things we can do. We all have unique skills and abilities that are worth exploring and developing. Take some time to think about what you can do and use that as a starting point. Celebrate your successes and take pride in your accomplishments.

With determination and hard work, you can achieve your dreams. You'll soon realize that the possibilities are endless! Embrace the things you can do and don't let anything hold you back. Everyone has their weaknesses and strengths. Make sure you focus on the strengths you have and what you bring to the table. Remind yourself that you are unique and an important asset. You bring value to the workplace. Your ideas and input are important, and you reached where you are today because you are capable of great things.

Start today, and you'll be amazed at what you can achieve just by believing in yourself and utilizing your talents.

Francesco Vitali

Your Notes for Success

191

"The struggles we endure today will be the 'good old days' we laugh about tomorrow." — Aaron Lauritsen

Today's struggles and challenges at work may seem like an insurmountable mountain to climb, but tomorrow it will be a thing of the past. With each step we take and every victory we secure, we are building a foundation of success and resilience that will serve us well in the future. Looking back at the challenges we face today will be the source of many future laughs, as we recall all that we have overcome and achieved. The struggles we endure today at work will be the "good old days" we laugh about tomorrow. It's easy to get bogged down by the challenges and hardships of the workplace, but what we may not realize is that in the end, these same struggles will shape us and make us more resilient in the long run.

Through our struggles, we learn how to work hard, stay focused, and develop the skills and knowledge we need to reach our goals. We also learn how to better manage our emotions and keep a positive attitude in the face of difficulty.

So, let's make the best of the struggles we face today and not forget that we are more capable, more amazing, and more incredible than we believe!

Francesco Vitali

Your Notes for Success

192

*"There are no secrets to success: don't waste time
looking for them. Success is the result of perfection,
hard work, learning from failure, loyalty to those for
whom you work, and persistence." — Colin Powell*

There are no secrets to success; success is the result of determination, hard work, and dedication.

Success is a journey, not a destination, and it is important to enjoy the process as much as possible. You should also remember to celebrate your successes and be proud of your achievements. With a positive attitude and perseverance, you can achieve anything you set your mind to. It takes effort and dedication to succeed, and to become successful you must be willing to put in the work and effort and be persistent. Learning from failure is an important part of success, as taking risks and making mistakes will help you to grow and learn, and will make you better equipped to handle future challenges.

Lastly, having loyalty to those you work with will help to create a strong, trusting and successful team. All these elements come together to create success—so don't waste time looking for secrets, and instead focus on putting in the hard work and dedication to be successful. You should also remember to celebrate your successes and be proud of your achievements. You've come this far because of your skills, talents, and abilities. You can take on anything and anyone!

Francesco Vitali

Your Notes for Success

193

*"Desire is the key to motivation, but it's determination
and commitment to an unrelenting pursuit of your
goal—a commitment to excellence—that will enable
you to attain the success you seek." — Mario Andretti*

Desire is the spark that ignites our ambition and drive. It is the key to motivation and a powerful tool for achieving our goals.

It is this desire that pushes us to take risks, try new things, and develop our skills in order to reach our goals. Desire can be a powerful force that encourages us to work hard and strive for excellence. It gives us the confidence to overcome obstacles and challenges that come our way. Desire is the fire that fuels our ambition and drive, and without it, we would be unable to reach our full potential.

But it also takes more than just desire to make our dreams come true. It takes determination and commitment to see it through. The pursuit of excellence is the cornerstone of success and requires an unrelenting dedication to our goal, no matter the obstacles and difficulties we may face along the way. These are the qualities that keep us striving for excellence, and pushing ourselves to reach the highest level of achievement.

With a steadfast commitment and unyielding perseverance, we can unlock the door to our goals and reach our highest aspirations. So, don't give up on your goals and dreams. Keep trying and keep believing in yourself, and you will get there before you know it!

Francesco Vitali

Your Notes for Success

194

"What do you mean I have to wait for someone's
approval? I'm someone. I approve. So I give myself
permission to move forward with my full support!"
— *Richelle E. Goodrich*

You don't need anyone's approval to move forward and make progress in your career. You are in control of your own success, and you are the captain of your own ship. You have the power to make life-changing decisions, and you don't need the consent of others to follow your own path. Don't worry about what others may think, because their opinions don't matter. You are the only one who can decide what is best for you, and you are the only one who can make your dreams come true. You are the only one who knows what is best for you and you should never let anyone tell you otherwise. Believe in yourself, trust your instincts, and you will never regret following your own path.

Never forget that you are your own boss. You have the power to make the changes you need to live a successful, happy, and fulfilled life. It is up to you to make the most of each day, make it count, and make decisions for yourself. Take ownership of your life and know that you have the potential to do great things and make a difference.

Francesco Vitali

<u>Your Notes for Success</u>

195

"Those who don't jump will never fly."
— *Leena Ahmad Almashat*

This quote is a great reminder that sometimes we need to take a risk in order to achieve our goals. Taking a leap of faith and attempting something new can often be difficult, but it is often the only way to achieve success. Those who don't take chances will never know the joy of experiencing what it's like to soar above the clouds. Bravely jumping into the unknown can be scary, but it can also be incredibly rewarding. Taking risks can open up a world of possibilities that can change our lives for the better.

Doing something new that you're not familiar with can be terrifying, but it also can be incredibly rewarding. By taking flight, you can discover a world of possibilities and new experiences. Taking risks can be frightening, but the rewards and experiences that come with taking a chance may be worth it. You never know what you may find and how far you may go. You never know where you'll end up. But it's the journey that matters the most.

So, take a chance, take a risk, jump, and take flight. You never know how far or how high you'll go.

Your Notes for Success

196

*"Who you are tomorrow begins with what
you do today." — Tim Fargo*

Today is the day to take action on the dreams and goals that you have set for yourself. Every action taken today will shape who you become tomorrow. You have the power to create the life you want, and it starts with what you do today. Every decision, every action, and every thought can lead you closer to becoming the best version of yourself and achieving your dreams.

So don't hesitate—to get started now and make the most of this day. What you do today will have a direct effect on who you will become tomorrow, and you have the capability to make tomorrow better than today. With dedication and hard work, you can create the life that you desire for yourself. Who you are tomorrow begins with what you do today. Taking small, consistent steps today will create a brighter tomorrow.

We can also choose to focus on positive outcomes, setting inspiring goals and rewarding ourselves for taking action. A positive attitude and a willingness to learn and grow can go a long way in creating a better future. By taking the time to invest in ourselves today, we can ensure that tomorrow brings us closer to our goals.

Francesco Vitali

Your Notes for Success

197

*"The most important thing is this: to sacrifice what you
are now for what you can become tomorrow."*
— *Shannon Alder*

The most important thing to remember is that sacrificing what you are now for what you can become tomorrow is essential for progress. It is often difficult to take risks and leave behind what is comfortable and familiar, but doing so is a necessary step toward achieving greater success. You will learn more, grow more, and become a better version of yourself by taking the leap and trusting that you will come out on the other side with a new perspective, confidence, and opportunities.

It is important to remain positive, stay focused, and keep pushing yourself to take the next step. Staying focused on your goals and objectives will help you stay motivated and make progress. Taking the time to think about what you want and what you can do to get there is also key to staying focused. Finally, pushing yourself to take the next step, even if it is hard, is the best way to ensure that you are making progress.

With this attitude, you will achieve more than you ever thought possible. Remember, you have what it takes to achieve greatness! Don't ever let anyone tell you you're not capable, because you can do anything you put your mind to!

Francesco Vitali

<u>*Your Notes for Success*</u>

198

"There's no reason to have a plan B because it distracts from plan A." — Will Smith

Having a plan B is often thought of as a way to prepare for the worst, but why waste time and energy on something that may never happen? Instead, focus your attention on plan A and trust that with the right effort and dedication, it will come to fruition. There's no need to worry about plan B because having faith in your plan A will bring you far more peace of mind and the rewards that come from achieving your goals.

It's important to be confident and never give up, for there's no telling what could happen if you remain focused on what's in front of you. Trust that you can accomplish anything you set your mind to. It may be difficult or challenging at times, but with determination and perseverance, you can stay the course and reach your goals.

Work hard, take risks, and don't be discouraged when you face obstacles. Believe in yourself and your goals and make sure you stay focused on the end result. Don't get sidetracked by outside influences or temporary setbacks. Just stay the course and you will succeed. Believe in yourself and your goals and you will be successful.

Francesco Vitali

Your Notes for Success

199

"The secret to success is constancy of purpose."
— *Benjamin Disraeli*

The secret to success lies in the power of constancy of purpose. When we are persistent and stay focused on achieving our goals, no matter how small or large, we are able to create a path that leads us closer and closer to our desired destination. With a strong mindset and the resilience to keep pushing forward, we can turn any dream into a reality. We can achieve the impossible.

Constancy of purpose is the fuel that keeps our goals alive and gives us the strength to keep going, no matter what the odds may be. By keeping our minds and hearts set on success, we can create a future of unlimited possibility.

Success is not something that is handed to us, it is something that we must actively pursue. We must set goals that challenge us and push us to our highest potential. By focusing our energy on the end goal, we can make steady progress toward our goals and eventually achieve success.

Additionally, it is important to stay positive and have faith in our abilities. Believing in ourselves and our potential can help us unlock our talents and create a life of abundance. When we remain focused and refuse to give up, success is within our grasp.

Francesco Vitali

Your Notes for Success

200

"Small shifts in your thinking, and small changes in your energy, can lead to massive alterations of your end result." — Kevin Michel

Small shifts in your thinking and small changes in your energy are like two pieces of the same puzzle that together create a powerful force. When you make small shifts in your thinking and small changes in your energy, you unlock a level of potential you never knew you had. You become aware of your inner strength, courage, and self-worth. You slowly start to feel empowered and more confident to take on whatever life throws at you. With each shift and change, you become stronger and more capable of achieving your goals. These shifts are the driving forces behind massive alterations of your end result.

By taking small steps to adjust the way you think and the energy you put out, you will be surprised at the tremendous impact it can have. If you focus on making small, incremental changes, you can create a ripple effect that will lead to massive transformation in your life.

You will find yourself in a much better place than you ever thought possible, with accomplishments that will make you feel proud and content. Small shifts in your thinking and small changes in your energy are powerful tools that can help you manifest your dreams and reach your full potential.

Francesco Vitali

Your Notes for Success

201

"Do not sit still; start moving now. In the beginning, you may not go in the direction you want, but as long as you are moving, you are creating alternatives and possibilities." — Rodolfo Costa

Do not sit still; start moving now. It's time to take action and start making progress toward your goals. Even if you don't know the exact direction you want to go in, the act of starting to move will help you figure out which direction is best for you. Taking action will open up possibilities and new paths that you may not have thought of before. It could also give you the motivation to pursue things that you never thought were possible, things that felt like a far-fetched dream.

It will also create new opportunities for growth and success. It allows you to take control of your destiny and live the life you have always wanted. Action is the only way to create the life you desire. Don't wait for the perfect opportunity, create it. Make the most of today, and move forward with confidence and ambition. Believe in yourself, and don't be afraid of failure.

Remember that actions speak louder than words. So instead of sitting still, take the initiative and start doing what you love. We don't know what tomorrow holds but we can make today count by making the most of it. So, don't put your dreams on the back burner; be proactive and go after them!

Francesco Vitali

Your Notes for Success

202

"Why be a man when you can be a success."
— *Bertolt Brecht*

Success is something that every person strives for and should strive for. Being a man is just one aspect of life, but being a success can be much more fulfilling. When you are a success, you have achieved something great, and it is something that can be admired and celebrated. Success can come in many forms, from business to personal accomplishments and everything in between. It can also be a source of pride, as you know that you have achieved something worthwhile.

It means that you are doing something that is meaningful and important to you, and that can be appreciated by others. It is a great feeling when you look back and see that you have accomplished something worthwhile.

You've made a positive change in the lives of your team members and you are a beacon of hope for them. They look up to you as the leader and role model they need. Success is the reward that comes from striving to be the best at something and it is a feeling that will stay with us for a lifetime. It is a feeling that can never be taken away and it is one of the most rewarding feelings in life.

So, why be a man when you can be a success?

Francesco Vitali

Your Notes for Success

203

"Beating the competition is relatively easy. Beating yourself is a never-ending commitment." — Phil Knight

Beating the competition is relatively easy. It often takes hard work, dedication, and determination to stay ahead of the curve. However, beating yourself is a never-ending commitment. It requires a focus on continual growth and improvement, with an eye on the future. Staying ahead of the competition requires a relentless commitment to self-improvement.

It means striving to be better than you were yesterday and pushing yourself a little harder each and every day. It means taking risks, thinking outside the box, and pushing the boundaries of what's possible. It means learning from your mistakes and using them as a catalyst for growth. It means having a vision for your future and taking the necessary steps to ensure that you're working toward achieving it.

Beating the competition is easy, but it's the never-ending commitment to beating yourself that will ensure success in the long run. The only person who you should be competing with is yourself. Strive to become better than who you were yesterday. If you compete with others, you'll never be able to improve. You'll always feel like you're lagging behind. But if you compete with yourself, you'll be able to take your time and work on turning your weaknesses into strengths.

Francesco Vitali

Your Notes for Success

204

"The distance between insanity and genius is measured only by success." — Bruce Feirstein

The distance between insanity and genius is often debated, but the truth is that one cannot measure the two by one another. Insanity and genius are both unique mindsets that can be seen in many people, but success is the only measure by which they can be accurately judged. It is true that genius often leads to success, but that success may come in many different forms. Geniuses have the ability to think outside of the box, solve problems, and create innovative solutions. This can sometimes be perceived as strange or insane by others. But when a genius's ideas are successful, they are celebrated and recognized as visionary.

Likewise, those deemed to be insane may also achieve success, albeit in a different way than genius. Ultimately, success is the one true measure that can be used to determine the distance between insanity and genius. It can be a great teacher, showing the potential of both mindsets, and it can also demonstrate the great rewards that come with hard work and dedication. Don't listen to what others have to say. You do you. You are the one in control; you are the master of your own destiny. Don't ever doubt yourself!

Francesco Vitali

Your Notes for Success

205

*"Success is the progressive realization of a worthy
ideal." — Earl Nightingale*

Success is the progressive realization of a worthy ideal and can be incredibly motivating. The idea of success is something that is personal to each individual, and the journey to achieving it is unique. Success is something that can be achieved through hard work and dedication, and it is an incredibly rewarding experience. It is important to have a purpose that is meaningful and inspiring, and to be willing to take the necessary steps to reach it.

The key to success is to remain focused on the end goal and celebrate each milestone along the way. Achieving success is a personal journey, and every person will have their own unique path. By taking small, achievable steps toward your end goal, and celebrating each milestone, you will be better able to stay focused and motivated. Celebrating successes, no matter how small, can be a great source of encouragement and a reminder that you are on the right track.

When we take the time to appreciate our successes, we can find the confidence and drive to continue toward our ultimate goal. Success is truly a journey and not a destination, and it is something to be embraced and celebrated.

Francesco Vitali

<u>*Your Notes for Success*</u>

206

"To earn more, you must learn more." — *Brian Tracy*

To earn more, you must learn more is an important mantra for success. Learning never ends, and the more you learn, the more opportunities you have to earn more. When you learn more, you become more valuable to employers, which can lead to higher pay and more job opportunities. With the right knowledge and skills, you can open up new sources of income, such as starting a business, selling products online, or freelancing.

Learning can also help you to become an expert in your field, which can give you an edge over your competition and make you more attractive to potential employers. Ultimately, learning more can help you to earn more and reach your financial goals.

Knowledge can provide insights on how to solve problems, how to make better decisions, and how to be more productive. It can also give you the skills to be a better leader and to stay ahead of the competition. With the right knowledge, you can be more successful in your career, in your relationships, and in life. Knowledge is the key to success, and the more you learn, the more successful you will be.

Francesco Vitali

Your Notes for Success

207

"Success is the doing, not the getting; in the trying, not the triumph. Success is a personal standard, reaching for the highest that is in us, becoming all that we can be."
— Zig Ziglar

Success is about doing, not getting. It's about putting in the effort, not the acclamation. It's about continuing to strive, even if we don't reach the top. It's about creating our own definition of success, and working to reach it. Having success isn't about the triumph, it's about becoming the best version of ourselves. Success is about pushing ourselves to our limits and continuing to grow. It's about staying humble and learning from our mistakes. It's about having the courage to try, even when the odds are stacked against us.

It's about having the perseverance to keep going, even when the going gets tough. Success is an individual journey. It's something we can each decide for ourselves. It's something that we can measure with our own personal yardstick. It's something that we can strive for and achieve. It is about taking the initiative and making the most of the opportunities presented.

Don't worry about reaching the finish line. Focus on the journey itself. There are so many experiences to look forward to, experiences that will teach you everything you need to know in order to succeed. So, don't pressure yourself to get things done quickly. Enjoy the moment and become the best version of yourself.

Your Notes for Success

208

"People can change anything they want to, and that means everything in the world." — Joe Strummer

People have the power to change anything they want to and become successful. With hard work and dedication, anything is possible. We can create positive change and break down any barrier if we put our minds to it. We must believe in ourselves and our abilities, and take advantage of any opportunity that comes our way. With the right attitude and determination, any challenge can be met. We must also take risks and not be afraid to fail, as this is often the best way to learn and grow. By taking ownership of our own careers, we can empower ourselves to create the life we desire. When we put our minds to it, we can accomplish anything and become successful.

We can strive to be the best people we can be for the benefit of others. We can use our resources and talents to help those who are in need. We can stand up for what is right and work for justice. We can be positive role models for others and be the change we want to see in the world. We can take the initiative to create the kind of world we want to live in. You have the power to change the world and make it better.

Francesco Vitali

Your Notes for Success

209

"Explore, experience, then push beyond."
— *Aaron Lauritsen*

Exploring enables us to step outside our comfort zone, to go beyond what we know, and to encounter new ideas, people, and places. It can open up a wealth of opportunities and the potential for personal growth. From exploring a new city to trying out a new activity, the experience can be truly life-changing.

However, the experience doesn't stop there. Once you have explored and experienced, it's time to push beyond. By pushing beyond, we can take the next step in our journey, building on what we have learned and discovered. We can take risks and challenge ourselves, further developing our skills and capabilities. We can make new connections, broaden our horizons, and open up exciting possibilities for the future.

Explore, experience, and then push beyond—it's a rewarding cycle that can lead to incredible things. By challenging ourselves and taking risks, we can develop new skills, gain a new perspective and even find a new passion. It is only when we push beyond our limits that we can find out what we are truly capable of. Taking the step to explore, experience, and push beyond our boundaries can allow us to reach new heights and grow in ways we never thought were possible.

Francesco Vitali

<u>*Your Notes for Success*</u>

210

"There's nothing in the world that breeds success like success." — Bob Ross

Success breeds success. It gives us the confidence, motivation, and self-belief to take on new challenges, to push ourselves further, and to strive for greatness. Success is a self-fulfilling prophecy. When we experience success, it gives us the encouragement to aim even higher and to develop our skills further. It also encourages us to take risks in pursuit of our goals, to persist in the face of adversity, and to keep our focus on our objectives.

Success gives us the strength to keep going and to eventually reach our goals. When we achieve success, we gain confidence and a sense of accomplishment. We feel like we have conquered a challenge and can now continue to push forward. Success motivates us to strive for more and to keep striving in life.

There's nothing in the world that breeds success like success, and it is something that should never be taken for granted. It is a powerful tool that can help us reach our dreams and make the most of our lives.

Your Notes for Success

211

"Once you bid farewell to discipline, you say goodbye to success." — Alex Ferguson

Once you bid farewell to discipline, it is akin to saying goodbye to success. Discipline is a crucial component of achieving success, as it helps us stay focused, stay motivated, remain organized, and work hard. Without discipline, it is all too easy to become distracted and lose sight of our goals. Discipline also helps us to become better at time management, which is an invaluable skill when it comes to success.

We have to be able to allocate our time appropriately to ensure that we are able to complete our tasks in a timely manner. Discipline also helps us develop self-control, which will prevent us from engaging in activities that could be detrimental to our success. Discipline is the foundation of success, and without it, achieving success is impossible. We need to understand that being disciplined with a goal in mind is the only way to succeed. There are numerous examples of successful people who have achieved success not just by using their skills, ideas, or technical expertise, but by being disciplined. Steve Jobs was disciplined and successful. Bill Gates used to be a heavy procrastinator and he admitted he became successful in life only after quitting this bad habit. You can do the same!

Francesco Vitali

<u>Your Notes for Success</u>

212

"Success is the best revenge." — Kanye West

Every path you choose is going to bring you face to face-with numerous challenges. You may find yourself alone standing by your beliefs and consistently pursuing your dreams. And there will come a time when you'll realize that you have all the support in the world. This will happen when you have finally achieved what you believe in. This will be your definition of success, and it, indeed, is the best revenge.

Success is the best revenge because it is the ultimate form of satisfaction. It does not matter what anyone else thinks of you, because, in the end, it is only your own successes that will bring you a sense of joy and pride. When you put in the hard work and effort to achieve success, you get a sense of accomplishment and satisfaction that no one can take away from you.

It is a reward in itself, and it is the best way to show those who have doubted or underestimated you that you are capable of great things. Success also gives you the confidence to take on bigger challenges and strive for even more success in the future. Success is the best revenge because it allows you to make your own mark in the world and prove that you can achieve anything you set your mind to.

Francesco Vitali

Your Notes for Success

213

"The price of success is to bear the criticism of envy."
— *Denis Waitley*

Success will always remain priceless to the people who have achieved their goals and realized their dreams. But there's a price attached to it. One that only the successful person knows.

The price of success is often misunderstood. On the surface, it can appear that success is easy to obtain and requires little effort. However, the truth is that success requires a great amount of hard work and dedication. Those who have achieved success understand that in order to get there, they must be willing to face criticism from those who are envious of their success. This criticism can be difficult to endure, but it is worth it in the end.

Those who are successful know that the price of success is to bear the criticism of envy. They understand that criticism is a natural part of life and it is a sign that they are doing something right. Successful people also know that the best way to deal with criticism is to stay focused on their goals and to stay motivated. It is with this attitude that they are able to rise above the criticism and continue on their path to success. If you embark on a path where you have big goals to achieve, then criticism of envy is the price you have to pay.

Francesco Vitali

Your Notes for Success

214

"Prepare yourself for success. You have to see it coming to get there." — Destiny Booze

The journey to success is not an easy one—but you'll get there with the right approach, discipline, and commitment to your beliefs when everything seems to be going in a different direction. You have to prove yourself again and again. There will be ups and downs. People close to you will tell you to give up. But to prepare for success, you need to block out all the negativity and focus only on your goals.

Preparing yourself for success is essential if you want to reach the top. It involves committing to hard work, developing the right skills and mindset, and having the courage to keep going even when things don't always go as planned. The first step is to identify your goals and create a plan to reach them. Set short-term and long-term goals and take the necessary steps to achieve them.

Make sure to have a timeline and track your progress. Then, focus on building the skills and knowledge necessary to succeed. Take classes, read books, and do whatever it takes to stay ahead. Finally, stay motivated and never give up. Have the confidence that you can achieve whatever you set out to do and don't let anything stand in your way. With dedication and commitment, you can make success a reality.

Your Notes for Success

215

*"It's no use saying, 'We are doing our best.' You have
got to succeed in doing what is necessary."*
— *Winston Churchill*

It's true that simply saying, "We are doing our best," isn't enough to get the job done. To succeed, we must take action. We must identify and focus on tasks that need to be done and take the steps necessary to complete them. We must stay organized and remain focused on the goal even when faced with obstacles and challenges. We must work together as a team and stay positive and motivated. With hard work and dedication, success is possible. We must remember that it's never too late to try and do better. To do this, we can set clear objectives and break them down into achievable steps. We can also reach out for help and support from our team and use the resources available to us.

Every effort we make brings us closer to our goal and eventual success. We need to be mentally prepared to do everything necessary to achieve our goals. Sometimes, self-doubt will engulf you and you may question the path you have chosen for yourself. But you cannot achieve success if you believe you are doing the best you can. Often, our definition of best is not enough, we need to go beyond it to achieve our goals.

Francesco Vitali

Your Notes for Success

216

"The ladder of success is never crowded at the top."
— Napoleon Hill

The ladder of success is not meant for everyone to climb. This is the reason it's not crowded when you reach the top. But to get there, you need to go step by step. The difficulties and challenges are part of the ladder. Staying strong, focused, and committed are the only things that can help you reach the top.

The ladder of success is never crowded at the top is a testament to the hard work and dedication one puts in to reach their goals. It is said that if you truly want something, you need to work hard and stay focused to reach the top. Being at the top of the ladder requires you to put in the hard work and dedication, which is why it's never crowded. It is important to remember that success isn't a destination, but rather a journey. It is important to enjoy the journey and not just focus on the destination. It's all about the journey and the lessons you learn along the way. With every step of the ladder, you learn something new and you become more prepared for the next step. With dedication and consistency, you can achieve anything and make your dreams come true.

Francesco Vitali

Your Notes for Success

217

*"Success does not consist in never making blunders, but
in never making the same one a second time."*
— Josh Billings

Success is not measured by the mistakes you make, but by how you handle them. Making mistakes is a natural part of life and a great way to learn and grow. The key to success is not to never make mistakes, but to never make the same mistake twice. By recognizing mistakes and learning from them, we can develop a better understanding of our strengths and weaknesses, allowing us to make more informed decisions.

When faced with a similar situation, we can use the information we've gathered to make a better decision. Mistakes can help us become more resilient and develop a more positive outlook on life. Success is not about being perfect, but about being able to recognize and learn from mistakes and use them as an opportunity for growth.

We should learn from our mistakes, as they are the best teachers one can have. Mistakes and failures become our lighthouses and guide us on our journey to success. Even if you become successful, you are bound to make mistakes. But to stay at the top, you need to embrace your mistakes, learn from them, and prepare a plan that doesn't involve repeating the same mistake.

Francesco Vitali

<u>*Your Notes for Success*</u>

218

"Even if you are on the right track, but just sit there, you will still get run over." — Will Rogers

It is important to remember that even if you are on the right track but just sit there, you will still get run over. This means that even if you have made the right decision and are headed in the right direction, if you do not take any action to move forward, you will not get anywhere.

To get somewhere, you have to keep running until you have reached your destination. Success, however, is not a mere destination but a journey—in order to achieve your goals and remain successful, you need to be on your toes all the time. You can't rest, thinking that you have achieved something—because that achievement can easily be taken away by someone or something else. The most valuable company in the world can go bankrupt. The achievements of the most successful athlete can be overshadowed by someone else in the same field.

This serves as a reminder that it is important to take action, stay focused, and push forward despite any obstacles that may come your way. Without taking action, it is impossible to make progress and reach your goals. Even if you are on the right track, it is important to remain active and keep moving forward in order to make progress and achieve success.

Francesco Vitali

Your Notes for Success

219

"Success goes to the ones who do. Get up.
Show up. Throw up if you have to. Do it afraid,
but do it no matter." — Toni Sorenson

Success goes to those who take action, no matter how afraid they may be. It's easy to talk about what you want to do, but it takes courage and hard work to actually do it. You have to get up and show up, even if at times, you'll feel like throwing up. You have to embrace the fear of the unknown, and take action anyway.

It's easy to talk yourself out of it, but it takes courage and confidence to push through and make it happen. Success doesn't come from sitting on the sidelines. It comes from taking risks, learning from mistakes, and never giving up. Success is something that you earn, and it's worth every ounce of effort you put in. So get up, show up, and take action, no matter how afraid you are. Success is yours for the taking.

To be successful, you need to change your mindset. No matter what you are going through, you have to show up in order to be successful. The world doesn't stop for anyone or anything—those who have tasted success know this very well. You need to keep going, even if all the odds are stacked against you. This is how you can be successful.

Your Notes for Success

220

*"Success is assured when a person fears the
pain of regret more than the pain of the process."*
— *Orrin Woodward*

Pursuing your dreams is a painful process—one that brings unprecedented challenges. We need to overcome our fears and passionately pursue what we desire. We need to fear the regret of not making the move more than what will happen if things go wrong. Success is indeed achievable when one realizes that the pain of regret far outweighs the pain of the process. Regret is a heavy burden to bear, as it can linger in our minds and hearts for a lifetime. By focusing on the long-term, we can more easily push ourselves through difficult and challenging times, knowing that the pain of failure will be much harder to bear than the effort we put in.

It's important to remember that all great successes require dedication and perseverance. The path to achieving our goals is often filled with obstacles, but we must remain focused on our end goal. The key to achieving success is to stay motivated and to remain positive throughout the journey. It's important to take the necessary steps to reach our goals, and to never give up, no matter how hard it may get. With the right attitude and mindset, success is assured.

Your Notes for Success

221

"If you always do what is easy and choose the path of least resistance, you never step outside your comfort zone. Great things don't come from comfort zones."
— *Roy Bennett*

If you are comfortable doing something and are afraid to try anything new, it is next to impossible that you will be successful. Success comes to those who are always willing to go the extra mile, accept new challenges, and step out of their comfort zone. The easy path with little to no challenges brings no reward. The proverb "high risk, high reward" aptly describes successful people. People who take risks are the ones who don't like to confine themselves in a specific zone where they feel comfortable.

If you always do what is easy and choose the path of least resistance, you will never be able to reach your full potential. Taking risks and challenging yourself is how you grow and develop as a person. Taking the easy route may feel comfortable in the short term, but in the long run, it can prevent you from achieving your goals.

Stepping outside of your comfort zone can be intimidating, but it can also be extremely rewarding. It can open you up to new experiences, knowledge, and opportunities. When you push your boundaries, you are able to discover new things about yourself and your capabilities. Taking the easy route may seem tempting, but it is essential that you challenge yourself and take risks in order to reach your full potential.

Francesco Vitali

Your Notes for Success

222

"No amount of reading or memorizing will make
you successful in life. It is the understanding and
application of wise thought that counts."
— *Bob Proctor*

Memorizing hundreds or thousands of books, concepts, and theories word by word makes no difference in determining success. To achieve your goals, you need to understand every word and the hidden meaning behind it. Knowledge is power only when you understand the situation you are in and know how to apply the acquired knowledge to navigate through challenges. There's more to success than meets the eye. It involves dedication, commitment, resilience, and risks.

Success in life involves far more than just the knowledge gained from books. It requires a deep understanding of the world, honed by the skills of critical thinking, problem-solving, collaboration, and communication. It is important to have a strong foundation of knowledge, but it is equally as important to have the skills to apply that knowledge to the real world.

Successful people recognize this and strive to continuously learn and grow. They understand that no matter how much they read, it is the ability to apply that knowledge that will make the difference. Successful individuals are also open-minded and curious, seeking out new ideas and perspectives to build upon their existing knowledge. They are also resilient, with the ability to adapt and adjust to overcome obstacles.

Your Notes for Success

223

"Since when is failure more appealing?
Never give up." — Richelle E. Goodrich

Failure can be a tough pill to swallow, but it should never be seen as an end. Instead, failure should be viewed as a chance to learn, grow, and develop. It can be a great opportunity to discover where you need to make improvements and come back stronger. Failure should never be seen as a sign of weakness, but rather a sign of resilience and perseverance.

Embracing your failures and moving on with life is all you need to be successful. It should only be treated as a learning experience, one that you can leverage to avoid repeating the same mistakes. Failure is often misconstrued as an end to your dream, but in reality, it is only an indication that you are heading in the right direction.

Failures are part of life, but accepting your defeat is a choice. It's important to pick yourself up, learn from your mistakes, and move forward. When you fail, use it as a chance to reflect and improve. Always remember that failure is an essential part of growth and progress. There is no shame in failure. No matter how hard things may seem, never give up and always keep striving for success.

Francesco Vitali

<u>Your Notes for Success</u>

224

"Fortunate are those who take the first steps."
— *Paulo Coelho*

You will never learn how to navigate through the storm if you choose to stay on the shore. The only difference between a successful and unsuccessful person is the first step. Those who give in to their fears and don't take the first step that can change their lives end up with regret. And those who take that first step go on to lead the world.

Taking the first step toward success is essential for achieving our goals. It sets the tone for the journey ahead and gives us the momentum to continue taking action. It is important to be proactive in defining our success and taking the initiative to move forward. We must be willing to take risks, try new things, and push ourselves out of our comfort zone.

This will allow us to discover new talents and skills that can enhance our path to success. Taking the first step also helps us to stay focused on our goal and take consistent action toward it. By taking the first step we can create an action plan that will guide us to success. We can also build our confidence and self-belief by seeing the progress we make with each step. Taking the first step is a courageous move, but it is essential for achieving our goals and becoming successful.

Francesco Vitali

Your Notes for Success

225

"Success is not the key to happiness. Happiness is the key to success. If you love what you are doing, you will be successful." — Albert Schweitzer

This quote encapsulates a profound truth about the nature of success and happiness. Often, people believe that achieving a particular goal or reaching a certain level of success will bring them happiness. However, this perspective is inherently flawed because it places happiness as a consequence of success. The quote suggests a different paradigm: that happiness itself is a powerful driver for success.

When you find genuine happiness and fulfilment in what you do, it fuels your motivation, determination, and creativity. Passion for your work makes you resilient in the face of challenges and setbacks. When you love what you do, the effort you put into it doesn't feel like a burden; it becomes a source of joy and purpose. This enthusiasm and dedication are what lead to true success.

Moreover, happiness enhances various cognitive functions, including decision-making and problem-solving skills. A positive mindset encourages innovation and fosters healthy interpersonal relationships, both of which are instrumental in achieving success in any field.

In essence, the quote emphasizes that success isn't just about material wealth or professional achievements; it's about leading a fulfilling and contented life. When you prioritize your happiness and align your actions with what brings you joy, you naturally become more productive, creative, and successful in your endeavours. Happiness, therefore, acts as the catalyst that propels you toward your goals and aspirations.

Francesco Vitali

<u>Your Notes for Success</u>

226

"My dreams are worthless, my plans are dust, my goals are impossible. All are of no value unless they are followed by action." — Og Mandino

Action speaks louder than words. There are over 8 billion people in the world and everyone has a dream. In a world where every individual desires to be something or someone, only a handful end up being successful. What makes them different is that their dreams, goals, and ambitions are backed by actions.

Dreams and goals without action are like a ship without a sail. Without action, dreams and goals are just idle thoughts. Taking action is the only way to make them come to fruition. Action is the bridge that takes you from where you are to where you want to be. It is the key to turning your goals into reality. Without action, dreams and goals are worth nothing more than the paper they are written on.

Action gives dreams and goals the power to shape our lives. It allows us to take control of our own destiny and move toward our desired future. Action gives our dreams and goals purpose and meaning. It shows that we are willing to do whatever it takes to make them happen. Every step taken in the right direction brings us closer to our goals and dreams. So take action and turn your dreams and goals into a reality!

Francesco Vitali

Your Notes for Success

227

"Success is a decision, not a gift." — Steve Backley

If you keep praying for success, it will never come to you. It is the result of hard work, dedication, commitment, discipline, and decisions. The decisions you make today are going to define your future. People who are successful never had it easy. They had to make some difficult, extremely risky decisions to be where they are today. It was not handed down to them, and it will never be handed down to anyone.

Success is a decision, not a gift. We all have the ability to take action and make our dreams a reality. It is a choice we make to dedicate our time, energy, and resources to achieving our goals. The key to success is to believe in yourself, develop a plan, be persistent, and never give up. When faced with obstacles, it is important to stay focused and keep working toward our goals.

Viewing success as a decision and not a gift allows us to take ownership of our lives, and take pride in our accomplishments. Success is something we all can achieve with dedication and hard work. Make the decision to be successful today, and you will be well on your way to achieving your dreams.

Francesco Vitali

Your Notes for Success

228

"If you want to be truly successful, invest in yourself to get the knowledge you need to find your unique factor. When you find it and focus on it and persevere, your success will blossom." — Sidney Madwed

The amount of time you spend watching movies, relaxing on a beach, hanging out with friends, or doing something that your heart desires will never make you successful. Time is precious— appreciate it while you still have it and make the most out of it. Instead of watching a motivational speaker telling you how to be successful, invest in upskilling yourself. Find your true calling and leave no stone unturned to learn it—by investing your time and money in yourself. This is the only way to achieve success.

If you want to be truly successful, invest in yourself and you will be rewarded with a wealth of knowledge. Embrace the opportunities that come your way and tap into the resources available to you. Start by educating yourself and learning all you can about what makes you special. Develop a positive attitude and an open mind. Take risks and dare to be different. Believe in yourself and your abilities.

Enjoy the journey, celebrate the victories, and learn from the setbacks. Cultivate relationships with mentors, peers, and experts to help you along the way. With the right attitude and dedication, you can unlock your potential and become successful. Make yourself a priority and take action to make your dreams a reality. Invest in yourself and you will be rewarded with success.

Francesco Vitali

Your Notes for Success

229

"Don`t allow ignorance to further enslave your destiny." — Jaachynma N.E. Agu

There's no such thing as fate. As humans, we are in charge of our destiny. We can decide where we wish to see ourselves in the coming years. If we leave everything to fate and do not take meaningful steps to correct our path, then success will always remain a distant dream.

Don't allow ignorance to further enslave your destiny. Instead, take control of your life and make it one of fulfillment and success. Utilize the power of knowledge and understanding to guide you on your journey. Open your mind to new possibilities and be willing to take risks in order to achieve greatness. Believe in yourself and have confidence in your abilities. Surround yourself with positive people who will encourage and support you. Be willing to learn and grow, and never be afraid to ask for help when you need it. Find joy and contentment in the small victories and celebrate your successes. Work hard and don't let anyone or anything stand in your way. Have courage and be strong in the face of adversity. Focus on the future and use past experiences to create a better tomorrow. Embrace the beauty of life and don't be afraid to make mistakes. Believe in yourself and never give up on your dreams.

Francesco Vitali

Your Notes for Success

230

"Get off the treadmill of consumption, replication, and mediocrity. Begin lifting the weights of creativity, originality, and success." — Ryan Lilly

If we keep on doing what everyone else does, we can never be truly successful. To achieve bigger things in life, it is vital that we don't settle down for mediocrity. We need to aim higher and take charge of our destiny. We need to make decisions based on insights and knowledge that we have acquired through education, experience, and life. We need to say goodbye to the comfort we are used to, and start taking on new challenges.

It is time to start crafting your own story and to pursue your own dreams. The world is your canvas, and the possibilities are endless. Dream bigger. Believe more. Fear less. Strive for excellence. Enjoy the journey and take risks. Have faith in yourself and your abilities. Be ambitious and inspired. Develop your own style and create something meaningful. Push yourself and be courageous. Have the confidence to stand out and be different. Believe in yourself and the power of hard work. Rejoice in the potential of what you can achieve.

Step away from the status quo and strive for innovation. Pursue the inner greatness that lies within. Tap into your unique gifts and talents. Unearth your inner strength. Revel in the power of self-expression. Take pride in your accomplishments. Embrace the beauty of originality!

Francesco Vitali

Your Notes for Success

231

"In order to grow, I promise you'll have to let go of
some habits. 10 times out of 10, they'll be the habits
you're most in love with." — Brandi L. Bates

To gain something in life, one has to let go of something. We have limited time in a day and if we don't quit the habits that are taking most of our time, we may never find time to pursue our dreams. This is the harsh reality. You need to sacrifice some things you love doing in order to achieve success. There's no other way around it.

In order to grow, you'll have to let go of some habits, but it will be worth it in the end. You have the courage and strength to let go, and you can look forward to a brighter future. Embrace the challenge and trust that the journey will be rewarding. Releasing the old will bring forth exciting new opportunities and experiences. It may be hard to release beloved habits, but you'll be better for it in the end. Celebrate what you are about to gain, and allow yourself to be optimistic about the journey ahead. Be brave, be strong, and be ready for a wonderful adventure.

You have the power to make positive changes in your life, and the potential for growth is limitless. Believe in yourself and the potential for greatness. You can do this. Let go and allow yourself to soar to new heights.

Francesco Vitali

Your Notes for Success

232

*"Don't grieve when people fail to recognize your ability.
Grieve for your lack of ability instead." — Confucius*

We humans tend to take emotions into our heads. We sometimes fall prey to how others, including our friends and family, judge our actions. We let emotions and words control us and, in the process, lose self-control. This defeats our chances of achieving our goals. If we keep getting distracted by how people judge us or our actions, then we will not be able to focus on achieving our goals and becoming successful.

Don't let discouragement get the better of you when others don't recognize your talents. Instead, use it as an opportunity to reflect and work on your weaknesses. Believe in yourself and focus on the positive aspects of your life. Your potential is boundless, and you should never let anyone tell you otherwise. Acknowledge your strengths, and work to improve your weaknesses. Find joy in the little things, and be proud of your accomplishments. You are capable of anything you put your mind to, so don't ever give up. Embrace your capabilities, and don't be afraid to take risks. Believe in yourself, and use setbacks as learning experiences. Persevere and stay focused on your goals. With determination, you can reach your highest potential.

Francesco Vitali

Your Notes for Success

233

"Whoever submits himself to a super-discipline can expect great triumphs." — Samael Aun Weor

The one thing in life that's the key to success is being disciplined. It does not have any cost associated with it and offers great benefits. From winning a battle or war to taking your business to new heights, discipline is important. This is the reason successful businesses and armies across the world focus on discipline first. If we are disciplined and align our day-to-day tasks in a way that we have time to focus on each task, then success will come to us eventually.

Whoever submits himself to super-discipline can expect great triumphs. It requires dedication, hard work, and determination to take on such a task. But the rewards of success can be extraordinary. With perseverance and ambition, one can achieve amazing heights. The feeling of accomplishment and pride that comes from attaining a goal can be incredibly rewarding. It is an opportunity to prove what one can do, to prove oneself, and to grow. It can lead to insights, self-discovery, and personal growth. It can also bring many opportunities and a sense of accomplishment. The satisfaction of having achieved something that seemed impossible can be exhilarating. It can be a life-changing experience, a journey of exploration and learning, and a path to a better future.

Your Notes for Success

234

"It's not so much what you accomplish. But what's more important is how far you've come to accomplish what you have. Success is the measure of not mere achievement, but also how hard one had to work."
— *Therone Shellman*

We all have some goals in mind and if we look back, we will realize that we have come a long way from where we started. This is all that matters. We should remain focused on working hard and doing better than yesterday. Gradually, the hard work will pay off and we may not be closer to achieving our goals yet, but we will be moving forward. The dedication and commitment required to achieve certain goals should be there—because that's how one can measure success.

Each step you take is a huge success and something to be celebrated. You should be proud of your efforts and the progress you have made. Despite challenges and obstacles, you have kept pushing and striving for greatness. You have worked hard and stayed determined to reach your goals. You have overcome every difficulty and emerged triumphant. You have taken leaps of faith and been brave enough to take risks. Your journey has been remarkable, and you have come so far. You have learned valuable lessons and developed into a stronger, more resilient person. You are an inspiration to everyone around you. You have persevered and achieved so much, and for that you should be exceedingly proud. You have demonstrated resilience, strength, and courage, and that is truly admirable.

Francesco Vitali

Your Notes for Success

235

"Determination, effort, and practice are rewarded with success." — Mary Lydon Simonsen

Determination, effort, and practice are the keys to success. When you apply yourself to any goal, you are more likely to reach it. Determination is the drive to keep going even when things get tough. Effort is the work you put in to make your goal a reality. Practice is the repetition of tasks to improve your skills.

When combined, these three actions can help you achieve anything you set your mind to. With determination, effort, and practice, you can overcome any challenge and reach any milestone. Success is attainable with the right attitude and the right mindset. Hard work and dedication can lead you to reach your goals and experience great rewards. Believe in yourself and never give up, and success will be within your reach.

The secret to success lies in staying determined, taking meaningful steps, and remaining focused on our goals. If you understand this basic formula and keep working hard, then success will surely come. It may not be in a month or a year, but it will come eventually. Being committed to your goals is all you need to achieve them. There's no shortcut to it. We have to go beyond the definition of doing our best to achieve success.

Francesco Vitali

Your Notes for Success

236

"The person who makes a success of living is the one
who sees his goal steadily and aims for it unswervingly.
That is dedication." — Cecil B. DeMille

Setting clear and realistic goals, dividing them into short-term and long-term goals, and working relentlessly to achieve them will bring you success. First you need to have a clear vision, which should be followed by absolute dedication to your goals, dreams, ambitions, or objectives. This is how you can live a successful and fulfilling life. We are responsible for our destiny and can steer our life in any direction, only if we dedicate our time, energy, efforts, and investment.

The person who makes a success of living is an admirable individual who exhibits true dedication. They have a clear goal in mind and strive to reach it relentlessly. This individual is ambitious, determined, and committed and is an inspiration to those around them. They are a leader and a motivator, encouraging others to strive for greatness. In this person we find hope, courage, and strength, traits that will help them reach their desired destination. They have a strong work ethic and are dedicated to their craft. Their qualities of ambition, resilience, and dedication are the foundation of their success, and will inspire future generations to take on their own challenges. They are a force to be reckoned with and will continue to reach greater heights.

Francesco Vitali

Your Notes for Success

237

"To be successful, you must decide exactly
what you want to accomplish, then resolve to
pay the price to get it." — Bunker Hunt

Success comes at a price. This is something we all should be aware of. Some pay the price of leaving the habits they love, and others have to dedicate their lives to achieving their goals. However, the definition of success varies for every individual. Success may mean growing your business to a global giant or it may mean achieving the senior management position that you wanted.

To be successful, you must decide exactly what you want to accomplish and then resolve to pay the price to get it. Success is achievable if you have the ambition, determination, and courage to see your goals through. You must be willing to invest your time, energy, and resources in order to obtain the results you desire. Set ambitious goals, and then make a plan to achieve them. Believe in yourself, and be persistent. Create positive affirmations and use them to stay motivated and focused. Cultivate a positive attitude, and stay optimistic. Nurture relationships with people who can help you reach your goals. Develop good habits, like hard work, positive self-talk, and goal-setting. Be open to learning new things, and be willing to make mistakes. Persevere, stay resilient, and remain confident. Have the courage to take risks, and have the courage to fail. Embrace the journey, and be thankful for the successes.

Francesco Vitali

Your Notes for Success

238

*"If you have time to whine then you have time
to find solutions." — Dee Dee Artner*

One of the key characteristics of successful people is that they spend time finding a solution rather than whining about it. Whining about anything will only bring you regret, as you will always find yourself surrounded by problems. Complaining about a problem or discussing the same thing again and again will not help you find any solution. The best it can do is to confuse you, and decisions based on confusion often result in disasters.

It's important to remember that when life throws you a curve ball, you can always work toward a positive result. Finding solutions is possible, it just takes a commitment of time and effort. Instead of worrying and complaining, focus on being proactive and looking for ways to improve the situation. It's amazing how a shift in attitude can lead to amazing results. Embrace the challenge and take this opportunity as an opportunity to grow and learn. Look for ways to rise to the challenge and be creative in your solutions. Believe in yourself and your ability to find solutions and you will be pleasantly surprised by the results. You can do it! Don't be afraid to believe in the power of positivity. Believe in yourself and the possibilities that a positive outlook can bring. With a little bit of effort and commitment, you can find solutions and be successful.

Francesco Vitali

<u>Your Notes for Success</u>

239

"Achieving success is a challenge but so is struggling so you may as well choose success." — Rob Liano

If you think working toward achieving your goal is a challenge, wait until you find yourself struggling to make ends meet. No matter what path you choose, challenges will always be a part of it. It is vital that we opt for the path to success no matter how big or inconvenient the challenges may appear. You just need to make the first move, and you will find the courage to overcome every challenge.

Achieving success is a challenge, but so is struggling, so you may as well choose success. It's not easy, but it's worth it. Success is not a destination; it's a journey, and the journey is filled with hard work, resilience, and dedication. Those who are successful understand that success comes from within and have the courage to keep pushing until they achieve their goals. Successful people are not afraid of failure; they use it as a learning opportunity to help them get closer to their goals. They have the ambition and determination to stay focused on the task at hand and never give up. When success is achieved, the rewards are plentiful and fulfilling. Success is a gift that can be shared with others, and it is a great feeling to know that you have worked hard and achieved something special. So, make success happen!

Your Notes for Success

240

*"You only have to doze a moment, and all is lost. For
ruin and salvation both have their source inside you."*
— *Epictetus*

You are the source of your salvation or ruin. Whatever you
wish to become, it all starts with you. You can opt for a life that
is filled with challenges and great rewards, or you can stay in your
comfort zone and depart from this world without making any
impact. The choice is and will always be yours.

You only have to doze a moment, and all is lost, yet there
is always the potential for salvation! Inside you are the power
to choose between ruin and renewal. You have the courage
to confront difficult situations and the wisdom to find positive
solutions. Your resilience, determination, and resourcefulness are
sources of strength and hope. You have the potential to create a
better future, no matter what happens in the present. You have
the capacity to manifest your dreams. You have the courage to
take risks and the fortitude to stay the course. With these qualities,
you are capable of achieving greatness and making a difference in
the world. You are a beacon of light, a true source of inspiration
and motivation. You have all that you need to make your mark on
the world.

Francesco Vitali

Your Notes for Success

241

"The secret code of success is patience, a virtue that cannot be replaced. It takes time to build great dreams."
— *Bernard Kelvin Clive*

No successful business came into being overnight. It takes time, patience, and the right strategy to grow a small business into a global conglomerate. Companies that are globally recognized today started very small. The case of successful individuals is no different—they had to struggle, but they succeeded only because they had patience and perseverance.

Patience is an invaluable virtue that allows us to keep striving for our dreams and goals in life. Patience is a sign of strength and wisdom, allowing us to take the time to make sure our goals are achieved in the best way possible. With patience, we can take our time to make sure that our dreams become a reality, allowing us to be passionate and hopeful. Patience is the key to unlocking our potential and achieving our goals. It is a powerful tool that allows us to remain positive and optimistic. With patience, we can trust the process even when the results are not immediately apparent. Patience allows us to stay focused on the long-term goal, no matter how difficult the journey may be. It gives us the courage and resilience to keep pushing forward, even when the going gets tough.

Francesco Vitali

Your Notes for Success

242

*"All we have to decide is what to do with the time
that is given us." — J.R.R. Tolkien*

We all have twenty-four hours in a day. The way we spend these precious hours ultimately decides our future. People who are successful also use the limited time they have to make an impact. They prioritize their day in a way that every important task is given its due attention. Using the time that's given to us wisely can make us successful.

All we have to decide is what to do with the time that is given to us. This is an empowering thought, as it reminds us that we have been blessed with time and it is up to us what we make of it. We can use our time to be productive, creative, and generous. We can use our time to learn something new, explore our passions, and share our gifts with the world.

We can be courageous, explore new ideas, and develop our own potential. There is so much potential for growth, happiness, and joy that comes with taking full advantage of the time we have.

We can use our time to make a positive impact and help others. The possibilities are endless and we can make the most of our time with the right attitude and focus.

Francesco Vitali

Your Notes for Success

243

*"We all make choices, but in the end,
our choices make us." — Andrew Ryan*

Our actions today define our future. The choices we make have a profound impact on making us successful or unsuccessful. This is the reason successful people consider all the possible outcomes of their choices before making any decisions. It is vital for every individual pursuing a dream or a goal to explore the possible outcomes—because what they choose today will ultimately have a positive or negative impact on their future.

We all make choices in life, and it's those choices that create our reality. Each decision we make brings us closer to our destiny and helps shape our character. When we make the right choices, it can lead to success, joy, and fulfillment. No matter what we choose, we have the power to create a better future for ourselves. We can make choices that are inspiring, courageous, and profound. We can choose to be kind and compassionate, to embrace life with enthusiasm, and to take action toward our goals. Even when our choices bring us difficult moments, in the end, they make us who we are. They remind us of our strength and resilience, and of the importance of making decisions that honor our values and beliefs. We all make choices, but in the end, our choices make us.

Francesco Vitali

Your Notes for Success

244

"It's not who you are underneath, it's what you do that defines you." — Bruce Wayne

It's not who you are underneath that defines you, it's what you do. Your actions and choices are what make you who you are. You have the power to choose your path and make your mark on the world. Being courageous, ambitious, and determined can take you far. You have the potential to be anything and everything you want. When obstacles arise, you have the strength to overcome them. You can be a leader, a role model, and an inspiration to others. You have the ability to make a difference and create a positive impact on the world. Your actions speak louder than words, and you have the power to make a difference. You embody courage, strength, and resilience. You have the power to make something of yourself, and you will be remembered for the good you have done. You define yourself, and your actions will determine your success. Be proud of who you are and what you do.

Our actions have meaning and consequences. What we do and how we do it matters the most. You may be an introvert who feels shy underneath, but when it comes to choosing success over staying in your comfort zone, you should always opt for the former. Success comes to those who work hard and understand how their actions, decisions, and choices will leave an impact.

Francesco Vitali

<u>*Your Notes for Success*</u>

245

"The future has not been written. There is no fate but what we make for ourselves." — John Conner

Future is nothing but the outcome of our decisions. Successful people don't really believe in fate—they know what they want to achieve and set their goals accordingly, as well as modify their lifestyle and habits. Our future is not written—we have the free will to act however we want. Be mindful of what you desire and work hard until you have it.

The future is filled with endless possibilities and opportunities. We have the power to create our own destiny, to make our dreams come true. We can choose to fill our lives with optimism, joy, and hope. With hard work, dedication, and determination, we can create our own success. We can have faith in ourselves and our abilities, believing that anything is possible. With courage and strength, we can take risks and make bold decisions that will lead us to an amazing, positive future. We can make the world a brighter, better place for ourselves and for others. The future is ours to create, and we can make it brilliant. With an open heart and mind, we can unlock a world of potential and make our dreams a reality. The future is a blank canvas that we can paint with success, prosperity, and happiness.

Francesco Vitali

Your Notes for Success

246

"Success requires no explanations.
Failure permits no alibis." — Napoleon Hill

The end justifies the means—this is absolutely true when it comes to success. If you are successful, people will never ask you for an explanation of how you achieved success; rather, they will seek guidance for themselves. However, if you are unsuccessful in your attempt, then no matter how concrete reasoning you may have, people may never accept it.

Success is an incredible feeling. It's a feeling of confidence, joy, accomplishment, and pride. It's a feeling that comes from hard work, dedication, and resilience. Success is about having a goal, believing in yourself, and maintaining a positive attitude regardless of the obstacles that come your way. It's about having the courage and determination to keep fighting and pushing forward, no matter the cost. Failure, on the other hand, can be a difficult thing to deal with.

But failure doesn't have to be viewed as a negative thing. It's a great opportunity to learn and grow, to become stronger and more resilient. It's an opportunity to develop the skills and knowledge necessary to reach the heights of success. So, while success requires no explanations, failure permits no alibis. We must accept our failures and use them as a learning experience and a stepping stone to success.

Francesco Vitali

Your Notes for Success

247

"Success is not the end of the journey. It is the beginning of the expression of your infinite potential."
— *Sakshi Chetana*

When we have achieved a milestone to become successful, what should we do? The simplest answer is that this will be the beginning of another adventure. It shows that you have great potential, and that you have to proceed to strengthen your position. As a successful business owner, you may want to capture more market share. If you have successfully achieved your goal of becoming a celebrity, the next adventure is to stay there while increasing your fan base across the globe.

Success is the start of a beautiful journey of growth and exploration. It is the motivation to reach for the stars, to strive for excellence, and to make a lasting impact. Success is the appreciation of hard work and dedication, a reward for taking risks and believing in yourself. It is the foundation for a life of joy, abundance, and fulfillment. Success is the spark that ignites our passions and encourages us to take action. By savoring the sweet taste of success, we are inspired to keep pushing forward and are empowered to reach for the highest heights. Success is a reminder that anything is possible and that with the right attitude, anything can be achieved. It is the embodiment of our dreams and a sign of the infinite potential that lives within each and every one of us.

Your Notes for Success

248

"The minute you start talking about what you're going to do if you lose, you have lost." — George P. Shultz

If you are planning to be successful and also thinking about losing and what your life may look like after that, you have already lost. Successful people tend to focus on their goals without considering what losing would do to them. Certainly, you will face many challenges and failures, but admitting defeat is not a trait of successful people.

The minute you start talking about what you're going to do if you lose, you have already opened yourself to losing. A positive attitude is key to any endeavor, and believing in yourself and your ability to succeed is a major part of achieving your goals. Instead of focusing on the possibility of failure, focus on the possibility of success. Believe that you can and will do it, and your confidence will lead you to success. Encourage yourself to take on challenges with enthusiasm and optimism, embrace the unknown, and believe in yourself and your abilities. There is nothing you can't do if you set your mind to it and work hard. Believe in yourself and your capabilities, and you will be unstoppable. Be brave, be courageous, and be confident. You can do it!

Your Notes for Success

249

"Your time is limited, so don't waste it living someone else's life. Don't be trapped by dogma—which is living with the results of other people's thinking. — Steve Jobs

We all have a limited time on this Earth, so why not make the most of it? Don't waste it living someone else's life, because you will never get that time back. Instead, create your own life and make your own dreams come true. Don't be hesitant or scared to take chances because you will regret it if you don't. Set achievable goals and take action to reach them. Believe in yourself and the power of your dreams. Recognize that it's okay to make mistakes and learn from them.

Don't be afraid to ask for help and advice from those around you. Know that each day is a chance to move closer to achieving your goals. Take time to celebrate your successes and learn from any failures. Surround yourself with positive and supportive people who encourage and motivate you. Stay focused and determined, and never give up.

Living your life to fit in the social fabric is the worst mistake, especially if you want to be successful one day. What people think of your ideas, beliefs, worldview, and plan to achieve success should never come your way of achieving success. If you start ignoring the suggestions of your social circle and start living your life the way you want it, only then can you truly be successful.

Francesco Vitali

Your Notes for Success

250

"If you look at what you have in life, you'll always have more. If you look at what you don't have in life, you'll never have enough." — Oprah Winfrey

Comparing yourself with others without realizing the hardships and challenges they had to go through will only bring you disappointment. It's never about a glass being half-full or half-empty; rather, it's about what you wish to do with the water you have. Appreciate the resources you have and if you want to achieve something, never make an impulse decision. Our definition of success should be exclusively ours. We need to define what it will take for us to feel successful and fulfilled.

When it comes to important lessons, one of the most valuable is the idea that if you appreciate what you have, you will always have more. It's easy to focus on the things we don't have, and it's human nature to want more. But when we take the time to really appreciate what we have and be thankful for it, we open the door to abundance. By counting our blessings, we tap into a positive energy that can bring us more of the same. When we look at what we have been able to achieve with gratitude and positivity, we attract more of the same into our lives. By looking at what we have, we can be sure that we will never lack.

So, start by appreciating where you stand, and you will go further.

Francesco Vitali

Your Notes for Success

251

"Don't judge each day by the harvest you reap but by the seeds that you plant." — Robert Louis Stevenson

All good things in life take time. We need to be patient, disciplined and focused. Our goals are the only thing that should be in our mind all of the time. It does not matter if we are taking small steps to achieve our goals, as long as we are making progress. Every small step counts and it will eventually help us achieve our goals.

We should strive to plant seeds of kindness, understanding, and compassion each and every day. In doing so, we will reap a harvest of joy and contentment. We should be patient. It may take time to see the fruits of our labor, but when we keep planting positive seeds, we will eventually reap the rewards.

We should not be discouraged if we don't always see the results of our actions right away. We need to keep our eyes on the future and have faith that the seeds we have planted will eventually bring us the joy and happiness that we seek. If we focus on planting the right kind of seeds, we will eventually have a harvest of peaceful and fulfilling days.

Just believe in the process. Give your 100 percent and you will achieve your goals!

Francesco Vitali

Your Notes for Success

252

"The future belongs to those who believe in the beauty of their dreams." — Eleanor Roosevelt

The future belongs to those who believe in the beauty of their dreams. Dreams are the essence of life, the source of our ambition, and our greatest motivator. With the right attitude, we can turn these dreams into reality. We can use our passion, determination, and hard work to make our dreams come true and create a better future for ourselves and the generations to come.

Dreams do come true with passion, commitment, and discipline. Dreams enable us to plan for our future, the kind of life we wish to live and how we are going to leave our mark. Dreams, along with actions, help us shape our future. They empower us to think about living a life that may seem impossible today.

The future will be full of opportunities for those who are willing to take a chance and put in the effort to achieve their goals. We can make our dreams come true if we have faith in ourselves and the power of our dreams. The future is bright and full of possibilities, and with a little bit of hard work, we can make it even brighter. It's time to believe in the beauty of our dreams and take the first step toward achieving them.

Francesco Vitali

Your Notes for Success

253

"Do not go where the path may lead, go instead
where there is no path and leave a trail."
— Ralph Waldo Emerson

The easiest thing to do is to follow other people. This, however, does not bring you closer to success in any way. We are responsible for our destiny, so it's unwise to allow the path to lead us. We should always explore unchartered territories. Do what people think is impossible, and prove them wrong with your success. We can silence those who question our approach only with success. This is why, to be successful, we must do things that challenge us and bring us out of our comfort zone.

The path the majority follows is the easy way out, but it won't bring you the rewards that forging your own way will. When you blaze your own trail, you will learn more and become a better person. You will see the world in a different light and you will gain a deeper understanding of yourself and your place in the world.

Taking the road less traveled is not only more rewarding, but it also allows you to explore more and be creative. You never know what you'll find when you step off the beaten path, but you're sure to be surprised. So, don't be afraid to take a chance and venture off the beaten path. You never know what great things could await you.

Francesco Vitali

Your Notes for Success

254

"You have brains in your head. You have feet in your shoes. You can steer yourself any direction you choose."
— *Dr. Seuss*

Life is like a vehicle and you are in the driving seat. You can steer it in any direction that you desire. You can choose your path and carve your own destiny. As long as you are alive, you can turn your life around. In the journey to success, you will see many roadblocks and find yourself taking the wrong turn. We all make bad decisions, but successful people are never afraid to turn around and step back if needed, before heading in the right direction again.

You have the power to steer your life in any direction you choose. You can create the career you have always dreamed of. Believe in yourself and your abilities. Set goals for yourself that will push you to become the best version of yourself. Surround yourself with people who encourage you, and can bring out the best in you.

When challenges arise, use them as an opportunity to learn and grow. Believe in your capability to make the right decisions and take the necessary actions to get you closer to your goals. If we don't take risks, we will never be able to reach our full potential. Don't let fear hold you back. Have the courage to make choices that will bring you closer to achieving your dreams.

Francesco Vitali

Your Notes for Success

255

"Behind every overnight success are years of hard work and dedication." — J. K. Rowling

Triumph conceals the roots nurtured in obscurity. While success radiates brightly, the nurturing soil remains unseen. When we marvel at the seemingly overnight achievements, we overlook the arduous journey that made them possible.

We extol visionary entrepreneurs who revolutionize industries yet disregard the failures that paved the way for hard-earned triumph. Artists enrapture audiences with effortless elegance, masking countless rehearsals behind closed doors. Champion athletes hoist trophies, their path to glory paved with setbacks and relentless training away from the spotlight. Within overnight success lies a foundation meticulously crafted through countless unseen hours and unwitnessed energy. Every realized dream stands on the bedrock of resilience, forged through doubt and defeat into unwavering determination. It is crucial to embrace the darkness that nourishes the light.

Welcome struggle as the crucible that forges true greatness. Understand that fulfillment stems from a commitment to the process, not instant outcomes. Cherish the steady progress made over time, no matter how small. Success is not a miracle but the natural blossoming of carefully sown seeds. When inspiration sparkles before you, remember the growth in the shadows and let your unwavering dedication flourish into remarkable achievements.

Francesco Vitali

Your Notes for Success

256

"The secret of success is to do the common thing uncommonly well." — John D. Rockefeller Jr.

Reinventing the wheel may get you nowhere—unless you reinvent it with a few modifications that are going to make the lives of the people easier. To be successful, often you only need to do things everyone is doing but better. For instance, a baseball player who helped his team secure the most wins might be revered as a legend. But if any other player does it better and breaks that record, that person will become a legend, one who has achieved something many thought was impossible.

This is an age-old proverb that is still true today: If you want to be successful, you have to go above and beyond what is expected. It means taking an extra step to ensure that your work is of the highest quality. It also means having a passion for what you do and never giving up. Successful people are those who have a commitment to excellence and never settle for average. They never compromise on their goals. They put in the extra effort and take the time to learn and grow. They are able to turn their passions into success.

By doing the common thing uncommonly well, you can achieve anything you set your mind to. This is the key to success and the secret to achieving your goals.

Francesco Vitali

Your Notes for Success

257

"Always bear in mind that your own resolution to
success is more important than any other one thing."
— Abraham Lincoln

Having a resolve of your own to achieve something is all you need. You need to have a commitment and it is something not to be taken lightly. People change the definition of commitment as per their convenience and this should not be the case. Being committed to your resolutions defines your character and ultimately helps you become successful. You need to steer clear of all the negativity in your surroundings and focus on only one thing—your resolution.

Always bear in mind that your own resolution to success is more important than any other thing. To achieve success, you must be determined and have a clear vision of what you want to achieve. It's essential to stay motivated and focused, setting goals and taking action to reach them. Success is a journey and it requires dedication, hard work, patience, and perseverance. You will also need to make sacrifices and be willing to learn from your mistakes. The most important thing is to believe in yourself and your abilities and never give up. Having a positive attitude and the right mindset will help you to overcome any obstacles and make progress toward your goals. With a little bit of effort and dedication, you can achieve anything you set your mind to.

Francesco Vitali

Your Notes for Success

258

"If you want to achieve excellence, you can get there today. As of this second, quit doing less-than-excellent work." — Thomas J. Watson

Excellence is not doing the best you can—it is doing the best there can be. Setting new standards, disrupting the existing norms, going beyond what is the standard practice, and providing value to your business, society, and people with every step is excellence.

If you want to achieve excellence, you can get there today. Excellence is not something that takes a long time to achieve, it is something that can be achieved right now. Excellence comes from hard work and dedication, and it is something that can be achieved with a few simple steps. Start by setting high standards for yourself and making sure to meet them. Take pride in your work, and strive to do better than you did the last time. Surround yourself with people and resources that will help you reach your goals. When you strive for excellence, you build confidence and become a master of your craft. It takes time and effort, but the results will be worth it. Excellence is not achieved overnight, but with dedication and hard work, you can create something that is truly special. You need to have the courage to take risks and try new things. With these steps and a positive attitude, you can achieve excellence today.

Francesco Vitali

Your Notes for Success

259

*"If you genuinely want something, don't wait for it—
teach yourself to be impatient."* — *Gurbaksh Chahal*

We have always been taught to not be impatient and to wait for the good things to come to us. This is not actually helpful. While success requires patience and following the plan you have developed, it also requires you to be impatient. Be impatient about taking on new challenges, discovering new opportunities, investing in yourself, and doing things differently. Success is a culmination of hard work, passion, dedication, commitment, patience, impatience, and a whole lot of other things.

If you want something, don't sit around and wait for it. Take the initiative to go out and get it. Impatience is the key to success. Don't be afraid to be aggressive in your pursuit to reach your goal. Take the necessary steps to learn and keep learning. Be creative and open to new ideas. Try out different approaches and don't be afraid to fail. If one approach doesn't work, try another. Keep pushing yourself and be persistent. Believe that you can achieve what you set out to do and take responsibility for your own success. Have faith in yourself, and it will help you make progress. Nobody else can give you what you want—you have to go out and get it yourself.

Francesco Vitali

Your Notes for Success

260

*"The only place where success comes before work
is in the dictionary." — Vidal Sassoon*

If we want to be successful, we have to work for it. This is the only way to achieve your goals and objectives. Just waiting or wishing for something to happen may work in a fairyland, but it does not happen in the real world. And even in the fairyland, you have to wish for it. You need to know exactly what you want to have. Having a clear goal is one thing, but achieving it requires hard work.

Success is a wonderful feeling that comes from hard work and dedication. It's a feeling of accomplishment that can't be beaten. The only place where success comes before work is in the dictionary, but in real life, success is something that is earned over time. Achieving success requires a lot of effort, focus, and persistence. It's important to set specific goals, stay focused on them, and put in the necessary work to get there.

It's important to stay motivated, remain positive, and keep pushing forward even when things get tough. With the right attitude, hard work, and a bit of luck, anyone can achieve success. It doesn't come easy, but it's worth it. So take the time to make a plan, stay focused, and put in the effort. Success is a wonderful feeling that comes from hard work and dedication.

Francesco Vitali

Your Notes for Success

261

"If you are not willing to risk the usual, you will have to settle for the ordinary." — Jim Rohn

If you are not willing to risk the usual, you will have to settle for the ordinary. This quote encourages us to take risks and try something new. It teaches us to not be afraid of failure and to take initiative. Risking the usual helps us to open ourselves up to new experiences and opportunities. It can lead to unexpected outcomes and greater satisfaction. It also helps us to expand our horizons and build self-confidence.

Taking risks can be intimidating, but the reward of achieving something extraordinary can be incredibly rewarding. Taking risks allows us to learn about ourselves and to grow in ways we may have never thought possible. It is a great way to challenge ourselves and strive for greatness. Doing so can help us to live a more fulfilling and meaningful life. So don't be afraid to take risks and challenge the ordinary. You never know what amazing things you may discover. You never know what you are truly capable of unless you step out of your comfort zone and push yourself beyond your limits. When you stop letting the fear of failure control you, that is when you will feel free. That is when you will be able to take on anything the world throws your way.

Francesco Vitali

Your Notes for Success

262

"Before anything else, preparation is the key to success." — Alexander Graham Bell

Before anything else, preparation is the key to success. Preparation involves setting goals, gathering resources, researching, and planning. Taking the time to properly prepare allows us to create a roadmap to success. It can also help us identify potential obstacles and plan for them in advance. Preparation provides us with the knowledge, skills, and resources needed to achieve our goals. It can give us the confidence and motivation to take on challenging tasks. Preparation also helps us to stay organized, focused, and on track.

By taking the time to prepare, we can maximize our chances of success and minimize potential risks. Preparation is an essential part of any successful endeavor, and it has the potential to make all the difference in our lives and careers. Preparation is always necessary to ensure that the objective is achieved. It involves researching the task at hand, understanding the requirements, gathering the necessary resources, and having a clear vision of what needs to be done. It also involves setting realistic goals and timelines and having a plan of action to ensure that the task is completed on time. So, before you start anything, make sure you're fully prepared!

Francesco Vitali

Your Notes for Success

263

"You miss 100% of the shots you don't take."
— Wayne Gretzky

You miss 100% of the shots you don't take. This phrase is a reminder that if you don't take risks, you won't succeed. It encourages us to take action and to be bold in pursuing our goals. This phrase is also a reminder that failure is part of the path to success and that it's okay to make mistakes. Instead of viewing failure as a negative, we should use it as an opportunity to learn, grow, and become better. Taking risks can help us reach our potential and create amazing things. We should be willing to take the shots, even if they don't always pan out the way we expected.

Taking the shot is the only way we can find out if it works and the only way we can progress and reach our goals. Don't be afraid to take the shot. It's the only way to make sure you don't miss out on something great. Though it may be intimidating to take shots that are out of your comfort zone, it is important to remember that you won't succeed unless you take the chance. If you don't take that shot, you'll miss out on 100% of your opportunities. So take the plunge and know that the rewards will be worth it!

Francesco Vitali

Your Notes for Success

264

"I have learned over the years that when one's mind is made up, this diminishes fear." — Rosa Parks

When one's mind is made up, fear can be diminished. When a decision is made, you know what to expect, and therefore, fear of the unknown is removed. Without fear, the individual can focus on the task at hand, which increases the chances of success. This can also free up emotional and mental space, allowing for creativity and focus. Having the courage to make a decision and stick with it can help build confidence, as you will be able to see the results of your choices. Knowing that you can make a decision, and that the decision can be successful can help to boost self-esteem and courage.

You will no longer be afraid to make decisions because you know that you can trust yourself. Standing firm by your decisions can lead to greater success, courage, and clarity. When we have a clear vision of what we want to accomplish, our fear is replaced with confidence and motivation. We become more resilient to setbacks and are better able to take risks and learn from failure. We become more empowered to take action and can achieve our goals. Our faith in ourselves increases, and we can become more successful in life.

Your Notes for Success

265

"Nothing is impossible, the word itself says,
'I'm possible!'" — Audrey Hepburn

Nothing is impossible if you work hard and never give up. Hard work and determination can help you to achieve anything and reach any goal you set your mind to. Success doesn't come easy, but it is attainable with a strong work ethic, dedication, and self-belief. Even when things seem hopeless, if you keep pushing and stay the course, you will find a way to achieve your goals. With the right attitude, you can make your dreams a reality.

You may stumble along the way, and there will be times you'll want to give up, but it's important to remember that failure is not the end; it's just a part of the process. Stay focused, stay positive, and never give up on yourself. With enough effort and perseverance, you'll reach for the stars. With the right attitude, dedication, and hard work, you can achieve whatever you set out to do. It is important to believe in yourself and never give up, even when the odds seem insurmountable.

You can achieve anything if you're determined enough. Remind yourself that you are here today because you have what it takes. And you will go even further because you are capable of achieving amazing things.

Francesco Vitali

Your Notes for Success

266

"The question isn't who is going to let me; it's who is going to stop me." — Ayn Rand

This is a powerful statement that inspires and motivates people to not give up and to reach for their dreams. It reminds us that no matter what obstacles come our way, we can overcome them and achieve our goals. It encourages us to believe in ourselves and be confident that we can make our dreams come true. It also reminds us to be persistent and never give up, no matter how hard something seems. We shouldn't let the opinions of others affect us in any way. They are, after all, opinions and not facts. They don't define us. They don't define what we are capable of achieving.

We must remember that the only person who can stop us from achieving our dreams is ourselves. We have the power to shape our own destiny and create the life we want to live. When we keep this in mind, nothing can stand in our way. Nothing and no one can stop us from achieving greatness. With perseverance and dedication, we can all strive to reach our highest potential and create a life of purpose and fulfillment. Let's keep believing in ourselves and our dreams, and never give up on our journey to greatness.

Your Notes for Success

267

"The only person you are destined to become is the person you decide to be." — Ralph Waldo Emerson

The only person you are destined to become is the person you decide to be. Life is full of choices and it's up to us to make the most of them. Each decision we make can lead us down a different path, and ultimately shape who we become. We have the freedom to choose our own direction and the power to create our own destiny. We can decide to be optimistic and kind, ambitious and driven. We can decide to work hard and make something of ourselves. We can decide to be generous and understanding and make the world a better place. If we strive to be our best selves, we can reach any goal we set out to achieve.

We have the power within us to reach our goals and fulfill our dreams. If we strive to be the best version of ourselves, we can make the most of our lives and achieve anything we set our minds to. It takes dedication and hard work, but when we put our hearts into it, we can overcome any obstacle and reach our goals.

The only person we are destined to become is the person we decide to be. Embrace the power of choice and create the life you want for yourself.

Francesco Vitali

Your Notes for Success

268

"I walk slowly but never backwards."
— *Abraham Lincoln*

It is important to always move forward, never backward. This mantra can be applied to life in many ways. Take walking, for example. If we move slowly, we can take time to appreciate our surroundings to take in the beauty of the world. We can pause and reflect on the journey while remaining focused on the destination. We can learn from our mistakes but never linger on them and never look back.

Mistakes are natural, and it is important to embrace them as part of our growth. Making mistakes is part of life, and can be a powerful tool for reflection and development. As long as we remain focused on the future and strive to learn from our mistakes, we will be able to make the most of our experiences and make positive progress in our lives.

Walking slowly but never backward is an important lesson in life, and one that can lead to great growth and understanding. Taking this approach can help us remain focused on our goals while still appreciating and learning from the journey. So, don't ever look back on the person you used to be or where you used to be. Focus on the person you will be in the future and where you need to be.

Francesco Vitali

Your Notes for Success

269

"The path to success is to take massive
determined action." — Tony Robbins

The path to success begins with one small step. Taking massive, determined action is the key to success. With dedication and hard work, the possibilities are endless. Every single action is like a brick that creates the foundation of your success. The more actions you take, the closer you get to success. You should tackle each challenge with optimism and confidence. Believe in yourself and your abilities, and you will be able to take the necessary steps to get closer to your goals.

Don't be afraid to take risks and make mistakes. It's okay to make mistakes as long as you learn from them, as they can help you become better and more knowledgeable. With determination and perseverance, you will be able to achieve success; you will be able to achieve success no matter what challenge you face. Success is within reach if you stay focused and never give up. Seize the opportunity and embrace the challenge to achieve success. With dedication and hard work, you can unlock your potential to reach your goals. Believe in yourself and don't let obstacles stand in your way. With commitment and dedication, you can achieve the success you desire.

Francesco Vitali

Your Notes for Success

270

"A strong positive self-image is the best possible preparation for success." — Dr. Joyce Brothers

Having a strong, positive self-image is the best way to set yourself up for success. If you doubt yourself, others will doubt you as well. When you feel confident in your abilities, it gives you the motivation to strive for your goals. It gives you the motivation to carry on after a tough day. With a positive attitude, you can take on any challenge without fear of failure. You can be secure in the knowledge that you have the skills and drive to reach your goals.

You are capable and you have the strength and determination to succeed. You are brilliant and deserve the success you desire. Self-belief is a powerful tool that will help you reach your goals and achieve success. It can help you stay focused, find solutions to problems, and make the most of every opportunity. It allows you to recognize your strengths and weaknesses and work on them while also recognizing and appreciating your own worth.

With a strong positive self-image, you can be the best version of yourself and create a strong foundation for success. This will allow you to strive for excellence and reach your goals.

Francesco Vitali

Your Notes for Success

271

"There are no traffic jams along the extra mile."
— *Roger Staubach*

Taking the extra mile in life is a choice that we make, and it is often the most rewarding one. It's a journey of self-discovery and a way to push ourselves to new heights. The extra mile is a road filled with many successes and little failures, but those failures will only make us stronger and more determined.

Choosing to take the extra mile is a sign of strength, courage, and commitment that will pay off in the end. Taking the extra mile is a unique opportunity to learn and grow, and it will be a rewarding experience that will stay with us forever. Success requires effort and dedication, and going the extra mile is a great way to show these qualities. It's a great way to show that you are serious about your future. It can lead to increased recognition, development opportunities, and ultimately, success. It also shows that you are dedicated to your goals and dreams. That you are willing to do anything to achieve them.

Life is too short to not take risks and aim higher, so why not take the plunge and explore the wonders that await us?

Francesco Vitali

Your Notes for Success

272

"Success does not come from physical capacity. It comes from an indomitable will." — Mahatma Gandhi

It is within us all to achieve greatness, no matter our circumstances. It is not about how much strength or skill a person has but about their drive and ambition to keep going, no matter the odds. This type of perseverance is what separates those who succeed from those who don't.

When faced with a challenging situation, those with an indomitable will see an opportunity to grow and learn, while those who lack this determination will give up. Possessing this quality is essential to achieving success in any endeavor, no matter how difficult it may seem. It is through this unwavering commitment and dedication to reach one's goals that true success is achieved.

With an indomitable will, success is within reach. With a strong determination and the right strategy, anyone can reach their goals and be successful. No matter the obstacles and challenges that may be encountered along the way, the strong-willed person will not be deterred. The power of a positive attitude and commitment toward a goal can be the difference between failure and success. Therefore, if we have the drive and the right attitude, we can achieve anything we set our minds to.

With this attitude, the sky's the limit and success is surely within reach.

Francesco Vitali

Your Notes for Success

273

"Every accomplishment starts with the decision to try."
— *John F. Kennedy*

Every accomplishment starts with the decision to try. If you hold back, you'll miss out on amazing opportunities. It takes courage and resilience to take the first step. But with the knowledge that it takes many tries to succeed, you can stay focused on the bigger picture.

When you make the decision to try, you open yourself up to all kinds of possibilities. You create a path toward success and make progress toward reaching your goals. Taking the first step toward achieving your goals can be intimidating and overwhelming. But when you make the decision to try, you are taking a leap of faith and investing in yourself. You are showing yourself that you believe in your skills and that you are capable of achieving great things.

Taking the first step is often the hardest part of any journey, but with the right mindset, we can find a way to make it happen. Putting in the extra effort and pushing ourselves out of our comfort zone can be daunting at times, but taking risks and believing in ourselves can pay off with amazing results. It is this kind of determination and courage that can help us build a better future for ourselves and those around us.

Your Notes for Success

274

*"If my mind can conceive it, and my heart can believe
it, then I can achieve it."* — *Muhammad Ali*

The power of the mind is an amazing thing. If you can
conceive something in your mind, and truly believe it with your
heart, you can achieve it. Your thoughts and beliefs become your
reality. Having positive thoughts and believing in yourself will help
you to manifest your dreams. With dedication and hard work, you
can achieve anything.

Success starts with believing in yourself and believing that
you can do it. No matter how difficult something may seem,
you can persevere and reach any goal with the right attitude and
determination. Believe in yourself, and don't be afraid to dream
big. You have the capability to do anything, so don't give up. If
your mind can conceive it, and your heart can believe it, then you
can achieve it. With a little bit of hard work and determination, we
can achieve anything we set our mind to, no matter how impossible
it may seem. This belief system can help us to stay motivated and
driven even in the face of adversity. It can empower us to reach our
goals and discover our full potential. Believing in ourselves is the
first step to achieving our dreams and living our best lives.

Francesco Vitali

<u>*Your Notes for Success*</u>

275

"You can never cross the ocean until you have the courage to lose sight of the shore."
— *Christopher Columbus*

Taking a leap of faith is a daunting concept, but it is also one of life's greatest adventures. To embark on a journey with no end in sight and no plan of where you might end up can be exhilarating. It can also be a humbling experience as you learn to trust in yourself and in the universe.

The courage to lose sight of the shore is the courage to be brave and explore the unknown. It is a leap of faith, but it is also a leap of hope, trusting that you will eventually find your way. It is the courage to take risks, to grow and to embrace the journey.

By having the courage to lose sight of the shore, you can open yourself up to new possibilities and experiences. You can never cross the ocean until you have the courage to lose sight of the shore, but with courage comes great rewards. The best decision you can make for yourself is taking that first step toward achieving your dreams. It all starts with a single step. Once you get past the difficult part, success is just an arm's reach away.

Francesco Vitali

Your Notes for Success

276

"Knowing is not enough; we must apply. Wishing is not enough; we must do." — Johann Wolfgang von Goethe

Knowing is not enough; we must apply. Wishing is not enough; we must do. This statement is so powerful and is a great reminder that in order to succeed, we must take action. Knowing what to do is one thing, but actually doing it is another. We must take the initiative and make things happen. We must be willing to put in the time, energy, and effort necessary to reach our goals. If we want something, we must be willing to go after it. We must be willing to chase it and give it our all.

When we apply our knowledge and take action, there is no limit to what we can achieve. Wishing for something is not enough. We must be willing to do the work and put in the effort to make it happen. Taking action is the key to success. Taking action is about being proactive and taking risks. It is about having the courage to make decisions and to continuously strive for improvement. It is about being willing to learn and grow, and to never give up. Taking action is the key to unlocking a world of possibilities and achieving success.

Your Notes for Success

277

*"All you need is the plan, the road map, and
the courage to press on to your destination."*
— *Earl Nightingale*

The most successful people are those who plan everything ahead of time; they envision their success. Having a plan helps to ensure that you have a clear path and a direction to follow. It serves as a guide, allowing you to stay focused on achieving your goals. Having a road map helps to keep you on track and can help you identify potential obstacles that may come up along the way. Lastly, having the courage to press on despite any difficulties or setbacks is key to reaching your destination. Having courage will help you to stay motivated and to take risks that may be necessary to reach your destination.

With the plan, the road map, and the courage to press on to your destination, you can reach your goals and dreams. Every step forward is progress, and every setback or obstacle can be overcome with perseverance. Even if it takes some time and effort, you will eventually reach your desired destination. It may not happen overnight, but with dedication and determination, you can achieve anything. With a strong and positive mindset, you can accomplish anything. So never give up on your goals and dreams, and you will be sure to reach them.

Francesco Vitali

Your Notes for Success

278

*"Only those who risk going too far can find out
how far one can go." — T. S. Elliot*

Only those who are willing to take a risk and push the boundaries of what they are capable of can discover how far they can truly go. It can be daunting to step out of your comfort zone, but when you do, you can open yourself up to a world of possibilities. With every risk you take, you can learn how much you are capable of and grow in strength, knowledge, and courage. It may be difficult, but the rewards of taking risks can be immense and can push you to reach new heights.

Taking risks can also lead to greater creativity and innovation. It allows us to pursue our passions, challenge ourselves, and open up new possibilities. Ultimately, taking risks is an essential part of growing and achieving our goals.

It gives us the courage to take on new opportunities that may have seemed impossible before. It also allows us to learn from our mistakes, and turn our failures into successes. Taking risks shows us that we have the strength and resilience to push ourselves beyond our comfort zone, and that no matter how difficult the situation may seem, we can still find a way to move forward.

Francesco Vitali

Your Notes for Success

279

"The successful warrior is the average man,
with laser-like focus." — Bruce Lee

The successful warrior is the average person with a laser-like focus. They are the person who sets their sights on their goal, and does whatever it takes to accomplish it. They are not deterred by their failures or setbacks, but instead they use them to propel themselves forward. They are focused, disciplined, and resilient. They know when to push themselves and when to take a break. The successful warrior is not extraordinary in any way, but rather, they are exceptional in their dedication to their vision. They stick to their plan, taking on every challenge that comes their way and never giving up. They know that success is the result of hard work and perseverance. They are a symbol of determination and an inspiration to us all. They show us that with a strong will and dedication, anything can be achieved.

By staying focused, the successful warrior is able to create the life that they desire. The successful warrior is an example for others to follow. They are the ones who are able to show that anything is possible when you focus and remain true to your goals. The successful warrior is the average person with an extraordinary focus.

Francesco Vitali

Your Notes for Success

280

"The ability to influence people without irritating them is the most profitable skill you can learn."
— *Napoleon Hill*

Having the ability to influence people without overwhelming them is a key to success. It is essential to be able to explain your point of view in a manner that will be heard and understood by others. When you influence without overwhelming, you create an environment of trust and mutual respect. You demonstrate that you value the opinion of the other person and that you are willing to take their ideas into consideration. This will help you to build strong relationships with colleagues and customers and create a better working environment. Knowing how to influence people in a positive manner will help you to achieve success in whatever endeavor you pursue.

If you can master the art of influencing people and communication, you will be well on your way to success. By learning the basics of communication and influence, you can create positive relationships and a successful career. You will be able to understand and articulate the needs of others and be able to build strong relationships. You will also be able to better understand the motivations of others and be able to use this understanding to create positive outcomes. With the right combination of communication, influence, and empathy, you can become an invaluable asset to any organization or team.

Francesco Vitali

Your Notes for Success

281

"They always say time changes things, but you actually have to change them yourself." —Andy Warhol

If you want to see changes in your professional life, you need to be willing to take the right steps to achieve them.

It is important to take action and do something to create the change you desire. You can take small steps toward your goals and eventually, you can make a huge difference. When you take responsibility for your actions and strive for improvement, you can ultimately create the change you want to see.

It is very empowering and gratifying when you look back and see how far you've come. Even when it seems like things aren't changing fast enough, it is important to stay motivated and keep taking one step at a time. With enough hard work and dedication, you will eventually make the changes you want to see in your life.

By setting realistic goals and taking consistent action, you will be able to move closer and closer to achieving the life that you've been dreaming of. Hard work and dedication will help you through the tough times and will give you the motivation to keep going when things get difficult. With a positive outlook and the right mindset, you will eventually make the changes you want to see in your life.

Francesco Vitali

Your Notes for Success

282

"The best way to predict the future is to create it."
— *Peter F. Drucker*

We have the power to shape the future to our own vision and make it as bright and successful as we wish. By embracing change, taking risks, and embracing new opportunities, we can create our own future. By setting goals, making plans, and taking action, we can turn our goals into reality. By being proactive and taking the initiative, we can make the future that we want.

By learning from our mistakes and past experiences, we can make the future even brighter. By looking ahead and planning for the future, we can see the possibilities and find the best course of action. By never giving up and working hard, we can make the future that we want for ourselves and for others. The best way to predict the future is to create it. Work so hard, and your dreams come true. By doing this, we can look confidently ahead and gain a greater sense of control over our lives, knowing that we can shape the future that we want to see. This is an invaluable mindset that can help us to become the best version of ourselves and lead us toward a better future.

Francesco Vitali

Your Notes for Success

283

"Experience is not what happens to you; it is what you do with what happens to you." — Aldous Huxley

Life is full of ups and downs, and each one of us has our own journey. What matters is how we react to the situation and what we take away from it. We have the power to turn our experiences into positive learning outcomes. For example, if we make a mistake, instead of beating ourselves up, we can use it as an opportunity to learn and grow. A positive attitude and outlook can help us to make the best of any situation and use it to our advantage. Experience gives us the wisdom and understanding of life that we need to become better and make the right decisions. It is how we face our experiences that make a difference. With the right attitude, you can turn any challenge into a victory.

It is important to remember that no matter how difficult the path may be, you have the strength and the power to overcome it. Having the right attitude can help us stay focused and motivated, so that we can face and overcome any challenge that may come our way. Having a positive outlook and seeing the good in every situation can help us stay on the path to success. There is no challenge too big or too small that cannot be conquered with the right attitude.

Your Notes for Success

284

"Thinking is the hardest work there is, which is the probable reason why so few engage in it." — *Henry Ford*

Thinking is arguably the most difficult task we can take on, yet it is also one of the most rewarding. Thinking deeply and critically can lead to greater understanding, creativity, and problem-solving skills. It encourages us to think outside the box and come up with innovative solutions. Thinking is a valuable tool that can be used to solve complex problems and make life easier. It can also provide us with the insight and perspective to better understand the world around us.

Despite its potential rewards, few people actively engage in this type of thinking. This is likely because it requires effort and dedication, which most people are not willing to give. However, those who do take the time to engage in critical thinking will reap its many benefits. So, when an idea or thought pops up, don't dismiss it; let your mind explore it!

Allowing yourself to explore ideas and thoughts can be a great way to expand your knowledge and grow as an individual. It can also lead to increased confidence and a more positive outlook on life. Ultimately, embracing new ideas and thoughts can be a great way to open your mind to the new possibilities out there and can be an incredibly rewarding experience.

Francesco Vitali

Your Notes for Success

285

"Don't go around saying the world owes you a living.
The world owes you nothing. It was here first."
— Mark Twain

Having a positive outlook on life is an important factor in success. No matter how challenging things may be at times, it is important to keep in mind that we can choose how we react and respond to our current situation.

Remember to be thankful for the opportunities and blessings that we have been given. Appreciating what we have and working hard to make the most of our resources can lead to wonderful outcomes and a more fulfilling life. It is possible to achieve great things with the right attitude and the willingness to take action. Don't be afraid to take the initiative and put in the effort to make your dreams come true. The world may owe us nothing, but we owe it to ourselves to make the most of our lives.

We must strive to do the best we can and make our mark on the world in whatever way we can. We must also take steps to ensure that our actions positively impact the lives of those around us. After all, our lives are not only about ourselves but about making a difference in the lives of others. With a positive outlook and determination, we can make the most of our lives and leave the world a better place than when we arrived.

Francesco Vitali

Your Notes for Success

286

"Pay no attention to what the critics say. A statue has never been erected in honor of a critic."
— Jean Sibelius

Pay no attention to what the critics say. Their job is to objectively assess and evaluate whatever it is they are critiquing. However, their words should not define our choices and actions. Rather, it's important to focus on our own inner voice and process and make decisions that reflect our own values.

A statue has never been erected in honor of a critic. Instead, a statue is a tribute to those who have achieved something extraordinary or made a lasting impact on society. So, it's important to take criticism into consideration and use it to our advantage, but ultimately, we must trust ourselves to decide the right course of action. We should not let the words of a critic dictate how we tackle challenges and work. Every challenge is an opportunity to learn and grow and to become stronger, wiser, and better. We should never let others affect how we view ourselves instead. We should look within and trust ourselves and our abilities to face them head-on. We should never forget that we are capable of achieving great things, even in the face of criticism. With courage, hard work, and resilience, any challenge can be overcome.

Francesco Vitali

Your Notes for Success

287

"A problem is a chance for you to do your best."
— Duke Ellington

A problem is an opportunity to do your best. It may be a minor inconvenience or a major challenge. Whatever it is, it's an opportunity to grow and improve. When you face a problem, you can use it as a chance to learn something new, to develop a skill, and to strengthen your existing abilities. Working through a problem can help you build confidence, resilience, and creative problem-solving skills. You can use the experience to become more resourceful, to think more critically, and to find innovative solutions.

A problem is a chance to push yourself to the limit and develop yourself in ways you might not have imagined. It's an opportunity to put your best foot forward, to make a positive difference, and to make the world a better place. By tackling problems, you can build confidence and resilience that will serve you well in the future. It's a chance to think outside the box, come up with creative solutions, and sharpen your problem-solving skills. Ultimately, a problem is an opportunity to learn and grow, and it can help you become a better version of yourself.

Your Notes for Success

288

"If your ship doesn't come in, swim out to it!"
— Jonathan Winters

If your ship doesn't come in, swimming to it shows an attitude of resilience and determination that should be admired and embraced. When we choose to take control of our lives and be proactive in our pursuits, we create opportunities for ourselves that may otherwise have been unavailable. Swimming to your ship is an indication of dedication and a willingness to take risks and try new things. It's a reminder that we can create our own destinies and don't need to wait around for something to be handed to us. It's an inspiring example of how, with hard work and dedication, we can turn dreams into realities, no matter how far away they may seem.

Also, remember that you are the captain of your own ship. You have the resilience and determination to overcome the obstacles that come your way and the ability to make wise decisions that will serve you well. You have the tools and the courage to take the risks necessary to reach your goals. You have the strength to face any challenge that comes your way and the wisdom to guide you through it. Your journey may be challenging, but you have what it takes to make it to the shore.

Don't give up!

Francesco Vitali

Your Notes for Success

289

"Success is falling nine times and getting up ten."
— Jon Bon Jovi

Success is an incredible feeling that often comes after making a lot of effort and hard work. It is true that failure can be a part of the journey, but it is only by learning from our mistakes that we can grow and become a success. This is why success is falling nine times and getting up ten. It is a reminder not to give up and to keep on pushing forward no matter how many times we may fail.

We must remember that failure is only temporary and that success is within reach; we just need to keep trying. Success is about resilience, determination, and never giving up. It is about striving and pushing ourselves to reach our goals and never giving up on them. Success is not an easy journey, but with perseverance, effort, and dedication, it is achievable.

With the right combination of dedication, hard work, and perseverance, anyone can achieve success. It is important to remember that success is not an overnight process and that it requires consistent effort and dedication. However, with the right attitude and effort, success is certainly within reach. So don't give up and keep on going—success is achievable with the right dedication and effort.

Francesco Vitali

<u>*Your Notes for Success*</u>

290

"Be like a duck. Calm on the surface but always paddling like the dickens underneath." — Michael Caine

Be like a duck: Calm on the surface but always working like wild underneath. This is a great way to approach life and its challenges. Ducks always look serene and tranquil, but beneath the surface, they are busy paddling away to reach their destination. This is a great metaphor for how we should approach life: We should strive to remain calm and composed on the outside but work diligently and persistently on the inside to achieve our goals.

This approach can help us maintain our peace of mind in difficult times and give us the strength to overcome any challenge. This way, we can tackle anything. We should be like a duck and remain focused and determined while keeping our composure and grace. This gives us the opportunity to think before we act, and to respond in a way that will best benefit us. When we remain calm, we are able to make better decisions, and we can better handle the situation. We may even be able to find a creative solution to the problem. Remaining calm no matter how tough the situation is can help us to be successful and to come out of the situation in a better position than when we went in.

Francesco Vitali

Your Notes for Success

291

"Whenever you see a successful person, you only see the public glories, never the private sacrifices to reach them." — Vaibhav Shah

Whenever you see a successful person, you rarely see the hard work, dedication, and passion that has been put into their pursuits. They have made the kind of sacrifices that are unknown to the public and have gone through the struggles and challenges that have helped them to reach their goals. It is often said that success is not achieved without great effort, and this is true in the case of any successful person. They have been willing to take risks, often without knowing the outcome, and have worked hard to overcome all the obstacles that have come their way. The rewards of their efforts have been great, and their commitment and determination have enabled them to achieve great things.

Whenever you see a successful person, remember this: They have likely put in countless hours of hard work and dedication to be where they are today. They have also likely made personal and professional sacrifices to reach their goals. It is admirable to witness the success of those who have persevered and worked hard to get where they are. It is a reminder that hard work and dedication can pay off, if we are willing to put in the effort. It is also a reminder that success comes in many forms and should be celebrated, regardless of how it is achieved.

Francesco Vitali

Your Notes for Success

292

"Opportunities don't happen. You create them."
— *Chris Grosser*

When you take the initiative to create opportunities for yourself, you can achieve great things. Opportunities don't just happen; you have to *make* them happen. You have to put yourself out there.

You can create opportunities by being open to new experiences, actively seeking out new ideas and approaches, and taking advantage of any chances that come your way. You can also create opportunities by putting yourself in the right place at the right time, networking with the right people, and using the resources available to you to their fullest potential. By taking the initiative to create opportunities, you can open new doors and find success.

With the right attitude and a willingness to take risks, the possibilities are endless. Don't wait for opportunities to come to you—go out and create them yourself. It will give you a sense of accomplishment and pride that you have taken control of your life and made a difference. Even if you are not successful at first, you will learn a lot and be one step closer to achieving your goals. So don't wait for opportunities, take charge and create them yourself. Your success will be determined by your hard work and dedication.

Francesco Vitali

Your Notes for Success

293

*"There is no easy walk to freedom anywhere, and
many of us will have to pass through the valley of the
shadow of death again and again before we reach the
mountaintop of our desires." — Nelson Mandela*

There is no easy walk to freedom anywhere, but with perseverance, dedication, and courage, anything is possible. Freedom is not an end goal but rather a journey of learning, growth, and self-discovery. We must accept that the journey to freedom will require hard work, dedication, and commitment. It is only through these efforts that we will be able to achieve our dreams and create the life we want for ourselves.

We must also remember to celebrate our successes, no matter how small, and to never give up. No matter how long and difficult the journey may be, there is always hope. With a positive attitude and the determination to succeed, there is no limit to what we can do. Freedom is within our reach, so let us take the first step and never stop walking!

If we remain determined and resilient, and work hard, we can overcome any obstacles and challenges that stand in the way. Despite the difficulty in achieving our goals, we can use our strength and courage to persevere and reach our desired destination. In the end, it is up to us to take the necessary steps to overcome our challenges and take control of our destiny. With determination, resilience, hard work, and a positive attitude, we can achieve anything we set our minds to.

Your Notes for Success

294

"The whole secret of a successful life is to find out what is one's destiny to do, and then do it." — Henry Ford

The whole secret of a successful life is to find out what is one's destiny to do, and then do it. This is a simple yet profound idea that has been echoed throughout history by wise men and women. It reminds us that our lives are not randomly determined but rather that we have the potential to shape our own destiny. Knowing one's purpose in life is empowering, as it allows us to direct our efforts toward the causes that bring about the most fulfillment.

Doing what one is meant to do can bring joy, a sense of satisfaction, and a sense of belonging. It can also bring about success and recognition, as we focus our energy on the things that bring out the best in us. With a clear understanding of our purpose, we can take the necessary steps to create a life of meaning. We can identify our goals and priorities, develop actionable plans, and create a positive environment for ourselves to grow and thrive. We can also be sure to make the most of our time, energy, and resources. Learning to recognize and follow one's destiny is the key to a successful life.

Francesco Vitali

Your Notes for Success

295

"If you're not stubborn, you'll give up on experiments too soon. And if you're not flexible, you'll pound your head against the wall and you won't see a different solution to a problem you're trying to solve." — Jeff Bezos

Being stubborn can be a good thing in certain situations, such as when it comes to experiments. If you're not stubborn, you may give up on experiments too soon. Being stubborn allows you to keep going, even when the results of an experiment don't seem to be going your way. It allows you to continue to search for answers, even when it may seem like there are none. It encourages you to keep pushing forward in the pursuit of knowledge, even when the odds may seem insurmountable.

By being stubborn in the face of adversity, you create opportunities for yourself to learn and grow in ways you may never have imagined. So, don't be too quick to give up when it comes to experiments—be stubborn and you'll be much better off in the long run. You will be able to stand up for yourself and your beliefs, and you will be more likely to take responsibility for your actions.

Being stubborn can also help you become more independent and confident, as you will be less likely to take no for an answer. In the end, being stubborn can often be the key to success, as it can help you stay on track and achieve your goals.

Francesco Vitali

Your Notes for Success

296

"The way I see it, if you want the rainbow, you gotta put up with the rain." — Dolly Parton

If you want success, you have to put up with difficulties. It is never easy to achieve success, but the rewards of hard work and dedication are worth the effort. Difficulties are just part of the process and should be embraced as an opportunity to grow and develop. With a positive attitude and strong resilience, you can emerge from any challenge as a better and more accomplished person.

With every difficulty, you will gain experience, knowledge, and strength. Don't be afraid to face the obstacles on your journey to success. You are capable of achieving great things and every difficulty is just a stepping stone to your ultimate success. Difficulties can be seen as a way to test our strength and courage. We may feel overwhelmed at times, but if we persist and never give up, we will eventually find success.

No matter how hard things may seem, we must always strive to stay positive and press forward. The feeling of being overwhelmed is natural, but it should not be a deterrent or a sign of failure. Instead, it should be seen as a challenge to push us further and motivate us to keep going. Through hard work and dedication, we can reach our goals and eventually find success.

Francesco Vitali

Your Notes for Success

297

"You must expect great things of yourself before
you can do them." — Michael Jordan

You must expect great things of yourself before you can do them. Believe in yourself and your abilities and have confidence that you can achieve whatever you put your mind to. Don't be afraid to try and strive for excellence. With a positive attitude and a strong work ethic, you can accomplish anything. You are capable and capable of greatness. Believe in yourself, be determined, and don't give up. With hard work, dedication, and the right mindset, you can achieve the goals you set for yourself.

Believe in yourself and your potential and you will be able to do great things. You have the power to make your dreams come true. Have faith in yourself, push yourself, and work hard to become the best version of yourself that you can be. Working hard and staying focused will help you reach those goals and be the best version of yourself that you can be. This is a great way to ensure that you are able to reach your full potential and live your best life. Having faith in yourself and pushing yourself to become the best version of yourself is a key step to success and fulfillment.

Francesco Vitali

Your Notes for Success

298

"There are two types of people who will tell you that you cannot make a difference in this world: those who are afraid to try and those who are afraid you will succeed." — Ray Goforth

Don't listen to the people who don't want you to succeed. Surround yourself with people who support you, who believe in you, and who want you to reach your goals. Believe in yourself, stay focused and motivated, and be willing to work hard. With the right attitude and determination, you can achieve anything you set your mind to. Success comes from within, so be sure to appreciate your progress and celebrate your successes.

Don't be afraid to take risks and put yourself out there. Believe that you can do it, and you will. With the right attitude, hard work, and a little bit of luck, you can achieve anything you set your mind to. You have the power to make your dreams come true. So, don't ever give up on yourself!

Nothing is impossible when you put your mind and heart into it, and have the courage to take the necessary steps. Don't let doubts and fears cripple your progress. Even when things seem daunting and difficult, just remember to keep going and never give up. With the right attitude, hard work, and dedication, you can achieve anything you want. So, don't ever give up on yourself! With your power and determination, you can make your dreams come true.

Francesco Vitali

<u>*Your Notes for Success*</u>

299

"I believe every human has a finite number of heartbeats. I don't intend to waste any of mine."
— *Neil Armstrong*

We all have only one chance in life, so it's important to make the most of it and focus on our own goals and dreams. Don't waste your chance on others who will not help you get to where you want to be. Instead, focus on your own success and work hard and smart toward achieving it. Set yourself clear, achievable goals and take actionable steps forward to make them a reality. Believe in yourself, stay motivated and surround yourself with people who will help and support you in your journey.

Don't be afraid to take risks and make mistakes—they are a part of the process of learning and growing. Believe that you can and you will, and your hard work will pay off. Make the most of your one chance and make it count!

When we make the most of our one chance and make it count, we can open the door to new experiences, discover our strengths and weaknesses, and create new pathways for our futures. We can create our own destiny and make the most of our one chance. By making the most of our one chance, we can create memories that will last a lifetime and achieve our goals.

Francesco Vitali

Your Notes for Success

300

"Don't limit yourself. Many people limit themselves to what they think they can do. You can go as far as your mind lets you. What you believe, remember, you can achieve." — Mary Kay Ash

Too often, we set boundaries on our potential, telling ourselves that we can't do something because it's too hard or too far out of our comfort zone. But when we limit ourselves, we miss out on the incredible opportunities that life has to offer. Instead, strive to push yourself beyond what you think you can do. Believe that you can take on any challenge that comes your way, and you will be amazed at what you can accomplish. When you remove the limits you set on yourself, you open yourself up to a world of possibilities. So don't be afraid to take risks and go beyond what you thought you could do. Life is full of exciting and rewarding experiences, and you can get more out of it if you don't limit yourself.

Always remember: don't ever limit yourself! We often hold ourselves back, thinking something is hard or outside our comfort zone, but guess what? We unlock incredible opportunities when we break free from those self-imposed limits. Embrace challenges confidently, and you'll be amazed at what you can do. So, take risks and chase your dreams with gusto. You're good, and the world's waiting for you! Keep pushing yourself, and you'll soar to new heights! Cheers to a life without limits!

Your Notes for Success

301

*"I find that the harder I work, the more luck
I seem to have." — Thomas Jefferson*

When you put in effort, you're more likely to succeed. You'll have a better chance of achieving your goals and reaching your full potential. Hard work is the key to success. You'll increase your knowledge and skills, build relationships, and identify opportunities. You'll also be able to better handle the challenges that come your way. Hard work will make you resilient and give you the determination to achieve your dreams.

With hard work, you'll have the dedication and discipline to stay focused and motivated. You'll also be able to take advantage of opportunities that come your way. With hard work, you'll have the confidence and determination to take on any challenge and make your dreams come true. Hard work pays off, and with it, you'll have the luck to make your dreams a reality.

To sum up, you have to work hard to succeed. But it's not just about putting in effort. It's also about being resilient, determined, and disciplined. Hard work will increase your skills, knowledge, and relationships and give you a better chance of handling challenges. Don't lose focus. Stay motivated and push forward. You'll make your dreams a reality with your hard work and luck!

Francesco Vitali

Your Notes for Success

302

"The only limit to our realization of tomorrow will be our doubts of today." – Franklin D. Roosevelt

The only thing standing between you and success is your self-imposed limitations. There's no such thing as an impossible dream. You can achieve anything you set your mind to, but this requires you to have the will to do what people believe is impossible. If we keep doubting ourselves or our capability to do something – then achieving a meager task of maintaining discipline in life will not be possible. However, if we start believing that we can do anything we want – then finding life on a planet hundreds of light years away from us is possible.

Things that were nothing but a dream a few decades back are now a reality. From video calling to artificial intelligence and telesurgery - all became a reality today only because people didn't put any limitations on their imaginations. We need to keep striving to achieve our goals while being oblivious to the negativity around us. Don't doubt yourself; everything will work out in the end. To hit the bullseye, you need to focus only on your objective – nothing else.

The only difference between you and the successful people is they stuck to what they believed in. And that should be your approach if you want to be successful.

Francesco Vitali

Your Notes for Success

303

"All progress takes place outside the comfort zone."
— *Michael John Bobak*

Progress is an essential part of growth, both personal and professional. It is important to push yourself out of your comfort zone in order to move forward. Taking risks and stepping out of your comfort zone can help you to learn and grow. It can open up new opportunities, create new experiences, and help you reach your goals. Stepping out of your comfort zone can be tough, but it can also be extremely rewarding. In order to make progress, you must be willing to take risks and put yourself in uncomfortable situations. Doing so can help you to discover new things about yourself and your capabilities.

It is through progress that you reach your full potential. It is during those times of uncertainty that you discover strengths and capabilities you didn't realize you had. You must be brave enough to step outside your comfort zone and explore the unknown. Be a part of the challenges. They're what make you grow. Don't shy away from taking risks because it's in the discomfort that you'll find the true essence of progress. Steps outside your comfort zone will lead you closer to your dreams. You're capable of doing great things, so make your mark on the world! Keep pushing forward, and let your journey be a testament to how magic happens when you embrace the thrill of progress.

Francesco Vitali

Your Notes for Success

304

"A dream doesn't become reality through magic; it takes sweat, determination, and hard work." — Colin Powell

The rewards of hard work and dedication can be far more rewarding than anything else. It's a great feeling when you can put in the hard work and see the results of your hard work paying off. It gives you a sense of accomplishment and pride. When we believe in ourselves and put in the hard work and dedication, we can achieve anything we set our minds to. Even if the dream seems too far away, with hard work and dedication, it can be achieved.

Hard work and dedication can take you places you never imagined. Having a dream and turning it into a reality is the most beautiful thing. It is the best reward for all of the hard work and dedication put in. Dreams do come true, and it takes hard work and dedication to make them happen.

A dream takes flight with hard work and dedication. It's a thrilling ride filled with ups and downs, challenges and victories. But if you're determined and driven, you'll soar to heights you've never dreamed of. You get moving toward your dreams with unstoppable momentum when you add fuel to your inner fire. The melody is a symphony of passion, resilience, and perseverance, playing with the joy of accomplishment. Keep believing in yourself, keep working hard, and get ready to see your dreams come true. Your unique brilliance is about to dazzle the world, so keep working hard!

Your Notes for Success

305

*"Only put off until tomorrow what you are willing
to die having left undone." — Pablo Picasso*

Putting off until tomorrow what you are willing to die having left undone is an excellent way to stay focused and purposeful in life. You can prioritize the tasks that are most important to you and use the extra time to relax or enjoy a hobby. You'll be able to make the most of the moments that you have, and you won't be weighed down by all the little tasks that can often distract you. By being focused, you can make sure that you are always making progress on the things that matter most to you. You can also take the time to reflect on your life and think about how you want to live it. This will help you stay motivated and stay on track with your goals. So, don't let the little things get in the way of your dreams and ambitions. Put off until tomorrow what you are willing to die having left undone, and you'll be living a much more fulfilling and meaningful life.

Staying focused will help you achieve your goals. Don't let distractions and insignificant tasks stop you from your dreams. Focus and intention can make your life more awesome. Don't let distractions or insignificant tasks stop you. It's crucial to keep your focus on what matters. Don't leave something undone until tomorrow. Start today and begin your journey!

Your Notes for Success

306

"Rarely have I seen a situation where doing less than the other guy is a good strategy." — Jimmy Spithill

If you want to succeed, never do less than the other guy. Putting in your best effort every single day is a surefire way to reach your goals. Doing more than what is expected will not only make you stand out, but will also give you an edge over the competition. Additionally, by doing more, you will be able to learn more, experience faster growth, and be more productive. Achieving success is a long, hard journey, and you need to focus on putting in 100% effort each and every day. When you constantly strive to do more, you will eventually reach the pinnacle of success. You will be where you've envisioned yourself to be.

So, never do less than the other guy, and you will definitely succeed. You can't afford mediocrity if you're trying for success. Keep going and set yourself apart by doing more than expected. It's the best way to go above and beyond so you'll stand out from the crowd. Push yourself to do more by constantly learning, growing, and pushing yourself to do better. Success is a challenging journey, but when you give 100% every day, you'll get there. Don't settle for anything less than the best. Keep pushing and keeping striving, and you'll reach your goals. Go out there and make it happen! You've got what it takes.

Francesco Vitali

Your Notes for Success

307

"Keep on going, and the chances are that you will stumble on something, perhaps when you are least expecting it. I never heard of anyone ever stumbling on something sitting down." — Charles F. Kettering

Keep on going, even when it feels like the odds are against you. The chances are that you will stumble on something, perhaps when you are least expecting it. There is an opportunity to be found in every situation, and with perseverance and a positive attitude, you can find it. You never know what may come your way, so stay focused and motivated and don't give up. You may just be surprised with the outcome. If you keep going, no matter what, you will eventually find something that you can turn into a positive and rewarding experience. There will be obstacles and failures along the way, but these are only there to help us learn and grow.

So don't give up. Keep on going and see what the future brings.

You've got to keep going when the going gets tough. Hidden opportunities often come up. Stay focused, stay motivated, and don't give up. Keep going, and you'll be pleasantly surprised by what's waiting for you in the future. Keep pushing forward, and you'll be pleasantly surprised by what happens next. Keep pushing forward, and watch your efforts become a rewarding experience. The best is yet to come!

Francesco Vitali

Your Notes for Success

308

"Change will not come if we wait for some other person or some other time. We are the ones we've been waiting for. We are the change that we seek." — Barack Obama

Change will not come if we wait for some other person or some other time. We are the ones we've been waiting for. We are the change that we seek. We have the power to bring about positive change in the world. Every day we have the opportunity to make small changes in our lives and in our communities that can have a lasting impact. We can reach out to our neighbors, volunteer in our communities, and be active in our local government. We can work together to create a better future. Change is within our reach, and it starts with us. We have the power to make a difference and create a better world. We are the agents of change, and together we can make the world a better place.

Don't wait for someone else or the right timing. We're the ones we've been waiting for, and we have the power to bring about the change we want. From small changes in our everyday lives, we can make a big difference. We can work together to build a brighter future by getting involved in our communities and local governments. Come together and let's make our world a better, more inclusive, and more compassionate place for all. Together, we can make a lasting impact.

Francesco Vitali

Your Notes for Success

309

"If you want to make a permanent change, stop focusing on the size of your problems and start focusing on the size of you!" — T. Harv Eker

If you want to make a permanent change, stop focusing on the size of your problems and start focusing on the size of you. Believe in yourself, your abilities, and your capacity to rise above and beyond any situation you find yourself in. Acknowledge all the challenges and obstacles you are facing, but also remember that you have the power to overcome them.

Be confident in your own strength and determination, and trust in yourself and your abilities. Take the initiative and take action, and don't be afraid to make mistakes. Believe that you are capable of anything, and be brave and courageous in the face of adversity. Believe that you are capable of creating a life you love and living a life of purpose and joy. A life of growth and fulfillment. A life of peace and harmony. Believe in yourself and know that you have what it takes to make the changes you desire.

No matter what your problems are, you have the strength, determination, and skills to overcome them. Take action with courage, embrace your abilities, and learn what you can. Trust yourself, be brave, and take initiative when faced with adversity. Believe in yourself, and use your mistakes as learning opportunities. Believing in yourself will unlock your limitless potential for positive change. You can make the changes you want.

Francesco Vitali

Your Notes for Success

310

"Let him who would enjoy a good future waste none of his present." — *Roger Babson*

Our future is determined by how we use our present. The present is the time for planning, dreaming, and taking action. Each and every moment of the present is precious and should never be wasted. Remember that time is of the utmost value and what matters is how we use the limited time we have. Each second counts. Every minute makes a difference. Every moment is monumental.

We should use our present moment to plan for the future and to take positive action that will lead us to the life we want to live. We should never procrastinate or delay our goals because tomorrow is never guaranteed. We should focus on the present and make the most of the opportunities that come our way. We should make wise choices and create a future that is full of joy and success. We should make good use of our present to ensure that the future we create is one that we can be proud of. By making the most of the present, we can create a future that is worth looking forward to—a brighter future not just for ourselves, but others who will follow.

Francesco Vitali

Your Notes for Success

311

"If you love what you do and are willing to do what it takes, it's within your reach. And it'll be worth every minute you spend alone at night, thinking and thinking about what it is you want to design or build."
— *Steve Wozniak*

Do what you love and love what you do. It may take time and hard work, but with dedication and passion, the rewards will be great. It's worth every minute you spend alone at night, thinking and dreaming about what it is you want to design or build. With focus and determination, you can make your dreams a reality.

You may encounter challenges along the way, but with a positive mindset and dedication to your goal, you can find solutions. You'll gain priceless experience and knowledge that will serve you for years to come. The journey will be fulfilling and the results will be rewarding. With the right attitude, you can achieve anything. So, take the plunge and be proud of the effort you put in. It will pay off in the end.

Make your heart sing by dancing to the rhythm of your passion and creativity. Stay unwavering in your focus, determination, and positivity even when obstacles arise. Do what makes your heart sing, and you'll see your unique designs or creations blossom. When you have the right attitude, each step of the journey will be fulfilling, and each milestone will be a sweet reward. Take the leap with pride, knowing you are creating a brighter future. Keep believing in yourself and watch your dreams emerge just the way you want them to.

Francesco Vitali

Your Notes for Success

312

"If you don't design your own life plan, chances are you'll fall into someone else's plan. And guess what they have planned for you? Not much." — *Jim Rohn*

Taking control of your life and deciding on your own future is the best way to ensure success and happiness. By setting goals and planning for the future, you can create the life you want. You can envision where you want to be and need to be.

Not only will you be in charge of your own destiny, but you will also have the satisfaction of knowing that you achieved your goals on your own. Additionally, taking the initiative to plan your life will help you to become more organized, efficient, and successful. With a life plan, you can be confident that you are working toward a brighter future. By taking charge of your life and creating a plan, you will be well on your way to achieving success and happiness.

Forge your own unique path to success and happiness by setting meaningful goals, making strategic plans, and visualizing your desired future. Having a plan will increase organization, efficiency, and success in your life. Planning your life will provide the fulfillment of knowing you achieved your goals on your own terms. With a solid life plan, you can confidently achieve your goals. Make your dreams come true by taking control of your life and creating your own destiny.

Your Notes for Success

313

"To be successful, you must accept all challenges that come your way. You can't just accept the ones you like."
— Mike Gafka

To be successful, you must accept all challenges that come your way. Success is not achieved by taking the easy route. Challenges are a part of life and the only way to grow and progress is to face them head-on. When you accept all challenges, you become resilient and can overcome obstacles that come your way. You also develop a mindset of determination and courage that can take you further in life. Accepting all challenges doesn't mean you can't make conscious decisions on the ones you take on. You can still weigh the pros and cons and decide if the challenge is worth pursuing. Taking on challenges also helps you develop your skills and knowledge and can open up new opportunities. So, don't shy away from any challenge that comes your way, because it could be the key to unlocking your success.

It's hard to succeed without overcoming challenges, so embrace challenges as stepping stones. They cultivate resilience, determination, and courage. You have the power to choose which challenges to pursue, considering the pros and cons. Embracing challenges gives you new opportunities and hone your skills. Don't be afraid of challenges—they may lead to your success. Make sure you don't let challenges get in the way of your goals, so face them with confidence and unwavering determination.

Francesco Vitali

Your Notes for Success

314

"If you put out 150 percent, then you can always expect 100 percent back." — Justin Timberlake

If you put out 150 percent effort, then you can always expect 100 percent back. When you are willing to go above and beyond what is expected, you will be rewarded. Your hard work and dedication will be noticed, and you will be rewarded with success. People will be drawn to your enthusiasm and energy, and you will be given the opportunity to do great things. You will also gain respect and admiration from those around you. Your willingness to put in extra effort will be appreciated, and you will be rewarded in many ways. You will be able to achieve big goals and create amazing outcomes. By putting in 150 percent, you will be able to reach heights you never thought possible.

You're going to set yourself apart as you go above and beyond, putting all your effort into it. Get ready to blaze your own path to success! You'll earn respect and admiration from people around you if you pursue excellence relentlessly. Get ready to achieve greatness and leave a legacy that inspires others by embracing the challenges, staying focused, and pushing forward. If you give your all, the possibilities are endless.

Francesco Vitali

Your Notes for Success

315

"Don't wait for extraordinary opportunities.
Seize common occasions and make them great."
— *Orison Swett Marden*

Opportunities are the key to success, and they don't just happen by themselves. You have to create them. It takes hard work, dedication, and creativity to make your own opportunities. It's important to take risks and be willing to fail in order to create opportunities for yourself. By thinking outside the box and taking initiative, you'll be opening yourself up to new ideas, projects, and chances to learn and grow. It's important to be proactive, to network, and to make sure you're always learning new skills. This way, when an opportunity arises, you'll be ready to take advantage of it. Opportunities don't happen without you creating them. Take the initiative, take risks, and take action. You'll be amazed at the opportunities you can create for yourself.

Make your own destiny by being the master of your own destiny! Don't wait for opportunities to knock; create them with unwavering dedication, ingenuity, and calculated risk. Never shy away from stepping out of your comfort zone, embrace a proactive mindset, and constantly learn and network. As you break barriers and create your own success story, you will be astonished at the boundless opportunities that unfold!

Francesco Vitali

<u>*Your Notes for Success*</u>

316

"No one can make you feel inferior without your consent." — Eleanor Roosevelt

You have the power to choose how you feel and how you respond to negative situations. You can choose to find the positive in any situation, no matter how difficult or uncomfortable. You can choose to stay strong and resilient in the face of adversity. You can choose to focus on the good in yourself and in others. You are in charge of your life and how you want to live it. No one can take that away from you.

When you focus on the good and stay positive, you will be able to find the strength and courage to overcome any obstacles that may come your way. And when you focus on the good, you will find that you are able to inspire and motivate those around you. So, don't let anyone make you feel you don't have any value. You have the power to choose how you feel and how you respond.

In the journey of life, you hold the reins to your emotions and reactions. Choose to embrace the positive amidst challenges, and stay resilient. Your choices shape your reality, and you have the power to focus on the good in yourself and others. You are the author of your story, and your positivity can be a beacon of inspiration to others. So, own your worth, make empowering choices, and let your positivity light up your path to success.

Francesco Vitali

<u>*Your Notes for Success*</u>

317

"If your actions inspire others to dream more, learn more, do more, and become more, you are a leader."
— *John Quincy Adams*

Leaders have the ability to influence, motivate, and empower others to reach their full potential. They have the power to create positive change in the world by inspiring others to strive for greatness. Leaders don't just talk the talk; they walk the walk. They lead by example and set the bar high. They have a vision and are passionate about it, and they aren't afraid to take risks to make it come true. They are passionate about the greater good and are willing to put in the hard work to make it happen.

A leader is someone who can rally people around a cause and get them excited about it. They can bring out the best in people and help them realize their true potential. Being a leader is not easy, but it is very rewarding. When you lead by example, you not only inspire those around you to be their best, but you also make the world a better place.

It is true that true leaders stand out in a world where leaders are defined by their actions. By setting high standards and inspiring others, leaders create a world that is better for future generations. They lead with unwavering determination, daring to take risks and achieve their vision.

Francesco Vitali

Your Notes for Success

318

"The biggest risk is not taking any risk … In a world that's changing really quickly, the only strategy that is guaranteed to fail is not taking risks." — *Mark Zuckerberg*

Taking risks can be intimidating, but every great accomplishment starts with a risk. The biggest risk is not taking any risk, as this can lead to missed opportunities and stagnation. By pushing yourself out of your comfort zone, you open yourself up to new experiences, new skills, and new ways of thinking.

Taking risks is essential for growth, both personally and professionally. It encourages you to push yourself, strive for improvement, and to think outside of the box. Taking risks allows you to challenge yourself, to try new things, and to test out new ideas. It encourages creativity and innovation and allows you to explore and experience new paths. Taking risks can be scary, but the rewards can far outweigh the risks. It's important to remember that taking risks can lead to great success if you are willing to be brave and face your fear.

Don't be afraid to take risks, embrace uncertainty, and push yourself beyond what you think you can achieve. Take calculated risks, dare to dream big, and leave an indelible mark. Your boldness will propel you toward incredible accomplishments.

Francesco Vitali

Your Notes for Success

319

"We become what we think about most of the time, and that's the strangest secret." — *Earl Nightingale*

The power of our thoughts is something that many of us don't fully understand. We become what we think about most of the time, and that's the strangest secret. By continually focusing our attention on what we want, we can create the reality that we desire. This simple but profound truth can be applied to every area of our lives. We can use it to improve our relationships, careers, finances, health, and even our spirituality. By directing our thoughts and energy toward our goals and dreams, we can manifest them into reality. No matter what we want to achieve, when we focus our thoughts and energy on it, we can manifest it in our lives. The strangest secret is that we create our own realities by the power of our thoughts.

In order to manifest our dreams into reality, we must consciously direct our attention toward our desires. Our thoughts shape our reality and determine our destiny. It applies to all aspects of our lives, from health to finances to relationships. Embrace the truth that your thoughts are the keys to creating your own reality. Your thoughts shape the world.

Your Notes for Success

320

"Though no one can go back and make a brand-new start, anyone can start from now and make a brand-new ending." — Carl Bard

It is never too late to make a change and start anew. With a positive attitude, hard work, and determination, anything is possible. It's important to remember that the past does not define us. Only the present does. We are all capable of creating a new beginning for ourselves and for those around us. With a little bit of effort and a lot of belief, we can turn our lives around and make something beautiful. Life is all about second chances, and we should seize every opportunity that comes our way to make a positive difference. It takes courage to start anew and make a fresh start, but it is well worth it in the end. So, let's take a step forward and start creating our brand-new ending today!

Take control of your destiny and leave the past behind. You hold the pen to write your own story, filled with fresh beginnings and limitless possibilities. Embrace the power of now, fueled by a positive mindset, relentless effort, and unwavering belief. Embody courage and let go of fear as you embark on a journey of self-reinvention. Every moment is a chance to shape a brighter future, so start authoring your unique and extraordinary ending today.

Your Notes for Success

321

"Frustration, although quite painful at times, is a very positive and essential part of success." — *Bo Bennett*

Frustration can be a difficult emotion to deal with, but it is an essential part of success. It shows that you are striving to reach your goals, and that you are pushing yourself to work hard and achieve more. If you never felt frustrated, it would mean that you are not challenging yourself and not doing anything that requires effort.

Frustration is a sign that you are growing, and it can be a motivating factor to keep you going. It means that you are pushing yourself to the limit and striving to reach your full potential. It is a positive sign that you are on the right track and working hard to reach your goals. Frustration can be painful, but it is a necessary part of the journey to success because it shows that you have goals and that you are working hard to achieve them.

In pursuit of excellence, frustration is a catalyst for growth, and it reminds you that you are challenging yourself. Embrace it as a catalyst for growth, and let it motivate your drive to overcome obstacles. Each step forward moves you closer to your dreams. So let frustration guide you on your path to extraordinary success.

Francesco Vitali

Your Notes for Success

322

"Successful people do what unsuccessful people are not willing to do. Don't wish it were easier; wish you were better." — Jim Rohn

Successful people are the ones who are willing to do whatever it takes to reach their goals. They understand that success takes hard work and dedication, and they are willing to put in the effort it takes to achieve it.

Unsuccessful people often don't want to put in the effort, and they may become discouraged when they don't see immediate results. However, successful people understand that success takes time and do whatever is necessary to reach their goals. They don't wish it were easier; they wish they were better. They understand that the most successful people are the ones who consistently work hard and put in the effort. They don't give up even when things get tough, and they keep pushing forward until they reach their goals. Successful people understand that hard work and dedication are the keys to success and are willing to put in the effort it takes to achieve it.

Essentially, success doesn't come to you for free, it's earned through hard work and unwavering determination. People who are willing to work hard and never give up will achieve their goals. Success may take time, but it's worth it. So, let's work harder, be better, and keep going until we get there.

Francesco Vitali

Your Notes for Success

323

"But you have to do what you dream of doing even while you're afraid." — Arianna Huffington

Dreams are what make life worth living. It is important to remember that it is okay to be afraid, but that shouldn't stop you from doing the things you want to do. Even when fear creeps in and you feel like giving up, it is important to take a deep breath and take a step forward. When you take risks and put yourself in new, unfamiliar situations, you will be amazed at the opportunities that come your way.

Fear can be a great motivator to do something amazing and make an impact. Taking risks, pushing through fear, and doing the things you dream of will not only make you a better and more confident person, but will also lead to a beautiful life. So, don't be afraid to take risks and follow your dreams; you are capable of more than you think!

While fear may try to keep us from taking risks, we must remember that magic happens when we do. Take steps toward achieving your dreams regardless of your fears. Fear doesn't have to stop you from living life to the fullest. Be bold, and brave, and chase your dreams!

Your Notes for Success

324

"If you do what you've always done, you'll get what you've always gotten." — Tony Robbins

If you keep doing what you always do, you will get nowhere. There is nothing wrong with maintaining consistency and working hard, but it is also important to take risks and push yourself. Change is inevitable, and sometimes, it is necessary to get out of your comfort zone and try something new. Embrace the challenge and be open to learning new things. When you take risks, you open yourself up to new opportunities and experiences. You will be able to explore the world in a way that you never thought possible and make real progress. When you take risks and work hard, you can achieve anything. With a positive attitude and an open mind, you can reach new heights and get closer to your goals.

To summarize, life is a canvas on which you can paint your own masterpiece. Make sure you embrace change and take risks, because growth and progress happen when you step outside of your comfort zone. Keep pushing yourself, take risks, and keep embracing new experiences. You'll be amazed at what you'll achieve if you embrace the challenges and opportunities that come your way. Take risks with a positive attitude, and watch yourself soar to success and fulfillment!

Francesco Vitali

<u>*Your Notes for Success*</u>

325

"Only those who will risk going too far can possibly find out how far one can go." — T. S. Eliot

This inspiring quote by T.S. Eliot highlights the importance of taking risks in order to grow and succeed. Those who are willing to step out of their comfort zone and explore the unknown often find great success. Taking risks can be intimidating, but it is often worth it.

Taking risks and pushing your boundaries can open new doors and allow you to reach goals you never thought possible. It is important to remember that failure is a part of the process, but learning from those experiences will help you grow and become stronger. Taking risks can be scary, but taking that leap of faith can lead to incredible opportunities that you would otherwise never discover. Only those who will risk going too far can possibly find out how far one can go.

Be brave, be adventurous, and keep pushing yourself to reach new heights. Be bold, be courageous, and be committed to pushing yourself further than you thought you could go. Take calculated risks, learn from failures, and keep encouraging yourself. You can achieve greatness by taking that bold step into the unknown, so be brave, be adventurous, and witness the magic unfold.

Francesco Vitali

Your Notes for Success

326

*"I always did something I was a little not ready to do.
I think that's how you grow. When there's that moment
of 'Wow, I'm not really sure I can do this,' and you
push through those moments, that's when you have a
breakthrough." — Marissa Mayer*

Doing something you're not ready to do can be intimidating and scary. However, by pushing yourself to take on a challenge, you open yourself up to the possibility of success. Taking risks and pushing your limits can help you gain new skills and knowledge, which can lead to success in many areas of life.

Overcoming your fear of the unknown can help you realize that you are capable of more than you think. You can learn to be resilient and gain a sense of pride and accomplishment by pushing yourself to take on something that seems overwhelming. By taking the chance, you open yourself up to the possibility of success and you can use that success to build more confidence in yourself and your abilities.

The best way to grow and succeed is to step outside of your comfort zone. Take risks, even if you're not completely prepared. If you push yourself to tackle challenges head-on, you'll be able to develop new skills, knowledge, and opportunities for success in many areas. Build resilience, embrace self-discovery, and be proud of your accomplishments. Your ability to accomplish greatness is limitless. You are capable of greatness beyond your imagination.

Francesco Vitali

Your Notes for Success

327

"Be humble. Be hungry. And always be the hardest worker in the room." — Dwayne Johnson

Be humble. Be hungry. And always be the hardest worker in the room. These are three essential pieces of advice that can help you be successful in anything you do. When you are humble, it allows you to be open to learning from others and stay humble even when you have achieved success. Being hungry encourages you to strive for more, to constantly seek out new opportunities, and to take risks.

Finally, when you are the hardest worker in the room, it shows that you are passionate and dedicated to what you do. This creates a positive attitude that will be noticeable and will help you stand out from the competition. Being humble, hungry, and the hardest worker in the room are key qualities that will help you reach your goals and be successful.

Don't forget these three pieces of advice: be humble, hungry, and work hard. It's about embracing humility, which allows you to continuously grow and learn. Get hungry for success by taking chances and looking for new opportunities. And last but not least, show off your unwavering work ethic and passion. These qualities will help you get where you want to be. Your success will soar if you keep pushing forward with determination!

Francesco Vitali

<u>*Your Notes for Success*</u>

328

"Often the difference between a successful person and a failure is not one has better abilities or ideas, but the courage that one has to bet on one's ideas, to take a calculated risk and to act." — Andre Malraux

Successful people have the courage to take risks, the willingness to learn from their mistakes, and the resilience to bounce back from any setbacks. They are not afraid of failure but use it as a stepping stone to success. It is their ability to take risks, to stay focused, and to keep pushing forward that makes them successful. They know that nothing great can come from playing it safe. They are willing to put in the effort and take the necessary steps to make their dreams come true. They have the courage to take calculated risks and the confidence to trust their own judgment.

Successful people are willing to put in the work and take the necessary risks to reach their goals. When they finally reach their desired destination, they are more than happy to share their success with others. Ultimately, it is their courage that sets them apart from the rest and helps them to achieve great things.

Successful individuals are fearless adventurers, embracing risks, learning from failures, and bouncing back stronger. Their unwavering confidence, relentless resilience, and passion for sharing inspire others to chase their own dreams and achieve extraordinary heights. Dare to be bold, learn from setbacks, and keep reaching for the stars!

Your Notes for Success

329

"Life is inherently risky. There is only one big risk you should avoid at all costs, and that is the risk of doing nothing." — Denis Waitley

Life is inherently risky. From the moment we are born, we are exposed to a multitude of unknowns and potential risks. However, rather than fear these risks and retreat from life, I believe we should embrace them. We should take risks, challenge ourselves, and strive for growth and development. Each risk taken is an opportunity to learn and grow, to become a better version of ourselves.

The only risk we should avoid at all costs is the risk of doing nothing. Doing nothing is a greater risk than any other, for it is guaranteed to bring no reward, no growth, and no progress. Instead, we should take risks, aim high, and live life to the fullest. There is no greater reward than the feeling of accomplishment that comes from taking risks and achieving our goals. So, let's take life's risks and live life without regret.

Let's embrace life's risks and challenges with courage and determination. Each risk taken is an opportunity for growth and learning, and the only risk to avoid is doing nothing. Let's aim high, live life to the fullest, and revel in the sweet taste of accomplishment. Embrace the unknown, take risks, and make life an adventure worth living!

Francesco Vitali

Your Notes for Success

330

"A ship in harbor is safe, but that is not what
ships are built for." — John A. Shedd

You can't expect success from your comfort zone. That doesn't mean you can't reach success. It means you must be willing to step out of your comfort zone. Doing so will bring about opportunities for growth and development. It can be scary, but it is worth it. Taking risks and putting yourself in uncomfortable situations will bring about greater rewards. When you take a chance, you can open up possibilities that weren't available before. You never know what could happen if you take a leap of faith and try something new. Taking risks can increase your chances of success. You don't have to be fearless to achieve success, but you do have to be willing to step out of your comfort zone. So, take a risk and believe in yourself. You have the power to reach success.

Success often lies beyond our comfort zone. Embracing discomfort and taking risks can lead to opportunities for growth and greater rewards. Don't be afraid to step out of your comfort zone and take a chance on yourself. Believe in your abilities and take that leap of faith. You have the power to achieve success!

Francesco Vitali

Your Notes for Success

331

*"If you don't value your time, neither will others. Stop
giving away your time and talents. Value what you
know and start charging for it." — Kim Garst*

If you don't value your time, neither will others. This simple
statement is incredibly powerful. Valuing your time is an important
part of life and is essential for setting healthy boundaries. When
you value your time, you recognize that it is a precious commodity,
and you use it to pursue your goals and dreams. You also set a
good example for others by showing that your time is valuable
and should be respected. When you take the time to prioritize and
value your own time, it shows that you understand the importance
of taking care of yourself. This in turn, will make others more
likely to respect and value your time too. So, remember to value
your time and set boundaries. It will pay off in the long run.

In a world where time is our most valuable currency, it's crucial
to recognize its worth and invest it wisely. Just like a precious gem,
our time should be cherished, guarded, and utilized to pursue our
passions and aspirations. By setting healthy boundaries and valuing
our time, we create a ripple effect that inspires others to do the
same. So, let's be time-savvy, prioritize ourselves, and watch as our
dreams flourish into reality, one moment at a time.

Francesco Vitali

<u>Your Notes for Success</u>

332

"Flaming enthusiasm, backed up by horse sense and persistence, is the quality that most frequently makes for success." — Dale Carnegie

When a person is enthusiastic, they are passionate and full of energy. They are driven to pursue their goals and have the courage to take risks. "Horse sense" is the ability to make wise decisions. It is the understanding of how to effectively use the resources at hand. Finally, persistence is the ability to keep going despite any obstacles that may arise. All of these qualities help a person continue to strive for their goals despite any setbacks.

Having these three qualities together creates a person who is unstoppable. They will have the mindset to stay focused and motivated to achieve any goal that they set for themselves. A person with flaming enthusiasm, horse sense, and persistence is sure to reach their goals and find success.

With unwavering enthusiasm, sharp horse sense, and relentless persistence, one becomes an unstoppable force on the path to success. Embracing passion, making wise decisions, and overcoming obstacles with determination, nothing can stand in the way of achieving their goals. So, let's ignite our enthusiasm, apply our horse sense, and persevere with unwavering determination to make our dreams a reality. Success awaits those who embody these qualities. Keep pushing forward, and watch your aspirations come to life!

Francesco Vitali

<u>Your Notes for Success</u>

333

"Worrying is like paying on a debt that may
never come due." — Will Rogers

If you want to get to the finish line, you have to keep going. It can seem daunting, but it is important to remember that you can achieve anything you put your mind to. With hard work and dedication, you will be able to reach your goal. It is important to stay motivated and to keep a positive attitude. Looking at each step as a success will help you to keep going and reach the finish line. Celebrate the small victories and obstacles that you have overcome. If you start to feel discouraged, take a break and refocus on the goals you have set for yourself. With perseverance and determination, you will be able to reach the finish line and will feel a great sense of accomplishment.

Stay committed, work hard, and keep a positive attitude as you work toward the finish line. If you feel discouraged, refocus and keep pushing forward with unwavering determination. Every step you take is a triumph, and every obstacle you overcome is proof of your perseverance. When you finally get there, the feeling of accomplishment will make all the effort worth it. Keep believing in yourself, and success will be yours to embrace!

Francesco Vitali

<u>*Your Notes for Success*</u>

334

"Don't stay in bed, unless you can make money in bed."
— *George Burns*

There is so much joy and satisfaction to be found in making the most of each day. After all, life is too short to waste away in bed. Get up and make something of yourself. Seize the day and make your dreams come true. Life is full of possibilities and opportunities. Take advantage of them and make your life extraordinary. Take risks, take chances, and make your life a positive and memorable experience. Make plans and set goals.

Every day is a new opportunity to make something of yourself and create a life you can be proud of. Don't stay in bed unless you can make money in bed. Get up and make something of yourself. With hard work, dedication, and a positive attitude, you can achieve whatever you set your mind to. So don't stay in bed; get up and make something of yourself.

Carpe diem! Take risks, seize opportunities, and strive for your dreams. Make each day count with open arms. Life is like a canvas waiting for your brush strokes of success and fulfillment. Set goals, make plans, and live your life to the fullest. Don't stay in bed; get up, and start building a brighter future with hard work, dedication, and a positive attitude.

Francesco Vitali

<u>*Your Notes for Success*</u>

335

"All the people who knock me down only inspire me to do better." — Selena Gomez

When people knock you down, take a look at the situation and use it as fuel to do better. Everyone experiences setbacks, but it's how you use them that will define your success. Each time someone puts you down, use that as an opportunity to learn and grow. Every time someone says you can't do something, use it as a challenge to prove them wrong. The people who knock you down can actually be your biggest motivators. Take it as an opportunity to learn, grow, and improve. You can use negative feedback as constructive criticism to help you work harder and become the best version of yourself. With the right attitude and determination, you can use all the people who knock you down to inspire you to do better.

Whenever you face setbacks or negativity, rise up and overcome. Use those challenges as stepping stones to push yourself forward. Learn, adapt, and show the world what you're capable of. Keep pushing toward your goals with unwavering determination, no matter what the doubters say. Your success is within reach, and every obstacle is an opportunity for you to prove your resilience. Keep going, and your relentless spirit will take you there!

Francesco Vitali

<u>Your Notes for Success</u>

336

"Whatever your life's work is, do it well. A man should do his job so well that the living, the dead, and the unborn could do it no better." — Martin Luther King Jr.

This simple phrase encapsulates the key to success and satisfaction. When you work with dedication, passion, and integrity, you will be rewarded with a sense of accomplishment. Doing your best at whatever you do, whether a job, a hobby, or a passion project, will give you a feeling of pride and joy. When you put in your best effort, you can be sure of achieving a positive outcome. Taking pride in your work and striving for excellence is a great way to ensure success. Doing your best in whatever you do will not only give you a sense of satisfaction but it will also set you apart from the rest. Doing your life's work well is the key to a life of success and fulfillment.

Always give your best. It's not just about the end result but also the journey and the effort you put in along the way. It's hard work, dedication, and commitment that will pay off in ways you can't even imagine. Never stop striving, stay true to your passions, and take pride in your journey. Enjoy the joy of doing your life's work well, and watch your fulfillment soar. Your best is just around the corner!

Francesco Vitali

Your Notes for Success

337

"Do what is easy and your life will be hard. Do what is hard and your life will become easy." — *Les Brown*

It's easy to choose the path of least resistance, but this will not take you far. You won't reach your goals and dreams this way. When you take on difficult tasks, you build a strong foundation for yourself to succeed in the future. You also build strong relationships with those around you and develop skills that will help you reach your goals. You will also gain a greater appreciation for the hard work that goes into achieving success.

By doing what is hard, you will create a life full of meaning and purpose. You will also learn valuable lessons that will help you become resilient and strong in any situation. Doing the hard things will bring you a greater sense of accomplishment and will help you reach your goals.

Don't forget success doesn't come easily. It is the challenges and difficulties that make us who we are. Embrace the tough tasks, push yourself beyond your comfort zone, and learn to grow. Taking on the hard stuff builds a strong foundation for a successful and fulfilling future. Don't shy away from challenges, take them on head-on, and watch yourself soar.

Francesco Vitali

<u>Your Notes for Success</u>

338

"Time can be an ally or an enemy. What it becomes depends entirely upon you, your goals, and your determination to use every available minute."
— *Zig Ziglar*

Time is a valuable resource. It is a gift that is given to us to use wisely. When we use every minute of our time wisely, we can be successful. We can achieve our goals and reach our highest potential. When we are mindful of our time and use it effectively, it allows us to stay focused and accomplish more in a shorter amount of time. We can maximize our efforts and be more productive with our time.

When we commit to using every minute wisely, we can create a positive impact in our lives. We can use our time to do things that are meaningful, and that will benefit us in the long run. By using our time wisely, we can find success and reach our highest potential.

Time is the currency of life, so let's invest it wisely. When we prioritize our time, we open doors to success. If we make sure we get the most out of each moment, we can achieve our goals, maximize our efforts, and make a positive impact on people's lives. So, let's take advantage of every minute, and make our dreams come true. Time is precious, so let's get to our dreams!

Your Notes for Success

339

"When gardeners garden, it is not just plants that grow, but the gardeners themselves." — *Ken Druse*

When you help others grow and blossom, you grow as well. Mentoring and supporting those around you is a truly rewarding experience, and it's one of the best ways to become a better person. By taking the time to listen, support, and encourage those around you, you can create a ripple effect of positivity and growth.

Whether it's offering friendly advice and guidance or simply lending a listening ear, being there for someone can be a powerful way to improve your own life. When you put your energy into helping someone else, you benefit from their growth and success. You learn from their mistakes and successes and gain insight into how you can improve yourself and your own life. People can grow and reach their goals together, and the rewards are mutual. Helping others is not only rewarding, but it's beneficial for your own growth and development.

If you listen, support, and encourage others, you spread positivity. Lifting others up is a rewarding journey. When you lend advice, or simply lend a listening ear, you improve your life. If we work together, we can achieve our goals, grow, and create mutually beneficial cycles of success. Giving and receiving help are equally rewarding.

Francesco Vitali

<u>*Your Notes for Success*</u>

340

"Most of the important things in the world have been accomplished by people who have kept on trying when there seemed to be no hope at all." — *Dale Carnegie*

Don't give up! You have what it takes to tackle any challenge that comes your way. Determination and perseverance are the keys to success. It may be difficult, but if you stay focused and stay positive, you can achieve whatever you set your mind to. Remind yourself that you are a champion.

You may have setbacks and experience some hard times, but that's when you need to stay strong and keep going. It's important to remember that no matter how hard it gets, there's always light at the end of the tunnel. Remember to take one day at a time and stay committed to your goals. Don't be afraid to ask for help along the way. It's okay to not have all the answers. With persistence, you'll get to where you want to be.

Keep going, champ! You've got what it takes to conquer any challenge. Determination and perseverance are your superpowers. Even when it gets tough, stay focused and positive, knowing that you're well on your way to success. Take it one day at a time, stay committed, and don't be afraid to ask for help. You're on the path to success, and you're destined to reach your goals.

Francesco Vitali

Your Notes for Success

341

"Success is the product of daily habits—not once in a lifetime transformation." — James Clear

Success is the product of daily habits and not a once-in-a-lifetime transformation. It is the result of small, incremental steps taken every day that add up to something big. It is the result of making good decisions and taking action. It is the result of creating routines that help you stay focused and on track. It is the result of being consistent and persistent in your efforts.

Success is not something that happens overnight; it is the result of steady progress. It is the result of a commitment to improving yourself and your circumstances on a daily basis. Success is achievable and can be had by anyone who is willing to put in the work and consistently apply themselves to their goals. The key to success is to make it a habit and to stay focused on the end result.

Taking small steps everyday will help you achieve success. Creating routines that keep you focused, making good decisions, taking action, and staying committed are not one-time changes, but daily habits that add up. Success is within your reach, and it's all about making it a habit and staying focused on your end goal. You're up to the challenge!

Francesco Vitali

Your Notes for Success

342

"The future has several names. For the weak, it is impossible; for the fainthearted, it is unknown; but for the valiant, it is ideal." — Victor Hugo

The future has several names, and for the brave and determined, it is ideal. Those who are not afraid of hard work, risk, and challenge can find success and satisfaction in the future. With a positive mindset and dedication, it is possible to shape the future into something that we want it to be. The future is a blank canvas, and with the right attitude and support, it can be painted with the colors of our dreams. It is up to us to make the most of it. With perseverance and dedication, we can make the future one that we would be proud of. We can make a future that is filled with hope, progress, and success. We have the power to determine our own destiny and create a brighter, more promising future.

Embrace the future and don't shy away from hard work, risk, or challenges. With a positive mindset and unwavering dedication, we can paint the future with hope, progress, and success. The future can be created, if we persevere and dedicate ourselves to it. Our journey to success begins here. So keep moving! Cheers to our brighter, brighter future!

Francesco Vitali

Your Notes for Success

343

"Luck is a dividend of sweat. The more you sweat,
the luckier you get." — Ray Kroc

Luck is an interesting concept; it almost feels like a reward for hard work, and it often is! The saying "luck is a dividend of sweat" is a great reminder that those who work hard and put in the effort will often be the luckiest. It's not a guarantee, of course, but it can certainly increase the odds. Working hard can make us more prepared for opportunities when they arise, and we're more likely to take advantage of them. We can also create our own luck by taking risks and trying new things. So, when it comes to luck, remember that it's not something that just falls into your lap, it's something that you have to work for. The more you sweat, the luckier you get!

We shouldn't just wait for luck to come knocking on our door. Getting lucky isn't just about luck, it's about putting in our own hard work and sweat. So, keep pushing yourself, take risks, and try new things. Let's make our own luck by being proactive and taking advantage of opportunities when they come up. Remember, the harder we work, the luckier we become. Don't give up, and your luck will soar!

Francesco Vitali

Your Notes for Success

344

"I had to pick myself up and get on with it, do it all over again, only even better this time." — Sam Walton

No matter how hard it can be at times, it's important to never give up. Picking yourself up and continuing on is the only way to reach the finish line. It's not always easy, but with the right attitude and a bit of determination, you can make it happen. It's important to remember that even if you don't make it the first time, that doesn't mean you won't make it the second time. And if you keep trying, eventually you'll reach your goal. You won't always be successful, but with persistence and hard work, you will get there. It's easy to get discouraged when things don't go as expected, but it's essential to remain positive and keep going. There's nothing more satisfying than achieving something you've worked hard for, and the feeling of success can be truly rewarding. So, don't give up, keep pushing yourself, and you will reach your goal.

Keep going with the right attitude and hard work, even when the road gets tough. Don't give up in the face of challenges. The taste of success will be worth it all, even if success does not come immediately. Keep pushing yourself, embrace the journey, and stay positive. Don't give up. Your perseverance will be rewarded.

Francesco Vitali

Your Notes for Success

345

"Singleness of purpose is one of the chief essentials for success in life, no matter what may be one's aim.."
— *John D. Rockefeller*

Having a clear and focused sense of purpose is the foundation to achieve success. Knowing what you want to achieve and having the motivation to stay on track will help you stay committed to your goals. It encourages us to stay focused and disciplined and to take the necessary steps to achieve success. It also helps us to manage our time efficiently, keep distractions to a minimum, and to stay organized.

Having a singleness of purpose ensures that we do not deviate from our aim and waste our energy and time on activities that do not contribute to our goal. It also helps us to be more productive and efficient by giving us clarity and direction which motivates us to take action and move forward. Singleness of purpose is an important aspect of success, and having it will help you to live a more fulfilling and successful life.

Having a clear purpose is paramount to success. By keeping our purpose in focus, discipline, and motivation, we can manage our time efficiently, minimize distractions, and stay organized. With a single purpose, we stay focused and don't waste time on irrelevant activities. Focus, clarity, and direction fuel our productivity.

Francesco Vitali

Your Notes for Success

346

"It is important to remember that there are no overnight successes. You will need to be dedicated, single-minded, and there is no substitute to hard work."
— *Mukesh Ambani*

It is important to remember that there are no overnight successes. The path to success is often long and winding and requires hard work, dedication, and resilience. It is not a matter of luck or chance, but of persistence and determination. Focusing on the small victories along the way is key to staying motivated and encouraged to keep going. While it can be easy to get discouraged by the lack of immediate success, it is important to remember that hard work and dedication will eventually pay off. Any success achieved will be much more meaningful and rewarding if it is done through hard work and perseverance. As the saying goes, "If it was easy, everyone would do it." So, keep working hard and stay focused—success is worth the effort!

It takes grit and perseverance to reach success. Understand that there are no shortcuts or overnight success. Celebrate the small victories along the way as they fuel your motivation to keep pushing forward. You're only able to succeed if you work hard and are dedicated. Stay focused, stay committed, and keep grinding. Your effort will be rewarded, and the taste of success will be sweeter than ever.

Francesco Vitali

Your Notes for Success

347

"If you are born poor it's not your mistake, but if you die poor, it's your mistake." — *Bill Gates*

If you are born poor it's not your mistake; it's simply the reality of the circumstances you were born into. However, if you die poor, it can be your mistake. It's true that some people are born into a life of poverty, but it's also true that everyone has the potential to better their lives, no matter their circumstances.

With a positive attitude, determination, and hard work, you can turn your life around. It's important to take advantage of available resources, such as educational opportunities, job training, and financial advice, to increase your chances of success. It's also important to focus on cultivating self-esteem and developing a strong sense of self-worth. With the right attitude, you can achieve anything. Don't let your circumstances define who you are; with the right mindset, you can create the life you want.

Although circumstances are out of your control, your mindset and actions are within your control. Take charge of your life and create the success you deserve. Be positive, work hard, and take advantage of the resources available. Don't let your past define your future. Take charge of your life and make a change. You can write your own success story at any time.

Francesco Vitali

Your Notes for Success

348

*"There is no royal road to a successful life, as there is
no royal road to learning. It has got to be hard knocks,
morning, noon, and night, and fixity of purpose."*
— *Charles M. Schwab*

Hard work and dedication are required to achieve any goal. If you want to achieve success in any field, you must focus on your work, invest your time and energy, and have a positive attitude. This is the only way to reach the top and stay there. Hard work and dedication are the keys to success. With these two things, you can achieve anything you set your mind to.

A successful life is the result of hard work, determination, and perseverance. If you want to succeed, you must be willing to put in the effort and dedication necessary to get there. The rewards of hard work and dedication are worth it in the long run, because success is something that can be enjoyed for a lifetime.

Getting ahead isn't just a dream; you've got to work hard and be dedicated. It's possible to succeed in any field if you focus on your goals, put in a lot of time and energy, and keep a positive attitude. Embrace the power of determination and perseverance, and you'll walk the way to a fulfilling and accomplished life. The journey might be tough, but the reward is worth it in the end. Keep pushing forward, and success will be yours to cherish for a lifetime.

Your Notes for Success

349

"In my experience, each failure contains the seeds of your next success—if you are willing to learn from it."
— *Paul Allen*

Failure is an inevitable part of life, and it's often hard to accept. But, it's important to remember that failure is also an opportunity. Every time you fail, it's an opportunity to learn and grow. Each failure teaches you something new and provides the seeds for your next success. It boosts your resilience and teaches you to be more creative and resourceful in your approach.

When you embrace failure and use it as a learning opportunity, it can be the catalyst for your next success. It's how you respond to failure that will determine your success. Each failure is an opportunity to reflect, grow, and move forward with a new perspective. With the right attitude and mindset, failure can be the stepping stone to your next success.

Failure isn't the end, it's a stepping stone to success. Learn, grow, and adapt to your failures. Every failure is an opportunity to improve, and if you have the right mindset, it turns into a catalyst for your next success. Don't fear failure, but rather see it as an opportunity to grow and succeed. Your success story awaits you, and failure is just a chapter in the book. Don't let failure get you down, and use it as a launching pad for your next big thing!

Francesco Vitali

Your Notes for Success

350

"When I started flirting with the hustle, failure became my ex, now I'm engaged to the game and married to success." — Lil Wayne

Hustle is the key to success. It is the drive and determination each of us has to put in the hard work and extra effort to achieve our goals. When we hustle, it means that we are willing to go the extra mile to make something happen. We are willing to put in the extra hours and effort to make sure we are doing the best job we can.

We are also willing to take risks and push ourselves to come up with creative solutions and ideas. Hustle is the fuel that drives us to success, and when we combine it with our creativity, ambition and hard work, it leads to amazing results. Hustle is the key to success, and when we put in the extra effort, we can achieve anything!

Don't stop hustling because it's what propels us forward! It's about putting in the work, taking risks and working hard to make our dreams come true. Hustle drives our creativity, ambition, and hard work, giving us incredible outcomes. With the right mindset and determination to hustle, we can do anything. Don't let your hustle stop you from unlocking your dreams and achieving limitless success!

Francesco Vitali

Your Notes for Success

351

"The journey of a thousand miles begins with one step."
— Lao Tzu

Taking that first step is often the most difficult, but it's also the most rewarding. Once we take that first step, the journey will become easier and more enjoyable. We will gain confidence, knowledge, and skills as we progress along the way. We will also learn how to better manage our time and resources, and become better problem-solvers. We will build relationships with those around us and make connections that will help us throughout our journey.

As we travel further, we will be presented with more challenges, but with each challenge, we will become stronger, more resilient, and wiser. With every step, we will gain more knowledge and become better equipped to reach our destination. The journey of a thousand miles will bring us to amazing places and incredible experiences, and it all starts with that first step.

You will gain a treasure trove of skills, experiences, and memories along your journey. So put on your favorite boots and take that first step. As you overcome challenges, you will grow in resilience and wisdom, unlocking new opportunities. Follow your passion and determination, and soon you'll stand at the summit, waving your victory flag with a smile that says, "I did it my way!"

Your Notes for Success

352

"If somebody offers you an amazing opportunity but you are not sure you can do it, say yes—then learn how to do it later!" — Richard Branson

By taking opportunities, we get to experience different aspects of life, explore our capabilities, and discover new things. Taking opportunities gives us the chance to gain new skills and grow as individuals. By learning to do them later, we can create long-term success and make progress toward our goals. Taking opportunities will help us develop a positive attitude and create a path to success. It teaches us to be brave and take risks, which can be beneficial in many areas of our lives.

Taking opportunities and learning to do them later can help us to open new doors and create new possibilities. We can also become more confident in our abilities, which will help us succeed in whatever we set out to do in life. Taking opportunities and learning to do them later is a great way to make the most of our lives and create a better future for ourselves.

Opportunities are like stepping stones to success, guiding us on a journey of self-discovery and growth. They challenge us to be brave, take risks, and learn along the way. Embracing them with an open mind and a positive attitude, we can unlock doors to endless possibilities and create a future that is uniquely ours. Let's seize every opportunity and make our lives a masterpiece of creativity, courage, and success!

Francesco Vitali

Your Notes for Success

353

"If opportunity doesn't knock, build a door."
— *Milton Berle*

If opportunity doesn't knock, building a door is a great way of motivating oneself to reach their desired goals. It encourages one to be proactive in their approach and to work hard to achieve success. It is a reminder that success does not come easily and that one has to work toward it.

This phrase serves as an inspirational reminder that a person should create their own opportunities instead of waiting for them to come knocking at the door. With hard work and determination, one can achieve anything one sets their mind to. It is a great way to boost morale and self-belief and to take control of one's destiny. It is a reminder that if you have a dream, go out and make it happen; don't wait for it to come to you.

Build your own path to success by remembering the mantra, "If opportunity doesn't knock, build a door." Be the architect of your own success. You need to embrace creativity, resilience, and innovation as you overcome obstacles and open up new possibilities. Be an entrepreneur, and dare to make opportunities where others don't exist. Let this phrase inspire you to design and build a future based on unwavering determination and unwavering belief in yourself.

Francesco Vitali

Your Notes for Success

354

"Motivation is the catalyzing ingredient for every successful innovation." — *Clayton Christensen*

Motivation is the catalyst for every successful innovation. It is what drives individuals to think outside the box and to push boundaries. It enables us to explore new ideas and to take risks. It is the fire that propels us forward, helping us to create something that can positively impact the world. It not only gives us the confidence to pursue our dreams, but it also allows us to stay focused and remain committed to our goals.

Motivation is a powerful force that can inspire us to achieve great things, and it can be a major driving factor in the success of any project. It encourages us to rise above our limitations and to strive for excellence. Without motivation, innovation would not exist, and our world would be much less exciting.

Your inner innovator will be fueled with motivation. It's the heartbeat of every great achievement, pushing you to break down barriers. With motivation as your compass, you can navigate the unknown, fueled by unwavering determination and a thirst for excellence. That's how dreams turn into reality and you succeed. Make your dreams a reality by embracing motivation and unleashing your limitless potential.

Francesco Vitali

Your Notes for Success

355

"Strength and growth come only through continuous effort and struggle." — Napoleon Hill

It's always important to remember that growth is never easy and won't be achieved without hard work. When times get tough, and it feels as though progress is slow, it's important to stay focused on the end goal and keep pushing forward. Challenges are inevitable, but they should be embraced as they provide the opportunity to learn and grow. With dedication, resilience, and tenacity, any goal can be achieved.

It's important to take the time to celebrate progress, no matter how small, and to recognize the efforts that have been put in. With self-motivation and belief in oneself, anything is possible. The strength gained from overcoming adversity is unparalleled, and it's important to remember that with each struggle and every challenge, strength and growth are just around the corner.

As you journey toward your goals, remember that growth comes from overcoming challenges. Embrace the struggles as stepping stones to success, and keep pushing forward with unwavering dedication. Celebrate each milestone, no matter how small, and believe in your own abilities. With resilience and self-motivation, you have the power to overcome any obstacle and achieve greatness. Keep going, and let your determination and perseverance light the path to your success story.

Francesco Vitali

Your Notes for Success

356

*"Decide what you want, and then act as if it
were impossible to fail."* — Brian Tracy

Making decisions and taking chances can be daunting, but when you decide what you want, and act as if it were impossible to fail, it sets you up for success. When you believe in yourself and your ability to succeed, you can push beyond your self-imposed limits and accomplish great things. It's important to remember that mistakes are part of the process and can be used as a learning experience.

If you focus on making decisions with a positive mindset, you will be equipped to face any obstacle that comes your way. With each successful decision, your confidence will grow and help you to push forward. By deciding what you want and acting as if it were impossible to fail, you will be one step closer to achieving your goals.

When you approach decisions with an unwavering belief in your own capabilities, the possibilities are limitless. Mistakes are stepping stones to learning and growth, not obstacles to be feared. With a positive mindset and confidence in your choices, you can overcome any challenge that arises. Keep pushing forward, guided by the conviction that success is within your reach. Believe in yourself, make decisions with purpose, and watch your dreams become reality.

Francesco Vitali

Your Notes for Success

357

"Every moment wasted looking back keeps us from moving forward." — Hillary Clinton

Every moment wasted looking back can be time lost. We should focus our attention and energy on moving forward to make the most of life. Instead of dwelling on the past, we should be looking to the future, building our dreams and making them a reality. We should focus on the positive and learn from our mistakes.

By taking control of our own destiny, we can make sure our future is filled with hope and opportunity. We can also take comfort in the fact that our experiences can help shape us, making us more resilient and better equipped for the future. Each day is a new chance to start afresh and make our dreams come true. Every moment wasted looking back is a moment we can spend moving forward and making a positive difference in the world.

The key to unlocking boundless opportunities is looking forward with unwavering optimism as we go through life. Our past may have lessons, but we should focus on the future we want. With control of our destiny, learning from mistakes, and embracing every day as a fresh start, we can change the world. Let's make every moment count, as we build a future filled with hope, resilience, and limitlessness.

Francesco Vitali

Your Notes for Success

358

"If a window of opportunity appears, don't pull down the shade." — Tom Peters

Opportunities in life don't come around often and can be hard to recognize. When a window of opportunity appears, it's important to take advantage of it and not pull down the shade. By seizing the opportunity, you can open yourself up to a world of possibilities, allowing you to grow and develop as a person. It may be scary, but it is worth taking the risk. You never know what you may learn or how you may benefit from the experience. Accepting an opportunity can make you more confident and resilient and can give you a greater understanding of the world. It can be a great way to develop new skills or to explore something that you are passionate about. So, don't be afraid to open that window and let the light in. It might just be the best decision you ever make.

Sometimes, opportunities are disguised as risks, so take a leap of faith when you see one. Take the leap, and let yourself experience new things as you embrace it. If you embrace opportunities, you might be able to uncover hidden talents, spark passions, and make a brighter future. You might find that opportunity to be a turning point.

Francesco Vitali

Your Notes for Success

359

*"When opportunity presents itself, don't be afraid
to go after it."* — Eddie Kennison

Opportunities provide us with an avenue to gain valuable experience, knowledge, and skills. Taking advantage of these opportunities can open up a world of possibilities and help us reach our goals. It can also help us discover our strengths and weaknesses, and provide us with a better understanding of our capabilities. Even if it's scary or uncertain, it's important to take a chance and trust that you can handle the situation.

Don't be afraid to take risks, because it's the only way you will truly grow. Embrace the opportunity and strive to make the most out of it. You'll never know what could come out of it if you don't try. Opportunities will come and go, so make sure you don't miss out on any of them. Seize the opportunity and make something of it!

They offer us a chance to discover our potential, learn new things, and widen our horizons. Opportunities are like hidden treasures, waiting to be discovered. Taking a leap of faith and seizing the opportunity is a great way to grow and develop. Don't let fear hold you back; take a risk and see where it takes you. You'll be glad you did that in the future!

Francesco Vitali

Your Notes for Success

360

"The difference between ordinary and extraordinary is that little extra." - Jimmy Johnson

The difference between successful people and ordinary ones is that successful people go the extra mile. They're always ready to give 110 percent. They know that even if they don't reach the moon, they will land on the stars. Go out of your way to cater to your clients and build a connection with them. *Listen* to them and figure out solutions that make things easier for them.

Go the extra mile with projects at work as well. Pitch in ideas, help your coworkers and make everything stress-free. The thing is, everyone can go the extra mile, but only a few of us choose to do so. Be *different*. Don't follow the masses. Work a little harder ignore naysayers, doubters, and others that are threatened by you. You may have to get up after you've been knocked down, put in more hours, make difficult decisions, be tired, and still do more. But in the end, when you reap the rewards of your hard work, you will be proud of how far you've come.

Nothing great comes without sacrifices, a conscious effort, and a strong mindset. Be the person who is not only an inspiration to others but to yourself as well. Remember that the most important thing to do is never give up because, with a little more effort, you can get to the finish line earlier!

Francesco Vitali

<u>*Your Notes for Success*</u>

361

"Success usually comes to those who are too busy looking for it." — Henry David Thoreau

Success usually comes to those who are too busy looking for it. These are the ambitious people who are never satisfied with the status quo and persistently strive to achieve more and better. Successful people always make sure to set lofty goals and then work hard to reach them. They are open to learning and never hesitate to ask questions or seek guidance.

They don't give up easily, and they never let failure discourage them. They understand that failure is part of the learning process, and they use it as a stepping stone to success. They are also willing to take calculated risks, which can often be the difference between success and failure. Ultimately, success is a result of hard work, dedication, and resilience. Those who are too busy looking for it will eventually find it.

Ready to ride the wave of success? Success isn't for the faint-hearted, but it's for dreamers, goal-setters, and hard workers. It's like a treasure hunt, where those who actively search for it will find its gems. Embrace challenges, learn from mistakes, and take calculated risks. Stay positive and keep pushing. Success isn't a destination but a journey of determination, innovation, and perseverance. So, gear up, ride the waves, and make your mark!

Francesco Vitali

Your Notes for Success

362

*"Success is liking yourself, liking what you do, and
liking how you do it." - Maya Angelou*

Success is peace of mind. It is a reward for the hard work
and dedication you put in to become the best version of yourself.
When you strive to be the best version of yourself, you are able to
find a sense of accomplishment in your achievements. You have
taken the time to work hard, learn, and grow. This can bring a
feeling of joy and pride that can be incredibly rewarding. Success
is not just about reaching the top of the mountain but about the
journey and how you got there. It is about having the courage
and conviction to continue to strive for excellence, to never settle
for mediocrity, and to always look for ways to improve. With this
mindset, success will soon become second nature, and you will be
able to enjoy a sense of peace and contentment.

Success is like a canvas waiting to be painted—and you
hold the brush! Each stroke of hard work, determination, and
self-improvement adds vibrant colors to your masterpiece. With
unwavering passion and creativity, you create a unique success
story that fills you with pride and joy. Embrace the canvas of
opportunities and paint your own extraordinary path to success.

Francesco Vitali

Your Notes for Success

363

"The only thing standing between you and outrageous success is continuous progress." — Dan Waldschmidt

We are our own worst critics. One thing we forget is that through hard work and commitment, we can keep improving. Don't be too hard on yourself—the important thing is to learn from your mistakes. Focus on being better than who you were yesterday. You are destined for great things. You have what it takes to achieve success. Don't let anyone else tell you otherwise. If you keep working hard, taking each failure as a lesson rather than a setback, and focusing your energy on preparing yourself for what is to come, you will reach the top.

What matters most is not where you stood yesterday but where you stand today and where you plan on standing tomorrow. Each failure is a chance to grow. It's a chance to work on ourselves and turn our weaknesses into strengths. No one is born without flaws. There's not a single person in the world who hasn't made a mistake. But what makes successful people stand out is that they use every failure as an opportunity to better themselves. They are always on top of their game.

The reward that comes with hard work is worth every struggle in the end. So strive to turn your dreams into reality!

Francesco Vitali

Your Notes for Success

364

"One secret of success in life is for a man to be ready for his opportunity when it comes." — *Benjamin Disraeli*

There are three key ingredients for success: Having the right attitude, a positive outlook, and being willing to take calculated risks. All are essential to maximize success. Having a clear vision of what one wants to achieve, setting realistic goals, and being prepared to work hard to achieve them is key. Being organized but also flexible is important to make the most of the opportunities that come your way. Finally, having the courage to take risks, having faith in oneself and one's abilities, and the willingness to learn from mistakes are qualities that can make a huge difference in the success of any venture. With these qualities, a person is well-prepared to take full advantage of the opportunities that come their way and to make the most of them.

The key to success lies in a positive outlook, a positive attitude, and taking calculated risks. The foundation is a clear vision, realistic goals, and hard work. Being organized and flexible is important to seize opportunities. Courage, self-belief, and being willing to learn from mistakes are the key. A person with these qualities will be able to take advantage of every opportunity and succeed in remarkable ways.

Francesco Vitali

Your Notes for Success

365

"The most common way people give up their power is by thinking they don't have any." — *Alice Walker*

Your thoughts are compelling and determine your business decisions, actions, and every part of your life that you can control. Your thoughts are one of the most powerful tools you will ever have in changing your business outcome. It is imperative to understand that you are no less than anyone else in this world. We all need to realize that the power is hidden within us. It is like a sleeping giant waiting for the moment we give the order to wake him up.

Realize that everything you need already resides within you. It takes nothing extraordinary to accomplish your goals, but simply your decision to feel empowered.

All power lies within your mind, and your thoughts and choices make magic happen. The more you trust yourself, the better your judgments will be.

We are all unique business minds. We all have unique strengths and superpowers as long as we believe we have them. Ultimately, it all depends on your beliefs. When you believe in yourself, you strive to make the impossible possible by trying every viable option. On the other hand, when we lose confidence in ourselves, it makes it harder for us to accomplish things that are more than possible. It's the mindset that determines our success. So set your mind to success, and soon you'll get there!

www.ingramcontent.com/pod-product-compliance
Lightning Source LLC
Chambersburg PA
CBHW070854120626
46546CB00001B/5